PROKOFIEV'S PIANO SONATAS

prokofiev's

Boris Berman

piano sonatas

A GUIDE FOR THE LISTENER
AND THE PERFORMER

Yale University Press • New Haven and London

Published with the assistance of the Frederick W. Hilles Publication Fund of
Yale University. Also published with assistance from the foundation established in
memory of Philip Hamilton McMillan of the Class of 1894, Yale College.

Set in Scala by The Composing Room of Michigan, Inc.

Printed in the United States of America.

Library of Congress Cataloging-in-Publication Data

Berman, Boris.
   Prokofiev's piano sonatas : a guide for the listener and the performer /
Boris Berman.
      p.   cm.
   Includes bibliographical references and index.
   ISBN 978-0-300-11490-4 (cloth : alk. paper)
   1. Prokofiev, Sergey, 1891–1953. Sonatas, piano.   2. Sonatas (Piano)—
Analysis, appreciation.   I. Title.
   MT145.P8B47   2008
   786.2′183092—dc22

                                                                2007030926

A catalogue record for this book is available from the British Library.

The paper in this book meets the guidelines for permanence and durability
of the Committee on Production Guidelines for Book Longevity of the Council
on Library Resources.

10 9 8 7 6 5 4 3 2 1

To my mother

contents

preface

Within the vast, virtually limitless piano repertoire, the piano sonatas of Sergei Prokofiev occupy a special place. Apart from Alexander Scriabin early in the century, Prokofiev was the only major twentieth-century composer to pay such consistent attention to the form, which had emerged in the eighteenth century, reached its pinnacle in the thirty-two sonatas by Beethoven, and was further developed through the masterpieces of Schubert, Chopin, Schumann, and Brahms. While other important twentieth-century composers, such as Rachmaninov, Bartók, Hindemith, Shostakovich, Stravinsky, Ives, Medtner, Barber, Ginastera, Boulez, Schnittke, and Carter, wrote occasional works in this genre, Prokofiev wrote nine piano sonatas, which became cornerstones of the piano repertoire. They are a constant presence in concert programs and are considered an indispensable part of the repertoire by almost every serious concert pianist. Piano students all over the world study them.

Prokofiev had a lifelong love of the sonata form. Ever since learning the basic rules during his childhood years, he strove to master them; a group of piano sonatas he wrote while a student at the St. Petersburg Conservatory reflect this interest. Prokofiev retained his fascination with the form for the rest of his life. In 1941, describing his Sonatinas op. 54 (1931), he remarked, "I liked the idea of writing a simple work in such a superior form as sonata."[1] One can learn a lot about the composer's growth by tracing his progress from the early sonatas, which cautiously dare to bend the textbook rules, to the masterful treatment of the form in his late works.

Prokofiev's piano music has always played an important role in my own work as both a performer and a teacher. While a student at the Moscow Tchaikovsky Conservatory, I had the privilege of studying with Lev Oborin. This remarkable pianist premiered both of Prokofiev's sonatas for violin and piano with David Oistrakh, preparing them under the composer's guidance. Prokofiev's works were heard very often in Oborin's studio, as well as in his own concerts.

In the 1990s, I undertook a mammoth project of recording Prokofiev's entire output for piano solo. It was released on nine compact discs by Chandos Records. As a matter of course, it encompassed all nine sonatas, including both versions of the Fifth Sonata, as well as the brief sketch of the beginning of the Tenth Sonata. This endeavor, coupled with the performing and recording of Prokofiev's concertos and chamber works, allowed me to deepen my understanding of the composer's style and its evolution, as well as his creative process. In my pedagogical work, I cherish the opportunity to discuss Prokofiev's oeuvre with my students in individual lessons, workshops, and master classes. This book is an extension of my work as a teacher and performer; it is from this dual vantage point that I examine the sonatas here.

While writing this book, I have kept two groups of readers in mind: music lovers who would like to enhance their enjoyment of Prokofiev's music, and piano students who are learning any of these works. This double purpose has determined the way the book is structured. Each sonata is discussed in a separate chapter, which opens with general information about the work, followed by a detailed discussion of the piece, in which I point out important details and features of the composition. I have tried to minimize the use of technical language in these sections, but some basic terms proved to be indispensable. Lay readers may find it useful to consult the glossary of musical terms provided as an appendix. Those readers who are able to read music can follow the discussion by consulting the sonata scores. For readers who do not have this ability, referring them to specific points in recordings seemed to be the way to go.

Because I present my personal and subjective views on the interpretation of this repertoire, it felt natural to use my own recordings as a reference source throughout the book. The precise timings provided throughout the book relate to my recordings of the Prokofiev sonatas issued by Chandos Records in a 3-CD set (CHAN 9637). This set is a remastering of my recordings of Prokofiev's complete works for solo piano, where individual sonatas appear as follows:

Sonata No. 1, op. 1: Volume 5 (CHAN 9017)
Sonata No. 2, op. 14: Volume 7 (CHAN 9119)
Sonata No. 3, op. 28: Volume 6 (CHAN 9069)
Sonata No. 4, op. 29: Volume 3 (CHAN 8926)
Sonata No. 5, op 38 (original version): Volume 9 (CHAN 9361)
Sonata No. 5, op. 38/135 (revised version): Volume 1 (CHAN 8851)
Sonata No. 6, op. 82: Volume 9 (CHAN 9361)
Sonata No. 7, op. 83: Volume 2 (CHAN 8881)
Sonata No. 8, op. 84: Volume 4 (CHAN 8976)
Sonata No. 9, op. 103: Volume 8 (CHAN 9211)
Sonata No. 10, op. 137 (fragment): Volume 9 (CHAN 9361)

The latter part of each chapter is titled "Master Class." I have written these sections with professional pianists in mind, discussing ambiguous passages, suggesting possible ways to interpret them, and giving detailed advice that I hope will help pianists in their work. In order to follow the discussion, readers will need to insert measure numbers in their copies of the scores, since no edition of the Prokofiev sonatas with printed measure numbers is available. Anticipating that many readers might turn to a chapter dedicated to a particular sonata without reading other parts of the book, I repeatedly discuss certain features of Prokofiev's music that may be pertinent to more than one sonata.

To precede the discussion of individual sonatas, an opening chapter offers a general overview of Prokofiev's music. Here I pay special attention to the circumstances that shaped the composer's life and influenced changes in his musical style. The following chapter examines Prokofiev's approach to the piano, both as a composer and as a performer of his own works. His playing is discussed as it emerges from reviews and memoirs of his contemporaries, as well as from his own recordings.

The abundance of available recordings of Prokofiev's sonatas has prevented me from attempting to evaluate or describe them. I have chosen to refer only to the performances of Prokofiev himself and of the two pianists who were entrusted by him to premiere the late sonatas: Sviatoslav Richter (Sonatas Nos. 7 and 9) and Emil Gilels (Sonata No. 8). In addition, Richter was the first, after the composer, to perform Sonata No. 6; he also started playing the Eighth Sonata soon after it was premiered by Gilels.

In spite of the many valuable books available today, the state of Prokofiev scholarship cannot be considered adequate: suffice it to say that the detailed catalogue of his works has not been updated since it was published in 1961.[2] At present, there is no edition of the Prokofiev sonatas free of errors. I have tried to do my best in pointing out some obvious mistakes, as well as certain doubtful readings. Many questions cannot be answered with certainty, as the manuscripts for some of the sonatas have been lost; those that have survived are not easily available for inspection. To get to some of them, I was fortunate to have the help of Russian colleagues in overcoming the restrictions of the current gatekeepers in Russia. As a result, some textual mistakes have been corrected for the first time in this book.

I would like to stress that the interpretive recommendations I make in this book should be viewed as my personal suggestions rather than objective truths. They aim at guiding listeners to appreciate the richness of the music and at helping pianists to build their own artistic concepts. I hope that my readers, professional pianists and music lovers alike, will find this book helpful.

acknowledgments

Three individuals have helped me immensely in bringing this book to its final shape: Barbara Goren, Ilya Poletaev, and Liam Viney. To them goes my sincere gratitude. Alexei Lubimov, a wonderful pianist and my friend of many years, has helped me to bypass the vestiges of the Soviet system and to obtain access to key sources in Russian archives.

I am also grateful to Adam Bloniarz, Alexander Rabin, and Andrew Resnick for their assistance; to Michael Friedmann for his advice; to my editor, Duke Johns, for his meticulous work; to Keith Condon of Yale University Press for his great help during various stages of preparing the manuscript; and to Leora Zimmer for formatting the music examples. I thank the Griswold Fund and the Frederick W. Hilles Publication Fund of Yale University for their assistance.

To my wife, Zina, my daughter, Daniella, and my son, Ilan, I am forever indebted for their loving encouragement and support.

Fig. 1 Prokofiev at the piano. Nikopol, 1910. Photograph courtesy of Sergei Prokofiev Family.

Prokofiev

HIS LIFE AND THE EVOLUTION OF HIS MUSICAL LANGUAGE

Prokofiev's creative path traversed many countries and was affected by wars and revolutions. Life brought him into contact with some of the most prominent and influential artistic figures of his time. Observing the magnificent panorama of Prokofiev's oeuvre, one sees that the composer's musical style evolved significantly over the course of his creative life. The reasons for the changes of direction have been much discussed and debated. Was a noticeable and undeniable mellowing of Prokofiev's musical language in his late works forced on him by political pressure, as some writers have claimed? Or was it—as others have asserted—a natural process of warming up in his mature years while shedding fashionable modernistic idioms? Did Prokofiev's return to the Soviet Union in 1936 deny him the opportunities for further experimentation that had rejuvenated his style in earlier eras and kept him in the creative forefront of musical modernism between the two world wars? Or were these experiments motivated by opportunism, calculated to keep him in the limelight, and not reflective of his genuine musical personality, which was grounded in more traditional idioms?

To answer these questions, we need to explore the circumstances of his life and how they influenced his compositions.

Sergei Prokofiev was born on April 11, 1891, in the village of Sontsovka in what is now Ukraine, where his father was the manager of a large estate and where the future composer spent the first thirteen years of his life. His musical gifts manifested themselves at an early age and developed in spite of his growing up in cultural isolation—his was the only educated family within a radius of dozens of miles. Though the Prokofievs undertook two visits to Moscow and St. Petersburg (in 1900 and again in 1901–2), where young Sergei was able to attend concerts and opera performances, his mother was his chief musical influence during these formative years. Mrs. Prokofiev, an amateur pianist of limited abilities and a traditional taste, was Prokofiev's first piano teacher. Under her guidance, Prokofiev became acquainted with the music of Haydn, Mozart, Beethoven, Chopin, and other masters. During the Moscow visit in the winter of 1901–2, Prokofiev met Sergei Taneyev, one of the most respected musicians of his time and the teacher of Rachmaninov, Scriabin, and Medtner. At Taneyev's suggestion, his student Reinhold Glière was engaged to spend two summers (1902 and 1903) in Sontsovka, supervising Prokofiev's music studies. Glière was a composer with a conservative outlook, and his instruction emphasized traditional aspects of musical language.

Nothing in Prokofiev's early music education—or in his early compositions, of which a sizable number have been preserved—gave any inkling of the future modernistic bent in Prokofiev's music. In fact, during the initial visit with Taneyev, the latter commented on the oversimplicity of young Prokofiev's harmonies. Yet certain traits of his later style, such as its rhythmic energy and penchant for a humorous, mischievous character, as well as a generally active (rather than reflective) emotional tone, can be discerned in his early works.

The psychological development of the adolescent Prokofiev was strongly influenced by his parents. He was their only child and the sole object of their love and devotion. Young Sergei was an affectionate and obedient son, accustomed to being the center of attention. He grew up without close friends; the few children who made up the circle of Prokofiev's playmates were of an inferior social standing and were treated as such. His parents, who emphasized industrious and serious studies (Prokofiev was homeschooled), supervised his studies and reading. They also encouraged their son's playfulness and natural curiosity, as well as the wholesome pastimes of long walks, horse riding, and swimming. In his autobiography, Prokofiev remembers various creative games as well as home theater performances, including the staging of his own opera *The Giant,* written at the age of eight.

His, however, was not a childhood of daydreaming, brooding, or incessant fantasizing. If he had any romantic urges, they were inhibited by a paucity of opportunities for social interaction and by firm parental control. Was this the reason why the lyrical side of Prokofiev's talent remained underdeveloped during his early years?

In 1904 Prokofiev was admitted to the St. Petersburg Conservatory, and he and his mother moved to the capital. Among his teachers were some of the best Russian musicians of the time: Nikolai Rimsky-Korsakov, Alexander Glazunov, and Anatoly Lyadov. The instruction in the conservatory did not challenge Prokofiev's conservative tastes, which had been cultivated by his mother and Glière. His compositions during these first student years, as well as his earlier attempts, did not show any interest in experimenting with a more radical musical language.

Prokofiev later looked back on his studies with the illustrious professors with disappointment. This is how he remembers, for instance, Lyadov's composition class: "Anyone who dared to depart from the conventional path was bound to incur his wrath. Thrusting his hands into his pockets and swaying back and forth . . . , he would say, 'I cannot understand why you bother to study with me. Go to Richard Strauss, go to Debussy.' He might as well have said, 'Go to the devil.'"[1]

Prokofiev seems to have learned more by attending concerts, as well as studying music that was previously unknown to him. In 1908 he began attending the "Evenings of Contemporary Music," an adventurous concert series organized by Alfred Nurok and Walter Nouvel. There he was able to hear the newest music written in Russia and abroad. (He himself presented there the Russian premiere of Schoenberg's Three Piano Pieces, op. 11, a manifesto of atonality.) He also was encouraged to bring his own compositions and prodded to use a more daring musical language. During the following years, Prokofiev presented several of his works at these evenings, such as

Four Etudes op. 2 (1909) and the pieces from op. 3 (1907–8) and op. 4 (1908–12). These performances helped to put Prokofiev on the map as one of the most promising and daring modernists in Russia. More important, the praise with which his experiments were met undoubtedly encouraged him to develop the modernist aspect of his musical language.

We can only marvel that, within a mere four years, this sheltered, provincial youth, conservative in his tastes and behavior, turned into a darling of the modernist circle. Here for the first time we find Prokofiev able, indeed eager, to modify his musical style in response to external forces. We will see such sharp turns repeatedly as we follow this composer's creative path.

Young Prokofiev was attentive to new musical trends. We can find traces of various influences in his early compositions. Some of the piano works from the set *Visions fugitives,* op. 22 (1915–17), are reminiscent of Debussy; the *Andante assai* section of the First Piano Concerto, op. 10 (1911–12), sounds like Rachmaninov; and the harmonies of the symphonic poem *Osenneye* (*Autumn* or *Autumnal Sketch*), op. 8 (1910), harken back to Scriabin. These, however, were rather passing influences. Others proved to be more enduring.

One of them was the fairy-tale streak in Russian music. Russians have always been fond of fairy tales, which to this day continue to be an important part of every child's upbringing. Setting fairy tales to music, Russian composers developed special musical idioms in response to recurrent themes: magical transformations, simple and fearless maidens, or equally fearless and mighty young men. (See such operas by Rimsky-Korsakov as *The Tale of Tsar Saltan, Kashchei the Immortal, Snow Maiden, The Golden Cockerel,* and *Sadko;* symphonic poems by Lyadov such as *The Enchanted Lake* and *Kikimora;* or Medtner's numerous *skazka* [fairy tale] piano pieces.) Prokofiev adopted the fairy-tale imagery of his older contemporaries and developed his own idioms, which are found in many of his piano works, such as some of the *Visions fugitives, Tales of an Old Grandmother,* and certain pages of Sonatas Nos. 3 and 4, or of Piano Concertos Nos. 2 and 3. (These idioms are discussed further in the next chapter; as examples, see Exx. 0.15a and b.)

Another significant influence was the Classical style. Prokofiev's childhood exposure to the Viennese classics was strengthened in the conservatory through his contacts with Nikolai Tcherepnin, who was his mentor in the conducting class: "Sitting beside me with the score at the innumerable rehearsals of our student orchestra, he would say, 'Now listen to that delightful little bassoon there!' and I found myself acquiring a taste for Haydn and Mozart, which later found expression in the *Classical Symphony*."[2] This symphony, his first (op. 25, 1916–17), as well as numerous short piano works written in eighteenth-century dance forms—gavotte, minuet, allemande—were the early manifestations of the neoclassical trend that can be traced through much of Prokofiev's creative life.

In his early operas *Maddalena,* op. 13 (1911–13), and *The Gambler,* op. 24 (1915–17, revised in 1927), Prokofiev honed his acute sense of the stage, which would serve him well in his later operas and ballets. The musical language of these two works was often strident, as the composer strove to find musical parallels to the dramatic tensions of the plot.

In the 1910s Prokofiev was also exploring two other musical topics under the inspiration of Sergei Diaghilev, a famous Russian impresario, the founder of the Ballets Russes and a formidable catalyst in the development of early twentieth-century music and dance. One was a barbaric, primitive style showcased in the *Scythian Suite,* op. 20 (1914–15), originally written for a projected Diaghilev ballet to be entitled *Ala and Lolly.* This powerful work is strongly reminiscent of Stravinsky's history-making *The Rite of Spring,* premiered by Diaghilev in 1913. The primeval style of the *Scythian Suite* is also heard in some of Prokofiev's other works written around the same time, such as his monumental Second Piano Concerto, op. 16 (1913, revised in 1923), or the cantata *Seven, They Were Seven,* op. 30 (1917–18). Such glorification of strong, savage emotions and the nostalgic revisiting of the distant and mythical pagan past were shared by many Russian creative figures of that time, such as the poet Alexander Blok (in his poem *The Scythians*) and the painter Nicholas Roerich. This mindset was developed concurrently with, and in opposition to, the refined, mystical art of Symbolist poets (the most prominent being the same Blok) and the music of Scriabin.

The other stylistic novelty, which Prokofiev developed in response to

Diaghilev's entreaties, was the folksy Russian style of his ballet *The Buffoon* (*Chout*), op. 21 (1915, revised in 1920). ("Please write me Russian music. . . . In your rotten Petrograd they have completely forgotten how to write Russian music," Diaghilev had admonished.)[3] The evocation of authentic Russian folklore—quite different from the renditions of Russian folk music by Glinka, Balakirev, Rimsky-Korsakov, or Tchaikovsky, who made the folk material conform to the Western musical tradition—did not come as naturally to Prokofiev as it did to Stravinsky in such works as *Les noces, Pribaoutki,* or *Renard. The Buffoon* remained the only "folkloristic" work written by Prokofiev, clearly motivated by the desire to please Diaghilev.

The beginning of the 1917 Revolution in Russia evoked Prokofiev's sympathy; his reaction was similar to that of many artists who aspired to artistic rejuvenation. However, the ensuing chaos and destruction caused him to leave the country in 1918. The new Soviet commissar of culture, Anatoly Lunacharsky, tried to dissuade Prokofiev from leaving ("You are a revolutionary in music, we are revolutionaries in life. We ought to work together," he said, as related by Prokofiev), but he helped the composer obtain a travel passport, nonetheless.[4]

Prokofiev spent the next eighteen years living outside Russia, first in the United States and then in Europe. These years were a struggle, initially for survival and later for recognition. But they were also much more. Settling in Paris in 1923, Prokofiev found himself in the world's center of new music. His works of the following decade reflect his continued efforts to define his musical language, as well as to remain relevant in light of the rapidly changing tastes of the Parisian and other European audiences, as is evident from the following passage from Prokofiev's autobiography. Having described the failure of the 1925 Paris premiere of his Second Symphony, op. 40, Prokofiev continued: "This was perhaps the first time it occurred to me that I might perhaps be destined to be a second-rate composer. Paris as the undisputed dictator of fashion has a tendency to pose as the arbiter in other fields as well. In music the refinement of French tastes has its reverse side— the public are apt to be too easily bored. Having taken up with one composer they quickly tire of him and in a year or two they search for a new sensation. I was evidently no longer a sensation."[5]

During this time Prokofiev tried his hand at many contemporary styles and techniques: he ventured into complex, dissonantly chromatic writing (Symphony No. 2; Piano Concerto No. 5, op. 55, 1932) and, conversely, into the diatonic style exemplified by the ballet *Le pas d'acier*, op. 41 (1925). Prokofiev remarked that, in the language of the latter work, the "radical change was from the chromatic to the diatonic . . . many of the themes were composed on white keys."[6] In the set of two piano pieces *Choses en soi*, op. 45 (1928), he "wished to indulge in a little musical introspection without trying to find some easily accessible forms for my ideas."[7] In other works, Prokofiev came close to expressionism (as in his opera *The Fiery Angel*, op. 37, 1919–27) or experimented with neoclassicism (Piano Concerto No. 4, op. 53, 1931). Sometimes it is hard to distinguish between Prokofiev's artistic searches and somewhat opportunistic changes of direction.

By the 1930s, Prokofiev's predilection for certain genres became clear: large-scale symphonic and stage works attracted his primary attention. He developed a particular affinity for ballet. His uncanny ability to create a memorable musical image within the first few measures was especially suitable for dance numbers, in which the first visual impact is particularly striking. The rhythmic vitality inherent in Prokofiev's music permeates many energetic, grotesque, or aggressive pages of his ballets. As for the portrayal of lyrical characters in his ballets, Prokofiev's long melodic lines seem to be born of the plasticity of the human body.

In 1927 Prokofiev undertook a concert tour of Soviet Russia, where he received a celebrity's welcome. This reception encouraged Prokofiev, and he became keen on restoring and strengthening ties with the music establishment of his native country. He made several subsequent trips to Russia (in 1929, 1932, and twice in both 1933 and 1934). Finally, by New Year's Eve of 1936, he moved back to Moscow for good.

Prokofiev returned to Russia in spite of the attempts of his friends, both in Russia and in the West, to dissuade him. His motives for this important step were hotly debated. Stravinsky believed that Prokofiev, having experienced financial difficulties in the West, was seduced by hopes of prosperity;* others hinted at entrapment of a sort. It seems to me that there were several reasons for this momentous decision, which altered Prokofiev's subsequent life. The years preceding the move saw Prokofiev's growing reattachment to his country and his interest in becoming involved in Soviet musical life. He might also have been attracted by the prospects of financial security in Russia, compared to the uncertainties of living in Europe between the wars. Having traveled several times in and out of Russia, he might have thought naively that he would be able to continue maintaining his "extraterritorial" status. Prokofiev had enjoyed being treated as a foreign dignitary during his visits to the Soviet Union and later, having settled there, he continued cultivating his "specialness" in everything. He had a foreign wife, wore foreign clothes, and brought home a car from his last concert tour in America at a time when hardly anybody in Russia had one. He was naive not to see how much resentment all this created, nor did he anticipate that his freedom of travel would soon be curtailed (his last trip outside the Soviet Union, mentioned above, was in 1938). In the words of Shostakovich, as related by Volkov, "He came to Moscow to teach them, and they started to teach him."[8]

In fact, the timing of his move back to Russia could not have been worse. The famous *Pravda* editorial "Muddle instead of Music," denouncing Shostakovich's opera *Lady Macbeth of Mtsensk,* was published in 1936, while the following two years, 1937 and 1938, witnessed Stalin's most terrible purges.

Having arrived in Moscow, Prokofiev lost no time in earning his credentials as a Soviet composer. The first work he completed in 1936 was a set of "mass" (popular) songs, whose texts exalted the life in collective farms and dealt with other similar Soviet topics. A much more ambitious undertaking was his *Cantata for the Twentieth Anniversary of the October Revolution,* op. 74. It was scored for two mixed choruses (a professional choir and an amateur

*"Prokofiev was always very Russian-minded and always anti-clerical. But in my opinion these dispositions had little to do with his return to Russia. The reason for this was a sacrifice to the bitch goddess." Igor Stravinsky and Robert Craft, *Memories and Commentaries,* vol. 1 (London: Faber and Faber, 1960), 72.

one), a symphony orchestra, a wind band, a percussion orchestra, and an orchestra of Russian folk instruments. The choice of texts by Marx, Engels, Lenin, and Stalin underlined the conspicuous political agenda. However, this attempt to glorify the revolution using unorthodox means was summarily rejected. It was strongly criticized at a closed audition and remained unperformed until 1966, long after the composer's death. Prokofiev still was under the illusion that revolutionary society needed and appreciated revolutionary art. In fact, the opposite was true: the tastes of the Soviet ruling elite, imposed on artists with an increasingly heavy hand, were thoroughly petit bourgeois. Composers were admonished to adhere to the principles of Socialist Realism* and to write music accessible to the people.

Prokofiev was aware of these expectations. For a while, he tried to be both cooperative and defiant. As early as 1934, he wrote an article for a Soviet newspaper in which he described his search for the "new simplicity." "What we need is great music, i.e., music that will be in keeping both in conception and technical execution with the grandeur of the epoch. . . . The danger of becoming provincial is unfortunately a very real one for modern Soviet composers. It is not so easy to find the right idiom for this music. To begin with, it must be melodious, moreover, the melody must be simple and comprehensible, without being repetitive or trivial."[9] Later, in 1937, he came back to the same subject: "I consider it a mistake for a composer to strive for simplification. . . . In my own work written in this fruitful year, I have striven for clarity and melodiousness. At the same time I have scrupulously avoided palming off familiar harmonies and tunes. That is where the difficulty of composing clear, straightforward music lies: the clarity must be new, not old."[10]

In part, these declarations seem to have been designed to throw the critics off his back, although lecturing his fellow composers about "the danger of becoming provincial" could hardly have earned Prokofiev many friends. His

*Much ink has been spent in efforts to define this sacrosanct term of dubious aesthetic value, without making it any clearer. Here is the definition that I remember learning during my studies at the Moscow Conservatory: "The art of Socialist Realism is one that is realistic in its form and socialist in its content."

music, however, did become more melodious, less dissonant and angular. Was Prokofiev simply adjusting to the demands of the market again? The answer is both yes and no. He must have been consciously moderating his musical language, although not to the extent that would please the conservative ears of the Communist apparatchiks. However, even before Prokofiev settled back in Russia, his music had begun to turn toward a much more melody-oriented style, departing from the complexity of some of his compositions of the 1920s and early 1930s. In works such as the ballet *Romeo and Juliet*, op. 75 (1935), he seemed to have attained a blend between modernism and traditionalism that felt natural to him.

Prokofiev was not alone among the leading composers of the twentieth century in changing his style repeatedly in the course of his career: Stravinsky, Schoenberg, Bartók, and others modified their musical language drastically at various stages of their creative lives. In Prokofiev's case, he always maintained certain stylistic facets throughout the transformations of his musical language. He himself identified several "basic lines" of his style:

The first was the classical line, which could be traced back to my early childhood and the Beethoven sonatas I heard my mother play. This line takes sometimes a neo-classical form (sonatas, concertos), sometimes imitates the 18th century classics (gavottes, the *Classical symphony*, partly the *Sinfonietta*). The second line, the modern trend, begins with that meeting with Taneyev when he reproached me for the "crudeness" of my harmonies. At first this took the form of a search for my own harmonic language, developing later into a search for a language in which to express powerful emotions (*The Phantom, Despair, Diabolical Suggestion, Sarcasms, Scythian Suite*, a few of the songs, op. 23, *The Gambler, Seven, They Were Seven*, the Quintet and the Second Symphony). Although this line covers harmonic language mainly, it also includes new departures in melody, orchestration and drama. The third line is *toccata* or the "motor" line traceable perhaps to Schumann's *Toccata* which made such a powerful impression on me when I first heard it (*Etudes*, op. 2, *Toccata*, op. 11,

Scherzo, op. 12, the *Scherzo* of the Second Concerto, the *Toccata* in the Fifth Concerto, and also the repetitive intensity of the melodic figures in the *Scythian Suite*, *Pas d'acier* [*The Age of Steel*], or passages in the Third Concerto). This line is perhaps the least important. The fourth line is lyrical; it appears first as a thoughtful and meditative mood, not always associated with the melody, or, at any rate, with the long melody (*The Fairy-tale*, op. 3, *Dreams, Autumnal Sketch* [*Osenneye*], *Songs*, op. 9, *The Legend*, op. 12), sometimes partly contained in the long melody (choruses on Balmont texts, beginning of the First Violin Concerto, songs to Akhmatova's poems, *Old Granny's Tales* [*Tales of an Old Grandmother*]). This line was not noticed until much later. For a long time I was given no credit for any lyrical gift whatsoever, and for want of encouragement it developed slowly. But as time went on I gave more and more attention to this aspect of my work.

I should like to limit myself to these four "lines," and to regard the fifth, "grotesque" line which some wish to ascribe to me, as simply a deviation from the other lines. In any case I strenuously object to the very word "grotesque" which has become hackneyed to the point of nausea. As a matter of fact the use of the French word "grotesque" in this sense is a distortion of the meaning. I would prefer my music to be described as "Scherzo-ish" in quality, or else by three words describing the various degrees of the Scherzo—whimsicality, laughter, mockery.[11]

To add to this self-analysis by the composer, I can mention that Prokofiev's lyrical material is of two general types. One includes contemplative, expansive melodies, usually of a considerable length and frequently using wide intervals, often accompanied by the counterpoint of secondary voices (see Exx. 0.12, 0.13a, 0.14, and 8.6). The other group consists of more intimate, simpler themes, sometimes related to the Russian folk melos, of a more symmetrical structure and often of a naive, even shy character (see Ex. 0.13b and the second theme of Sonata 3 in Ex. 3.1).

The active passages of Prokofiev's music, his "toccata line," are based on relentless movement of similar rhythmic values, usually non legato; they often contain an ostinato motive. Emotionally, they range from fierce and aggressive to vigorous, and from mysterious to humorous (see Exx. 0.4a, 0.5a, 0.5b, 0.5c, 0.7b, and 0.9).

Humor, in particular, comes in many shades, encompassing gentle teasing, a hearty joke, or cruel and grotesque mockery. In the preceding quotation, the composer expressed his disapproval of the word "grotesque" applied to his music; such a strenuous disavowal seems to reflect a wish to disassociate himself from any characterizations that smacked of the bourgeois West. Sarcastic, unsparing humor is very much a part of Prokofiev's emotional vocabulary, especially in the music of his earlier years. Let us recall the last work in the set of piano pieces *Sarcasms*, op. 17 (1912–14) (Ex. 0.7b). The program for it—not included in the musical score but revealed in the composer's autobiography—shows Prokofiev's understanding of humor's psychological richness and ambiguity: "Sometimes we laugh maliciously at someone or something, but when we look closer, we see how pathetic and unfortunate is the object of our laughter. Then we become uncomfortable and the laughter rings in our ears—laughing now at us."[12] To express a broad gamut of humorous emotions, Prokofiev built an impressive vocabulary that included incisive rhythms, wide melodic leaps or panting, stuttering melodies, and sharp dynamic contrasts.

Later, responding to the official agenda, Prokofiev developed yet another facet of his music, which can be termed his "patriotic style." It was exemplified by the cantata *Alexander Nevsky*, op. 78 (1938–39), a reworking of his music to Sergei Eisenstein's movie of the same title (see Ex. 0.1). This bold, virile style can also be found in his later works, such as the opening and closing scenes of the opera *War and Peace*, op. 91 (1941–52), or in the so-called War Sonatas (Nos. 6–8) for piano.

In these works we also find a frequent use of sonorities imitating bells. Chimes are a common attribute of Russian music, especially in works imbued with a national character. Hearing them, we realize that we are being presented with a momentous (often calamitous) event. (This is how Mussorgsky uses bells in his operas, to give but one example.)

The "Russianness" of this style was sometimes emphasized by Prokof-

Ex. 0.1 Alexander Nevsky, *"Alexander's Entry into Pskov"*

iev's use of unusual time signatures, such as $\frac{5}{8}$ or $\frac{7}{8}$, typical of Russian folk music. Such asymmetrical meters were often employed by Russian composers of the nineteenth century in music with a national flavor. (There are various examples in many operas by Rimsky-Korsakov, including a chorus in the opera *Sadko* written in $\frac{11}{4}$. See also the five "Promenade" movements in Mussorgsky's *Pictures at an Exhibition*.) In the same spirit, Prokofiev uses such special time signatures in the last movement (see Ex. 0.2) of his Sonata No. 1 for Violin and Piano, op. 80 (1938–46). This trend, however, had little in common with the Russian style of his earlier folkloristic ballet *The Buffoon,* in which a heroic look at Russian melos was simply not on the agenda.

Examining the musical language of Prokofiev in a more detailed way, we must acknowledge that for him melody was always the most important element of music, one that determined the quality of the composition. This value system can be clearly viewed through his criticism of the music of others, as expressed in his letters and diaries. In such notes, he may have remarked on interesting harmonies or effective orchestration but would frequently add that the material of the work was weak or insufficient. The context of such comments leaves no doubt that for him the "material" was primarily melody.

Prokofiev's music is usually based on a firm sense of tonality. Whatever tonal uncertainty and ambiguity one experiences, mainly in developmental passages, they are mostly short-lived. His treatment of functional harmony

Ex. 0.2 Sonata No. 1 for Violin and Piano, mvt. 4

Ex. 0.3a Rondo op. 52, no. 2

Ex. 0.3b

includes expansion of the areas of tonal instability, enriching them with nonchordal tones and alluding to distant tonal centers in order to create contrast with the clear resolution into an unambiguous tonic. In a polyphonic texture, different voices often arrive at such a resolution not simultaneously. Another frequently employed device is transposing segments of the musical flow a half step up or down from their expected level. It often creates the feeling that fundamentally traditional music has undergone a stylistic facelift. I recall Prokofiev's younger son, Oleg, remembering that Prokofiev frequently referred to the need to "Prokofievize" a newly composed work. As an example of this, compare the beginning of the Rondo, op. 52, no. 2 (Ex. 0.3a) with my own attempt to "de-Prokofievize" it in Example 0.3b. As one can see, returning the transposed part to the original tonality greatly diminishes this music's peculiar Prokofievian charm.

Prokofiev had a particular aptitude for combining previously composed material with new music into a coherent whole or for regrouping old material in a new way. His chess player's mind (he played and studied chess all his life) saw the possibilities for new combinations of different fragments, some of them quite small. Here is how he describes his work on creating *Four Portraits and Dénouement from "The Gambler,"* op. 49 (1931):

> I was planning a symphonic suite based on the music of *The Gambler*. But I could not make much headway with it. The close interweaving of the music and the text resulted in an intricate pattern from which it was hard to pick any thread for a single symphonic line. In the end I discarded the idea of a suite in favour of portraits of the individual characters. This, however, was not so simple either, inasmuch as the music of the different characters was scattered throughout the opera. I devised the following method: I took the score apart, picked out everything relating to a given character and spread the sheets out on the floor. Seated on a chair, I studied the pages for a long time until gradually the unrelated episodes began, as it were, to coalesce. This gave me sufficient concentrated material to work with.[13]

Later in this book, we will see evidence of Prokofiev's working this way in the first movement of Sonata No. 8 as well as in the draft of Sonata No. 10 (see respective chapters).

Piano Sonatas Nos. 6 (op. 82), 7 (op. 83), and 8 (op. 84) are universally recognized as Prokofiev's greatest contribution to the piano repertoire. They are often referred to as the "War Sonatas" and described as reflecting the tumult of wartime. World War II was indeed a cataclysmic event that profoundly affected Prokofiev's life. For Russians the war started in June 1941, when German troops invaded the country. (Russian historiography refers to the war fought by the Soviet Army in 1941–45 as the Great Patriotic War.) Before then, very little news of the war in Europe was public knowledge in Russia. The Soviet leadership, which had signed the nonaggression pact with Germany in 1939, played down both the atrocities of the war and the ominous signs of a possible attack. This is why the shock of invasion was so devastating for the Soviet people.

However, with regard to the three piano sonatas, all of their ten movements had been started in 1938, and the Sixth Sonata finished in 1940, before the beginning of the war's Russian phase. Could the nervous atmosphere of the Sixth Sonata's outer movements and their dramatic juxtaposition of the energetic and lyrical have been born out of the uncertainty of the prewar years, reflecting both what was happening in western Europe and the awful purges that were taking place in Russia? (Similarly, Shostakovich's Seventh Symphony ["Leningrad"] is commonly assumed to reflect Hitler's invasion of Russia. In reality, this symphony was conceived and begun long before the war and may have been influenced by the powerful evil forces of domestic origin.)

The war interfered mightily in Prokofiev's life and work. Along with the whole nation, he was deeply affected by both the suddenness of the events and the quick deterioration of the situation. Together with many creative artists, he was relocated to the south of the USSR, away from the approaching front line. Subjected to many deprivations in his living conditions, Prokofiev nevertheless was caught up in a patriotic fever. He wrote music for several war-theme movies, as well as the symphonic suite *Year 1941*, op. 90 (1941). He also worked on some of his most significant compositions, such as the ballet *Cinderella*, op. 87 (1940–44), the opera *War and Peace*, the Fifth Symphony, op. 100 (1944), music for Eisenstein's movie *Ivan the Terrible*, op. 116 (1942–45), and the Piano Sonatas Nos. 7 and 8. Always an eager traveler, he was energized by the sights of the Caucasus and central Asia. His sojourn in Nalchik, the capital of the Kabardino-Balkarskaya Autonomous Republic, gave birth to the Second String Quartet, op. 92 (1941), based on Kabardinian folk tunes.

The wartime coincided with a significant change in Prokofiev's private life: he left his wife and two sons to join a younger woman—Mira Mendelson, who later became his wife. Many of Prokofiev's friends observed a dramatic change in his character and the way he treated other people; they attributed it to the influence of his new partner. "We were astonished," wrote one of them. "What had happened to the carelessly condescending attitude toward others? He was simple and kind with everyone."[14] His music, too, became warmer and simpler, continuing the trend of a few years back. Much of his most memorable lyrical music was written at this time.

The strain of the war years proved to be detrimental to Prokofiev's health. In January 1945 he had his first severe attack of hypertension, which ultimately caused his death eight years later. The illness significantly reduced the speed of Prokofiev's work and caused a noticeable decrease in the energy of some of his compositions. One could cite the Ninth Piano Sonata, op. 103 (1947), as an example of Prokofiev's quieter, simpler writing, lacking the visceral excitement of his earlier works.

In 1948 came another momentous event for Prokofiev, as well as for Soviet music in general. A political attack on the opera *The Great Friendship* by the minor composer Vano Muradeli was quickly expanded to target nearly every Soviet composer of note, including Prokofiev, Shostakovich, Khachaturian, Myaskovsky, and Shebalin.* They were all accused of "formalism," a political libel in the guise of an aesthetic term. Defined as a tendency to exaggerate the formal aspects of a work of art at the expense of its content, it had a particularly ominous ring, since it could be applied to any deviation from the tastes of the ruling elite. Dissonances, complex polyphony, a melody that could not be remembered immediately—all these were characterized as formalist tendencies. "Formalists" were blamed for writing "anti-people" works and deliberately depriving their audiences of simple, tuneful music.

The works of offending composers, including Prokofiev, were immediately forbidden to be performed or broadcast. Prokofiev took these punitive actions to heart, asking his wife, "Can it be that I will never hear any of my compositions again?"[15] Undoubtedly, the events of 1948 contributed to the deterioration of the composer's already fragile health.

In response to attacks like this, repentance was expected. Prokofiev, like

---

*A notable absence was the name of Dmitri Kabalevsky, who, "having discovered in advance that his name was to be included in this list, succeeded in the last minute in having it removed, and substituting that of Gavriil Popov instead." Elizabeth Wilson, *Shostakovich: A Life Remembered* (Princeton, N.J.: Princeton University Press, 1994), 208.

many of his colleagues, did offer the required "self-criticism," promising that his opera in progress, *The Story of a Real Man*, op. 117 (1947–48), would have "clear melodies and a harmonic language which is as simple as possible."[16] This opera was one of the succession of works written in a deliberately impoverished and simplistic style: these included the cantata *Flourish, O Mighty Land*, op. 114 (1947); the young pioneers' cantata *Winter Bonfire*, op. 122 (1949); and the oratorio *On Guard for Peace*, op. 124 (1950). It is remarkable that some of the compositions written at this time, such as the Sonata for Cello and Piano, op. 119 (1949), and the Seventh Symphony, op. 131 (1951–52), although marked by the same self-conscious "simplicity," still show Prokofiev's individuality and genius.

Mira Mendelson-Prokofieva wrote:

In the last months of his life . . . Prokofiev worked on seven compositions at the same time. A few days before the end . . . , Prokofiev asked me to inscribe the titles of these works in the list of his compositions . . . :

Op. 132—Concertino for Violoncello and Orchestra, in three movements;

Op. 133—Concerto No. 6 for Two Pianos and String Orchestra, in three movements;

Op. 134—Sonata for Unaccompanied Cello, in four movements;

Op. 135—Fifth Piano Sonata, new version, in three movements;

Op. 136—Second Symphony, new version, in three movements;

Op. 137—Tenth Sonata for Piano, in E minor;

Op. 138—Eleventh Sonata for Piano.

Only one of these works, the new version of the Fifth Piano Sonata, was completed before he died. Much of the Concertino for Cello and Orchestra . . . was written. The Concerto No. 6 . . . and Sonata for Unaccompanied Cello had only been roughly sketched;* he had just begun the Tenth

---

*According to information kindly provided by Prof. Alexander Ivashkin, the first movement of the Sonata for Unaccompanied Cello has been completed and published by the Russian composer and musicologist Vladimir Blok. Another movement of this composition, the Fugue, was completed by Prokofiev himself. The manuscript of this work, unknown to anyone except its dedicatee, Mstislav Rostropovich, was kept in the cellist's private archive.

Sonata for Piano—he had written one and a half pages. The Eleventh Sonata for Piano was not even started.[17]

It is significant that, interspersed among the new projects, Prokofiev's re-working of two of his earlier works could be found: the Second Symphony, the most complex and recherché of his symphonies, and the Fifth Piano Sonata, the only one of the sonatas representative of the modernist style of his years spent abroad. (The extant fragment of the Tenth Piano Sonata is also based on the Sonatina in E Minor, op. 54, written in Paris.) Prokofiev seemed determined to streamline these earlier works, hoping to fit them into the musical language of his last years. It may not be too much of a stretch to say that the late style of Prokofiev connected with, and responded to, the traditional musical tastes he imbibed during his formative years.

Prokofiev's insistence on including all these titles of unfinished works in his catalogue must have been caused by a superstition, as if this act would somehow assure their completion. It did not come to pass: Prokofiev died on March 5, 1953. His death went almost unnoticed by the public, overwhelmed by the shattering event that occurred the same day: the death of Joseph Stalin.

It is impossible to say whether or not Prokofiev's musical style would have metamorphosed once again in the climate of the cultural thaw that followed Stalin's death. As we have seen, the periodic changes in his musical language often reflected or were prompted by the great historical events to which he was a contemporary. Prokofiev's music remains a testament to his tumultuous times.

Prokofiev the pianist

The piano plays a central role in Prokofiev's oeuvre. Not only are his works for piano solo or piano with orchestra numerous, but they also rank among his more important compositions. The piano was the first instrument Prokofiev heard and the only one he mastered.

Early in his creative life, Prokofiev developed a highly individual way of writing for the piano. Though the differences between the piano textures of his early and late works are palpable, the main qualities of his piano writing are recognizable throughout.

One can easily discern two types of piano texture particularly favored by Prokofiev: motoric, driven (usually fast) passages and meditative, lyrical (mostly slow) ones. His fast music is always rhythmically active; it often employs a uniform motion of running fast notes, frequently in scalar patterns. Usually it is based on well-articulated, active fingers, often playing non legato (Exx. 0.4a, 0.4b, 0.4c). The wrist is frequently employed as well, with textures ranging from non legato single notes to double stops to chords (Exx. 0.5a, 0.5b, 0.5c). The resulting sonority is quite dry and transparent. When Prokofiev aims for a more powerful sound, he usually turns to scales and arpeggios, often spanning a wide range of the keyboard (Exx. 0.6a, 0.6b). Chordal harmonic writing reminiscent of Rachmaninov's can be found mostly in Prokofiev's earlier works (Exx. 0.7a, 0.7b), along with octaves, a mainstay of piano virtuosity in the nineteenth century (Exx. 0.8a, 0.8b).

Ex. 0.4a Scherzo, op. 12, no. 10

Vivace

Ex. 0.4b Concerto No. 4 for Piano (left hand), mvt. 1

Allegro inquieto

Ex. 0.4c Sonata No. 7, mvt. 1

Ex. 0.5a Concerto No. 1

Ex. 0.5b Toccata, op. 11

Ex. 0.5c Concerto No. 5, mvt. 3

Ex. 0.6a Sonata No. 6, mvt. 4

Ex. 0.6b Sonata No. 7, mvt. 2

Ubiquitous, on the other hand, is the kind of chordal writing in which a single voice carries a melodic line or a brief ostinato motive while the other voices either move continuously, often chromatically, or repeat the same pitches. This texture can be found throughout his piano output, from the early *Suggestion diabolique,* op. 4 (Ex. 0.9), to the last movement of Sonata No. 7 (Ex. 0.10). Big, audacious leaps and jumps are characteristic of Prokofiev's music throughout his oeuvre (Exx. 0.11a, 0.11b).

In his slow music the texture can be quite different. The most striking feature is a long, curvy melodic line that often evokes the lyrical pages of Prokofiev's ballets (Ex. 0.12). Equally frequent are pure, naive, lyrical melodies presented in an utterly simple fashion, often with two hands playing

Ex. 0.7a Concerto No. 1

Ex. 0.7b Sarcasms, op. 17, no. 5

Ex. 0.8a Concerto No. 1

Ex. 0.8b Concerto No. 2, mvt. 4

Ex. 0.9 Suggestion diabolique, *op. 4, no. 4*

in unison with a merely rudimentary accompaniment (Exx. 0.13a, 0.13b). Prokofiev's lyrical pages of a more outspoken, openly expressive kind are often suggestive of orchestral sonorities. The writing can encompass a vast range, sending the melody very high and making it difficult for a pianist to produce a singing tone (Ex. 0.14). The texture of these lyrical passages is often polyphonic; the melodic line is frequently passed from one voice to another in different registers of the piano.

Many pages of Prokofiev's oeuvre continue the important tradition of Russian music based on fairy tale–inspired imagery. Prokofiev often employs opposite ends of the piano range or sustains the same type of texture or

Precipitato (♩♩♩)

Ex. 0.10 *Sonata No. 7, mvt. 3*

Ex. 0.11a *Concerto No. 3, mvt. 2*

Ex. 0.11b Sonata No. 6, mvt. 1

Ex. 0.12 Sonata No. 7, mvt. 1

uniform rhythmic patterns for evoking the feeling of a spell or an enchant-
ment, as well as for creating a mysterious, frightening atmosphere (Exx.
0.15a, 0.15b).

   The Russian tradition of suggesting the sonority of church bells in emotionally charged moments is also well represented in Prokofiev's piano mu-

Ex. 0.13a Sonata No. 6, *mvt. 1*

Ex. 0.13b Vision fugitive, *op. 22, no. 10*

sic, especially in each of the "War Sonatas" (Ex. 0.16). This goes hand in hand with the "epic" quality mentioned by Heinrich Neuhaus (see below), a feature of Prokofiev's later style.

Finally, the neoclassical streak of Prokofiev's music is expressed in mock Baroque or Classical textures, such as an allusion to Alberti bass in the finale of Sonata No. 5 (see Ex. 5.2a). Anti-Romantic austerity is sometimes expressed by unaccompanied, or barely accompanied, running passages (Ex.

Ex. 0.14 Sonata No. 6, mvt. 3

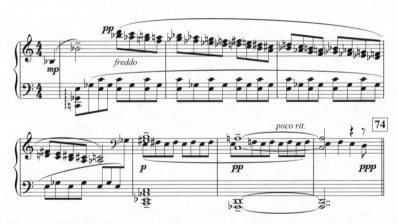

Ex. 0.15a Concerto No. 3, mvt. 2

0.17), or with both hands playing in unison two or three octaves apart (Ex. 0.18).

Prokofiev was universally recognized as an accomplished pianist. This is, in fact, surprising, given the lack of professional guidance during the early years of his studies. Reinhold Glière, his music tutor during the summers of 1902 and 1903, remembered that, as a youngster, Prokofiev "played the pi-

Ex. 0.15b Sonata No. 4, mvt. 2

Ex. 0.16 Sonata No. 7, mvt. 2

Ex. 0.17 Sonata No. 6, mvt. 4

Ex. 0.18 Concerto No. 5, mvt. 5

ano with great ease and confidence, although his technique left much to be desired. He played carelessly and he did not hold his hands properly on the keyboard. His long fingers seemed very clumsy. Sometimes he managed rather difficult passages with . . . facility but at other times he could not play a simple scale or an ordinary arpeggio. . . . Seryozha's chief trouble was the incorrect hand position. Technically his playing was careless and inaccurate, his phrasing was poor and he paid little attention to detail. . . . I must say that he was rather obstinate."[1]

Having entered the St. Petersburg Conservatory in 1905, Prokofiev became a piano student of Alexander Winkler. He later remembered that, at his first lesson, Winkler "said that for some two weeks I would have to play only exercises aimed to strengthen the fingers and to develop the wrist. . . . At last, I have been harnessed: until then I played everything but did it rather carelessly, holding my fingers straight, like sticks. Winkler insisted on my playing accurately, holding my fingers in the rounded shape and putting them down with precision."[2]

In 1909 Prokofiev entered the studio of Anna Esipova, the leading professor of piano at the conservatory. She remained his teacher until 1914, the year of both his graduation and Esipova's death. Their relationship was not easy, as Prokofiev himself testified:

At first we got along very well. Esipova even boasted outside the class that she had pupils who wrote sonatas (I completed Sonata, Op. 1, and played it to Esipova, who took it home and inserted pedaling). But before long trouble began. Esipova's method of teaching was to try to fit everyone into a standard pattern. True, it was a very elaborate pattern, and if the pupil's temperament coincided with her own, the results were admirable. But if the pupil happened to be of an independent cast of mind Esipova would do her best to suppress his individuality instead of helping to develop it. Moreover, I had great difficulty in ridding myself of careless playing, and the Mozart, Schubert and Chopin which she insisted on were somehow not in my line. At that period I was too preoccupied with the search for a new harmonic idiom to understand how anyone could care for the simple harmonies of Mozart.[3]

On her part, Esipova recorded that her student "has assimilated my method only to a limited extent. He is very talented, but rather crude."[4] According to Glière, "Once, in a fit of anger, Esipova declared, 'Either you will place your hands properly on the keyboard or leave my class.'"[5] In spite of these frictions, Prokofiev made a great deal of progress, culminating in his winning the conservatory's piano competition upon his graduation.

While still a student, Prokofiev started to appear as a pianist professionally, primarily as a performer of his own works. Later, during the years he spent outside Russia, piano performances played two critical roles: putting food on his table and popularizing his own music. In the beginning of his stay in the United States, Prokofiev was making his name (and income) primarily as a pianist, much to his distress. He certainly could not have appreciated the caption that appeared in *Musical America* under his photo with Stravinsky: "Composer Stravinsky and pianist Prokofiev." Although occasionally he performed works by other composers (Chopin, Mussorgsky, Rachmaninov, Myaskovsky, Schoenberg, Scriabin, and Tchaikovsky, among others), his repertoire consisted mainly of his own compositions. Prokofiev was well aware of his persuasive powers as a pianist in advocating for his music. According to his first wife, Lina: "Many pianists got interested in his

Fig. 2 Prokofiev's hands. Photograph courtesy of Sergei Prokofiev Family.

music only after they heard the composer's performance—such as Borov-sky, Horowitz, Gieseking, Rubinstein and many others."[6] Yet Prokofiev always knew that his main vocation was composing, and he frequently felt that his concertizing got in the way of it.

Prokofiev stopped performing publicly soon after he returned to the Soviet Union. The performances of the Sixth Sonata in the winter of 1940–41 were the last occasions for him to premiere his works. Mira Mendelson-Prokofieva testified that "in 1942 he told me about his intention to stop appearing in concerts, as the preparation for them took too much of his time. According to [Prokofiev], he learned pieces 'relatively slowly' and 'memorization took more time than technique.' Prokofiev used to say that he is fully satisfied with the excellent performances of his works by our pianists, namely by such wonderful artists as Sviatoslav Richter and Emil Gilels."[7] Heinrich Neuhaus remembered that "when [Prokofiev] had already ceased to give concerts, . . . I told him how much we musicians would have liked him to give a recital of his piano compositions. To which he quite reasonably replied, 'Yes, but that would cost me half a sonata.' There was no answer to that."[8] His last public performance was on April 26, 1943, in Alma-Ata (now Almaty in Kazakhstan) at an evening commemorating the thirteenth year of the death of poet Vladimir Mayakovsky. He played a few short pieces that Mayakovsky had heard him play in 1916 or 1917: the Prelude from op. 12, the Gavotte from the Classical Symphony, and the March from *The Love for Three Oranges*.

There are numerous reviews and descriptions of Prokofiev's performances that help to inform us as to what kind of pianist Prokofiev was. Let us survey them chronologically.

Alexander Glazunov made the following notes while adjudicating one of Prokofiev's piano exams at the St. Petersburg Conservatory: "An original virtuoso of a new kind with original technique, he is trying to produce the effects, which are often beyond the piano's abilities, often at the expense of beauty of the sound. A tiresome affectation, not always sincere."[9] The review in the *St. Petersburg Gazette* on the first performance of the Second Concerto in 1913 mentioned Prokofiev's "sharp, dry touch."[10]

Prokofiev was especially active as a pianist during his years in the United States. The titles of numerous reviews seem to refer as much to his compositions as to his performances: "A titan of a pianist," "Volcanic eruption at the keyboard," "Russian chaos in music," among others. Some of the critiques reveal an astonishingly arrogant lack of musical understanding: "When a dinosaur's daughter was graduating from the conservatory of her time, she had Prokofiev's music in her repertoire." A *New York Times* reviewer wrote regarding his performance of the First Concerto: "The duel between his ten mallet-like fingers and the keys ends with the beautiful sonority being killed. . . . The piano stinks, wails, shouts, fights back and seems to bite the hands which assault it."[11] Prokofiev recalled a review after his New York recital: "Of my playing they said that it had too little gradation, but that I had 'steel fingers, steel wrists, steel biceps and triceps.'"[12]

In 1927 Prokofiev toured the Soviet Union for the first time since leaving the country almost ten years earlier. For many of his old friends and colleagues, this was an opportunity to compare both his music and his playing with what they remembered. His former conservatory classmate Boris Asafiev, who had become a respected musicologist, published two reviews under the pen name "Igor Glebov," in which he noted

high rhythmic tension, virile unwavering energy, technical *brio* and brilliancy of accents. . . . In general, Prokofiev's playing became softer and more rounded . . . because of . . . strikingly touching and emotionally rich phrasing, as well as his outstanding ability to mold and carry on the melodic line. . . .[13]

What is striking in Prokofiev's playing is the outstandingly convincing expression and uncommon rhythmic plasticity. . . . One should especially note a very original use of accents. There is an endless range of them: from hardly audible and scarcely noticeable pushes to pricks and passing-by stresses to temperamental and powerful strokes. The accent in Prokofiev's performance becomes the most valuable shaping element, bringing sharpness, capriciousness, and a special dry spark to his playing. Regular metric stresses disappear behind rhythmically refined and dynamically rich accents. This makes the phrasing especially clear and intensely vital. . . . [Prokofiev's] reserve does not imply dryness or indifference: Prokofiev knows how to control his emotions, but does not shy away from the touching, gentle lyricism. He is not interested in pompous pathos. He found something better: simplicity and naturalness. . . .

Prokofiev plays simply, clearly, and sensibly. Calmly, but without coldness of an over-confident virtuoso, brilliantly, but without showing off his marvelous technique. . . .

Melodic line is an important structural element. It determines the direction and character of the musical motion and gives . . . musical shape to the rhythmically organized texture. Because of this, Prokofiev's playing has a beautiful singing quality, without ever being sweet. Because of this, each piece in his performance has an uncommon finish and completeness. From the beginning till the end, it is perceived as a purposeful unfolding of the material and as a dynamically intensive development of musical ideas.[14]

For the younger generation of Russian musicians, the tour of 1927 was a first opportunity to get to know the new compositions as well as the piano playing of their celebrated compatriot. David Oistrakh remembered Prokofiev's performance in Odessa:

What struck me about Prokofiev's playing was its remarkable simplicity. Not a single superfluous gesture, not a single exaggerated expression of emotion, no striving for effect. The composer seemed to be saying, "I refuse to embellish my music in any way. Here it is. You may take it or leave it." There was a sort of inner purity of purpose behind the whole performance that made an unforgettable impression.

He played his Toccata with great inner force (while outwardly appearing perfectly calm and unmoved). . . . The tempestuous, defiant Prokofiev at [lyrical] moments became as touching as a child. The fact that Prokofiev could be poetic and moving came as a surprise to many.[15]

Sviatoslav Richter, who was twelve during this visit of Prokofiev to Odessa, recalled the same concert: "I remember being struck by his way of playing virtually without any pedal. And his manner was so polished."[16]

Pianist Yakov Milshtein described Prokofiev's concerts in Moscow: "We encountered a pianist who played not only with the incredible will and rhythmic energy, but also with warmth, poetical finesse, and the ability to carry a melodic line flexibly and gently. . . . Those who think, according to an obscure tradition, that Prokofiev played in an angular, dry way, with incessant accents thrown around here and there, are mistaken. No! His playing was poetic, childishly innocent, astonishingly pure and modest."[17]

The famous pianist and pedagogue Heinrich Neuhaus heard Prokofiev's playing before the composer left Russia, as well as after he resettled there. Remembering his impressions of Prokofiev as a pianist, he noted:

Energy, confidence, indomitable will, steel rhythm, powerful tone (sometimes even hard to bear in a small room), a peculiar "epic quality" that scrupulously avoided any suggestion of over-refinement or intimacy (there is none in his music either), yet withal a remarkable ability to convey true lyricism, poetry, sadness, reflection, an extraordinary human warmth, and feeling for nature . . . were . . . the principal traits of his pianism. His technique was truly phenomenal, impeccable. . . .

He played quite differently at home than on the concert stage; it was as though he stepped on to the stage clothed not only physically but emotionally in formal dress. . . . Notwithstanding his outspoken contempt for what is known as "temperamental" performances, he had enough temperament to prevent his playing from sounding dry or emasculated. True, at times he played with such reserve that his performance amounted to a mere exposition; here is my material, he seemed to be saying, understand it and feel it as you please. . . . The ease (the result of confidence!) with which he tackled some of the most breathtaking passages was truly amazing; he did indeed seem to be "playing" in the literal, almost "sporty" sense of the word (no wonder his enemies called him the "football pianist"). The remarkable clarity and preciseness of the entire musical texture was based on supreme mastery of all the necessary technical media. . . .

As for his virtuosity, he displayed astonishing technique in the leaps no matter how big, never missing the right note, and some extraordinary wrist-work and staccato. . . . The faint whisper . . . was rarely heard in his playing.[18]

In his book *Fortepiannoye tvorchestvo i pianizm Prokofieva* (Music for Piano and the Pianism of Prokofiev), Victor Delson sums up the principal qualities of Prokofiev's piano playing:

His sound was material, real . . . without any illusionary airiness or weightlessness . . . sometimes it was dry and, when playing fortissimo, somewhat harsh. His mastery combined dynamic impetuousness and willful power of intellect; youthful freshness, spontaneity and concentrated seriousness. His phrasing was simple, clear and definitely precise, but not mechanical, as claimed by some critics. True, it had not a hint of improvisatory quality (in this regard, Prokofiev's piano playing parted ways with the Romantic performing style), but his agogics were vivid, flexible, sometimes even courageously free. . . .

Prokofiev fully understood the magical power of rhythm. . . .

In lyrical sections, his always strict playing was filled with inner warmth . . . and incomparable *directness* of expression. At the same time, Prokofiev, as if afraid of being excessively open, . . . limited his expressivity, made it appear restrained, neutral, even severe. . . . He never allowed himself to be sentimental and even used to say that he felt "ashamed" noticing it in the playing of other pianists. Sometimes it was as if he simply presented what is written in the score. . . .

He was absolutely enchanting in interpreting the episodes of fairy tales or mysterious legends, so typical for his music. . . . Prokofiev was not so much painting as telling a story with his playing. (Not by chance, *narrante* was one of his favorite remarks.) . . . Prokofiev's virtuosity was very impressive. Leaps, clear staccato touch, scales and double-stop runs, octaves and chords, powerful *fortissimo* and gentle *piano*—everything was "in its place," everything was played to the last note without any sign of fatigue and with inconceivable precision. . . .

Expression of humorous, grotesque, sarcastic characters held an important place in his playing.[19]

One senses a certain contradiction in the reports of Prokofiev's playing being, on the one hand, hard and aggressive and, on the other, shyly understated. It may be that the impression of aggressiveness was born more of the music than of the playing itself. However, Delson is probably right in saying that "a 'lyricist-pianist' coexisted perfectly well with a 'destroyer-pianist,' both were merely different sides of the same multifaceted performer."[20]

To form our own opinions about the qualities of Prokofiev's pianism, we can turn to the recordings of his playing. Prokofiev's earliest recordings were made on piano rolls for the Aeolian Company. In 1919 he signed a contract to produce five recordings a year. Between 1919 and 1924 he recorded the following compositions: Prelude, op. 12, no. 7; March, op. 12, no. 1; Rigaudon, op. 12, no. 3; Scherzo, op. 12, no. 10; *Sarcasms,* op. 17, nos. 1 and 2; Toccata, op. 11; the Scherzo and March from *The Love for Three Oranges,* op. 33 (the March had not been released); and the *Tale of an Old Grandmother,* op. 31, no. 3. He also recorded works by Rachmaninov, Glazunov, Scriabin, Mussorgsky, Myaskovsky, and Rimsky-Korsakov.[21]

Prokofiev's later recordings were done for His Master's Voice (HMV) using much more advanced electrical recording technology. In 1932 he recorded his Third Piano Concerto with the London Symphony Orchestra, with Piero Coppola conducting. In 1935 he continued with a series of solo works: *Visions fugitives,* op. 22 (nos. 9, 3, 17, 18, 11, 10, 16, 6, 5); *Suggestion diabolique,* op. 4, no. 4; *Tales of an Old Grandmother,* op. 31, nos. 2 and 3; Sonatina pastorale, op. 59, no. 3; *Paysage,* op. 59, no. 2; Etude, op. 52, no. 3; the second movement of Sonata No. 4; the Gavotte from the Classical Symphony, op. 25; and another Gavotte, op. 32, no. 3.

Prokofiev seemed to take the HMV project much more seriously than the Aeolian Company's. He carefully planned the program for each face of the record, which could take only about four minutes of music, and he felt apprehensive about the difficulty of the task. "During the four minutes that the disc is being made you can't afford to hit one wrong note," he wrote in a letter to Myaskovsky.[22] Upon the project's completion, he reported, "I did my work with much attention and perseverance and I hope that the results from the standpoint of playing will be satisfactory."[23]

The picture that emerges from Prokofiev's recordings can give us but a limited impression of his playing. The primitive recording techniques involved, particularly that of the rolls, are unable to capture nuances of sound and touch. Even in the areas of rhythm and tempo, which are supposed to be reflected faithfully, these recordings leave us with some questions: Is the noticeable unsteadiness in the Toccata op. 11 correctly reflective of his playing, or is it the result of unsteady traction on the part of the roll? Was the surprisingly fast tempo of the *Andante assai* of the Fourth Sonata caused by Prokofiev's desire to fit it within the time constraints of the 78 rpm record? (It occupied one and a half sides, with the remainder filled by the Gavotte, op. 32, no. 3. In Prokofiev's recording, four minutes were reached in time for a formal caesura before m. 54.) Prokofiev's concern about not hitting wrong notes is, most probably, the reason for the otherwise inexplicable *subito meno mosso* in the passage with difficult jumps in variation 2 of the second movement of Concerto No. 3 (rehearsal number 60).

With all the limitations of an imperfect medium, there are several observations to be made listening to Prokofiev's recordings. His technical accuracy and velocity are very impressive (listen to the Etude, op. 52, no. 3, *Paysage,* op. 59, no. 2, and *Suggestion diabolique,* op. 4, no. 4). We find works played in a conspicuously mechanical way (*Vision fugitive,* op. 22, no. 11) or with an unexpected atmospheric rubato (*Vision fugitive,* op. 22, no. 9). Several recordings display a considerable unevenness (*Sarcasm,* op. 17, no. 1; Toccata op. 11), but this may be a result of the shortcomings of the piano roll technology, as noted above. In dance pieces, his playing can be very free (Rigaudon, op. 12, no. 3), but, generally speaking, his delays in the upbeats or cadences of such pieces are considerably smaller than those to which we have become accustomed (Gavotte from the Classical Symphony, op. 25; the slow waltz *Vision fugitive,* op. 22, no. 18).

Prokofiev's playing of lyrical music is especially noteworthy. His phrasing can be exquisitely beautiful in its dynamic molding (second theme of the *Andante assai* from Sonata No. 4; the middle section of *Vision fugitive,* op. 22, no. 11), and his polyphonic voicing can be clear and expressive (Sonatina pastorale, op. 59, no. 3). He does not use any rubato in these compositions, although there are infrequent examples of rhythmic freedom elsewhere

Ex. 0.19 Vision fugitive, *op. 22, no. 5*

among his recordings. He also appears to be highly sparing in using the pedal. The opening of the second movement of Sonata No. 4 is played without pedal, thus creating a stark, severe character. In *Vision fugitive,* op. 22, no. 5, Prokofiev's performance even disregards his own indication *Pedale al Fine* (pedal until the end), which is intended to create a polytonal sonic haze for the last twelve measures of the work (Ex. 0.19).

A comparison between Prokofiev's performing style and that of present-day interpreters of his music reveals some important differences. While Prokofiev's drive could be quite relentless (*Suggestion diabolique,* Concerto No. 3), today's listener is struck by the absence of aggressive "in-your-face" playing, to which we are accustomed now. The composer played with a sober matter-of-factness, with an understatement that could be described as refined at times, rather than with the crushing impulsiveness of pianists of younger generations. In the lyrical passages, there is no heart-on-the-sleeve expressivity, heavily lubricated by rubato; instead, Prokofiev's playing maintains an objective reserve.

Though Prokofiev stopped performing publicly in 1942, he in no way removed himself from the preparation for premieres of his new works in the later years of his life. Among pianists, he worked most often with Sviatoslav Richter, who premiered his Sonatas Nos. 7 and 9, the Sonata for Flute and Piano, and the Sonata for Cello and Piano, and who was the first pianist, after the composer, to play Sonata No. 6 and Concerto No. 5. Prokofiev also worked with Emil Gilels, who premiered Sonata No. 8, and with Lev Oborin, who premiered both the First and the Second Sonatas for Violin and Piano. The composer also made himself available to other performers who wanted to play his works for him. Reportedly, in all such encounters Prokofiev was brutally frank. Richter described an episode when "a pupil was playing him his Third Concerto, accompanied by his teacher at a second piano, when the composer suddenly got up and grabbed the teacher by the neck shouting: 'Idiot! You don't even know how to play, get out of the room!'"[24]

Of all the pianists with whom Prokofiev worked during the Soviet period of his life, he clearly preferred Richter. One of the testaments to this, described here for the first time, is a note in Prokofiev's handwriting preserved in Richter's archive. It seems to be a draft of a congratulatory cable—the text lacks punctuation marks—that says, "Warm salute to pianist best in Soviet Union and round whole globe the Prokofievs."

The playing of Soviet pianists of the younger generation differed significantly from the composer's performing style, as discussed above. (Here I am referring to the generation of Richter and Gilels or younger, as opposed to Prokofiev's coevals such as Neuhaus and Samuil Feinberg, who also had Prokofiev's works in their repertoires.) Since we know that Prokofiev appreciated their playing, does it mean that he accepted their approach? Should we regard the new generation's playing as a distortion of the composer's intentions or as a natural evolution of interpretive style?

I believe that Prokofiev, having been exposed to the new performing style of the Soviet pianists, accepted at least some of its qualities. We can mention assertive muscular playing, open expressivity, and a gripping commitment to the music among those traits that brought recognition to Soviet pianists and assured their success in the international arena. These characteristics were concordant with the evolving compositional style of Prokofiev, whose later works became both more virile (often heroic) and expressive in a warmer and more open way. Perhaps Prokofiev the pianist had also started to change in the years before he stopped performing? Doubtless Neuhaus's description of a "peculiar 'epic quality' that scrupulously avoided any suggestion of over-refinement or intimacy" suits Prokofiev's late music. The composer's own recorded playing from earlier years gives us enough evidence of such refinement. Moreover, benefiting from their knowledge of the composer's later style, performers may be expected to project it on his earlier works. After all, our approach to the early works of Beethoven or Chopin is constantly being colored by our knowledge of their later compositions.

Prokofiev's music has become an integral part of the piano repertoire. As with other masters of the past, each new generation of pianists is likely to create its own approach to Prokofiev, discovering and emphasizing those facets of his music that are concordant with its tastes. Discussing historically informed performance practice in relation to Prokofiev's music may sound premature now, but the time for such an approach will come. When it does come, the facts presented in this chapter may prove useful in formulating the direction of the new inquiry.

Sonata No. 1 in F Minor, op. 1

Composed in 1906–9, premiered by the composer on March 6, 1910, in Moscow. First published in 1911 by P. Jurgenson. Dedicated to Vassily Morolyov.[1]

The First Sonata is Prokofiev's reworking of the first movement (Allegro) of a three-movement sonata from his student years. Prokofiev describes in his *Autobiography* the summer of 1906, when he was fifteen:

> That summer I decided to write a long piano sonata. I was determined that the music would be more beautiful, the sonata interesting technically, and the content not superficial. I had already sketched out some of the thematic material. In this way I began to work on the F minor *Sonata No. 2*, in three movements, and wrote a good deal of it in a very short time. It proved to be a more mature work than my other compositions of that period, and for several years it towered above them as a solid opus. Later I discarded the second and third movements, then reworked the first and made it into *Sonata No. 1, Opus 1*. But alongside my serious numbered works, this sonata seemed too youthful, somehow. It turned out that, although it was a solid opus when I was fifteen, it could not hold its own among my more mature compositions.[2]

Elsewhere Prokofiev referred to this work somewhat apologetically: "As a rule the publication of his first opus is a landmark for the composer, a sort of dividing line between his early work and his mature compositions. With me it was different: the Sonata No. 1, a naïve and simple little piece, marked the end of my early period; the new began with the Etudes, Op. 2. Both works I performed during my first appearance in Moscow on March 6 . . . , 1910."[3] This was not Prokofiev's only turning to his earlier sonatas, of which there were no fewer than six: "'I don't think you ought to bother numbering your sonatas,' Myaskovsky once said to me with a smile. 'The time will come when you will cross out all the numbers and write "Sonata No. 1."' That is exactly what happened, although some of the material from these early sonatas did go into later sonatas (No. 2 after some changes became No. 1, Op. 1; No. 3 remained No. 3; No. 4 and No. 6 were lost; No. 5 was incorporated in No. 4, Op. 29."[4]

The First Sonata was met sympathetically by Prokofiev's piano professor, Anna Esipova, as vividly described in the composer's diary (entry of November 20, 1909):

Once, leaving her class, I heard her calling:
—Prokofiev!
I turned back.
—When are you going to play your compositions for me?
—Anna Nikolaevna, I did not know that they interest you.
She nodded.
—Besides, I play them like a composer, not like a pianist.
—This is all right, play like a composer.
—In this case, allow me to bring it to you next Friday.
—Please.
I began studying my Sonata . . . in a very thorough way. For the first time in my life I practiced each hand separately. On November thirteenth I took the Sonata . . . to her. . . . Esipova was following with the score.
—This is very interesting music, she said,—but I would like to hear it performed not by you. One can make accents, but it is impossible to play everything fortissimo. Besides, you slam on pedal without any relief. Leave it with me—I will mark the pedal. . . .
Some five days later, Esipova smiled very nicely upon seeing me and said that she had time to mark the pedal only on four pages. . . . But when a week later (today!) I, again, had a lesson at her home and played

Beethoven, she gave me back my Sonata so heavily marked with pedals that I gasped with admiration. She even added that if there were places where the pedaling was not to my liking I should tell her and she would change it.[5]

Curiously, not a single pedal marking can be found in the printed score.

The musical language of the First Sonata is traditionally Romantic. Victor Delson finds similarities between it and the "music of Medtner (and 'through Medtner' with Schumann) and, to some degree, of Rachmaninov and early Scriabin."[6]

Listening Closely

ALLEGRO (DISC I, TRACK I)

Analyzing the thematic material of the sonata, one notices that all of the work's themes are related to each other; they all are based on ascending or descending tetrachords, as shown in Ex. 1.1. This feature brings a sense of unity to the music.

The work begins with a four-bar introduction, which immediately sets the piece's tumultuous tone. This short section plays an important role—its intonations are used later in the sonata. Compare m. 3 (00:05) and m. 14 (00:28) and later, m. 28 (00:56), and m. 4 (00:07) and m. 15 (00:30). In addition, the descending chromatic motion in the bass in m. 1 is recalled at the end of m. 24 (00:48), while the bass line of m. 2 serves as the foundation for that of mm. 5–6 (00:09–00:13).

In m. 5 (00:09), the first theme begins. A narrative melody is supported by the emotionally charged accompaniment in triplets. This texture resembles sections of the Third Sonata. The melody is presented in three paragraphs, each of them starting similarly. The third of these phrases appears in *forte*, exhibiting a more passionate, soaring expressivity. This structure and the general mood of the theme bring to mind the first theme of the opening movement of Schumann's G-Minor Piano Sonata.

In m. 26 (00:53), the bridge theme arrives. Presented in triplets and punctuated by pauses as if catching breaths, its material elaborates upon the emotional content of the first theme. Both its restless mood and the structure are reminiscent of the bridge section in Sonata No. 3 (m. 27, 00:42, Disc 1, Track 6). As the music evolves, the perception of meter changes from $\frac{4}{4}$ to that of $\frac{3}{4}$ in m. 34 (01:05).

The second theme in A-flat major is introduced in m. 42 (01:21). It consists of two bars of a proud and stately character, followed by two parenthet-

Ex. 1.1 Sonata No. 1

Ex. 1.1 *Sonata No. 1*, cont.

ical bars built on the motion of triplets, like much of the preceding music. In m. 58 (01:53), the theme is repeated in a louder dynamic while the "asides" are presented in a more elaborate imitative texture. (These asides are essentially diminutions of the theme's ending.)

The closing section consists of two contrasting parts. The first (m. 74, 02:25) has a long singing line that bears a relation to the first theme. Tonally, it vacillates between the home key of F minor and the parallel key of A-flat major. The second part (m. 82, 02:38) is of a stormy, yet commanding nature and is based on fanfarelike calls. Later, in m. 93 (02:58), the succession of chords brings the exposition to a majestic close in A-flat major. Such chords have appeared previously in the second theme (compare with mm. 54–57, 01:45–01:52, and mm. 70–73, 02:17–02:25).

The development (m. 94, 02:59) is clearly separated from the exposition by a pause. (A clear separation between exposition and development is typical of most of Prokofiev's subsequent sonatas.) Returning to the home key of F minor, it starts in a searching *pianissimo,* in contrast to the intense dynamics of the preceding section. The left-hand part is based on the material from the bridge section, while the right develops the intonations of the second closing subject. A volatile emotion surges unexpectedly, but then subsides quickly. The initial four bars of the development are repeated in the subdominant key of B-flat minor (mm. 100–103, 03:10–03:16).

In m. 104 (03:16), a buildup starts; the perception of meter changes to $\frac{3}{4}$, the way it had happened in m. 34 (01:05). When *forte* is reached in m. 116 (03:36), the development is focused on the initial motives from both the first and second themes. In m. 134 (04:15), the pedal point of C in the bass (the dominant of the home key of F minor) signals the beginning of a retransition. Here the passionate melody initially sounds as a return of the first theme. After the first two bars of the theme are heard, however, they are repeated two more times, each time climbing up sequentially. The section ends with a climactic arpeggiated dominant ninth chord, as if with a rhetorical question mark.

The recapitulation begins in m. 146 (04:49) in an unusual way. The first theme is drastically reduced to six bars, compared to twenty-one in the exposition. It sounds vague and indecisive—in a slower tempo and in *pianis-simo*—and wanders in a descending chromatic sequence away from the home key. As a result, we realize that the recapitulation is under way only when the bridge section reappears in m. 152 (05:05),* albeit in C minor rather than in the expected tonic key, and the main tempo returns. Compared to the exposition, the bridge is more extensive in the recapitulation: the composer visits several keys before bringing in the second theme, which is heard now in D-flat major (m. 174, 05:42).

In m. 194 (06:21), the closing material is recapitulated. It begins in F minor and is presented in a long and passionate melodic line. Starting with m. 202 (06:33), the first part appears exactly as it sounded in the exposition, fluctuating between A-flat major and F minor. The tempo broadens prior to m. 218 (07:00), indicating the arrival of the coda, which is based on the material of the closing section. The expanded first part is followed by a heroic second part in m. 226 (07:38). At this point, the tempo quickens and the music becomes even more agitated.

Toward the end, powerful chords add gravity to the volatile mood. The codetta of the last five bars (07:38) brings back the material of the introduction. It is followed by a reminiscence of the closing section and by the determined, weighty concluding chords.

Master Class

The first two bars need to be played as one statement. The phrasing in each of these measures—and in much of the sonata in general—extends from the second beat to the next downbeat. In m. 4, let the bass line (B-flat–A-flat–G) be heard.

The long melody of the first theme (m. 5) should be played with warmth, paying attention to the descending bass line and to the inner voices. In mm.

---

*One can say that part of the recapitulation's function has been relegated to the retransition section of the development (m. 134, 04:15), or that thematically the retransition and recapitulation are fused together.

19–23, the four-note chromatic motive at the end of each of these bars (in the left hand) must be treated melodically.

In the beginning of the bridge section (m. 26), the pauses in the melodic line bring in a feeling of breathlessness. Do not allow them to break the melody, though, and listen to the bass line as well. Starting with the middle of m. 27, feel a single harmony unfolding in the left hand over one and a half bars. A similar extended harmony occurs in m. 32.

In mm. 34–36, feel the meter as changed to $\frac{3}{4}$. The left-hand part in mm. 38–39 and 40–41 again contains the unfolding of a single harmony, proceeding in two waves from top to bottom. This is the dominant of A-flat major, which ushers in the second theme. All through this passage, the pianist should strive to achieve a singing tone in the melody, carried by the fifth finger of the right hand.

The second theme (m. 42) can be felt either as a warm meditative melody or as a proud majestic statement. The rhythm of consecutive dotted quarters should not sound square; rather, it must soar expressively. Do not allow the accompaniment in the left hand to cut the melodic flow. Two bars into the theme, it is interrupted by a parenthetical "aside," which should be played lightly but melodically and should not be articulated excessively. The chords in mm. 54–57—and later in mm. 69–73—need to carry the melodic line; do not let them sound too separate from one another.

When the theme is repeated *fortissimo* in m. 58, give it a feeling of noble grandeur. The parenthetical bars (mm. 60–61 and 64–65) now contain imitations in the left hand; they need to be heard. Play the first part of the closing section (m. 74) expressively and with a singing tone, but stay in *piano* to create a contrast with the second part in m. 82.

In the beginning of the development, the big swell toward *forte* in m. 96 and later in m. 102 will sound more impressive if you stay in *pianissimo* for as long as marked in the score. The perception of meter in mm. 104–15 changes to $\frac{3}{4}$ again. Pay attention to the chromatically moving bass line: from C (m. 102) to C-sharp (m. 110) to D (m. 116). In m. 119, bring out both the low voice in the right hand (a continuation of the melodic line started in the preceding bar) and the top voice. (The same needs to be done in m. 123.)

In the ensuing four bars (mm. 124–27), fragments from the first and second themes that pass from one hand to the next should each have a distinct character.

Pay attention to the bass line in mm. 128–34, which determines the harmonic progression of the passage. Descending every half bar (G-sharp–F-sharp–F–E-flat), it lingers on C-sharp [D-flat] before establishing a harmonic pedal on C in m. 134. Play the *fff* in mm. 140–45 powerfully but without forcing the sound, and follow the melodic lines in every voice.

The recapitulation of the first theme in m. 146 is hesitant and tentative in character. Listen to the moving inner voices. Starting with the bridge section (m. 152), the rest of the recapitulation moves along the lines of the exposition. A dynamic indication of *piano* for the second theme in m. 174 opens the possibility of giving it a different mood from the exposition, where it is marked *mezzo forte*.

At the end of the recapitulation and through the coda, which starts in m. 218, the excitement mounts. The pianist needs to build emotional intensity gradually, from the *forte* in m. 210, to the *fortissimo* in m. 218, to the *Più mosso* in m. 226, to the imposing stretching of the tempo prior to the return of the introduction material in the *Meno mosso* of m. 240. The three-note motive in mm. 241–42—and its inversion in the left hand—should be played very expressively. Make the concluding chords sound in a gravely determined way.

Sonata No. 2 in D Minor, op. 14

Composed in 1912. First performed by the composer on February 5, 1914, in Moscow. First published in 1913 by P. Jurgenson. Dedicated to Maximilian Schmidthof.[1]

Only a few years separated the Second Sonata from its predecessor. During this short time the young composer further defined his musical language, writing several works, including *Suggestion diabolique,* op. 4, no. 4, Toccata op. 11, and the Piano Concerto No. 1, op. 10, that hold their own with his later, more mature compositions.

Sonata No. 2 gives us a chance to see how the main stylistic traits of Prokofiev's music, outlined in the opening chapter, play out within the context of a sonata. Prokofiev's language in this composition is not particularly novel. Many of his themes sound quite traditional. Both the first and second themes of the first movement begin in a conventional Romantic way. The third movement builds upon the tradition of fairy-tale imagery so important in the music of Prokofiev's older Russian contemporaries—Rimsky-Korsakov, Lyadov, and Medtner. Instead, the novelty is in the way Prokofiev treats his material.

Compared with the conservatively homogeneous music of the First Sonata, the Second astonishes with its huge variety, even incongruity, of styles, presented in a paradoxical, carnival atmosphere. In fact, this work pushes the limits of contrasts more than any other Prokofiev sonata. It covers a huge emotional range: from Romantic lyricism to aggressive brutality, from Schumannesque soaring to a parody of the cabaret or of musical automatons. Musicologist Givi Ordzhonikidze coined the term "polypersonalia" to describe the extraordinary multitude of characters in the Second Sonata.[2] Indeed, polypersonalia lies at the very core of Prokofiev's irreverent treatment of musical material in his early years. In this music one often feels that there are no sustained emotional values to be relied upon. What has been treated with compassion and tenderness becomes an object of mockery a few short bars later. In the aesthetics of early Prokofiev, not much attention is paid to the cornerstone of the Romantic sonata—emotional development of the material. Instead, a variety of textures, superimposition of different themes upon one another, and unexpected dissonances and accents discredit the emotional veracity of the thematic material and prevent our identification with any part of it.

Regarding the circumstances of the writing of this sonata, Prokofiev observes the following: "The piano compositions of this period [1912] include . . . two one-movement sonatinas, one of which was subsequently lost and the other took the form of a sonata Allegro that, in turn, grew into a Sonata in four movements, op. 14 (completed in August 1912)."[3] The sonata is dedicated to Maximilian Schmidthof, Prokofiev's Conservatory friend, who committed suicide in 1913.

Listening Closely

FIRST MOVEMENT: ALLEGRO, MA NON TROPPO
(DISC I, TRACK 2)

The strong contrasts typical of this sonata manifest themselves as early as its opening, when the impatient, Schumannesque first theme is interrupted by harsh dissonances and a recurring chiming motive in the left hand (m. 8, 00:08). The diatonic beginning has been "contaminated" by dissonances to such a degree that the tonal direction is completely lost. The music has to stop and to be started all over again in m. 20 (00:20). This time the harmonic procedure is reversed. The theme is presented together with angular and dissonant counterpoint; the chromaticism diminishes, however, and the harmonic direction is clarified before stopping by a mighty subdominant chord in the bass register (m. 31, 00:31). Against the background of this chord's resonance, the bridge material is introduced in the key of G minor (m. 32, 00:34). This theme is built similarly to the chime motive that precedes it: three adjacent notes (a half tone down and back) and a bigger leap. This writing is reminiscent of late Baroque and Classical textures.

One can interpret the bridge section as a dreamy, fairy tale–like passage. I am more inclined, however, to see it as "puppet music," related to the middle section of the second movement (m. 27, Track 3, 00:34). The melodic material of the latter is built upon an octave followed by a minor second.

In m. 48 (00:44), the pleading intonation of a descending second appears in the middle voice and is repeated several times. It gives birth to a lyrical, somewhat plaintive second theme in m. 64 (00:57) in the Phrygian E minor. Delson believes that this theme derives from the lyrical passages of Rimsky-Korsakov.[4] However, the theme has a waltzlike quality—not a typical Rimsky-Korsakov feature—resulting from the lingering on the first beat of most bars. The Chopinesque arpeggio accompaniment in the left hand introduces another traditional element, hardly typical for Prokofiev; this throws an ironic light on the procedure. The theme is repeated in m. 72 (01:09), with a weaving chromatic line added to it. We feel the approaching cadence in F major at the end of m. 81 (01:26); this would be a "correct" key for the end of an exposition in a D-minor sonata. At the last moment, however, the direction changes, the tempo slows down, and the mood becomes sadder (the composer's remark is *tristemente*—sadly) as we arrive in E minor (m. 85, 01:34), the key a half step lower than the "legitimate" F major.

The closing section is a stern affirmation of the E-minor chord, interspersed with a quick motive, derived from the bridge theme. The limping chords, however, add the comical effect of a waltz that cannot get started.

The development begins in m. 103 (01:59) with the reappearance of the second theme. The accompaniment has changed, and the quality of the theme has changed with it. Now it sounds more like a lied—another association with traditional writing, as if the music longs to be taken seriously. The generally dark mood becomes even sadder in m. 105 (02:02), with the reiteration of a pleading four-note motive related to the bridge theme. The upper voice weaves its line above this motive.

Just when the listener has begun to emotionally identify with the soulful music, the mood changes at once in m. 115 (02:17). The opening gesture of the bridge—which has also been used in the closing section—is heard again. For two bars it sounds light and whimsical (Prokofiev's marking here is *scherzando*), but within just one bar of a sudden intrusion (recalled from m. 7 of the exposition), the mood turns willfully stubborn. Here the familiar motive sounds twice as slow. In m. 121 (02:24), the same motive has a light and visionary character, but again not for longer than two bars. It is then replaced by another augmented version of itself, which sounds insistent, even demanding. All these kaleidoscopic changes make a dizzying impression.

The next section (m. 127, 02:33) moves us into a genuinely troubled dramatic atmosphere. The same material is heard simultaneously on three different levels: the familiar motive forms an ostinato accompaniment, its fast version appears in the treble, and the plaintive intonation of a descending second is heard in the middle register. These all are combined with the chromatically rising melodic line of the upper voice. In m. 143 (02:47), two other important elements are brought in from the exposition: the upper voice presents the second theme in augmentation, while the middle voice intones the descending bell-like motive that was first heard in m. 8 (00:08). These two new additions create a feeling of ever-mounting tension. The melody moves up a tone in m. 159 (03:01); it steps up another tone in m. 175 (03:15), and after that is developed further. A characteristic accompanying rhythm of the chords, which was introduced for the first time in m. 8 (00:08), is brought into the development in m. 159 (03:01).

The ending of the first theme (see m. 27, 00:27) reappears in augmentation in m. 187 (03:27); here it affirms the key of C-sharp minor, a half step down from the home key. Back in the exposition, these decisive chords had been followed by the delicate sonority of the bridge section (m. 32, 00:34). Now the first bar of the bridge material, which had been the basis for the accompaniment through much of the development, appears in the low register (m. 197, 03:37). It changes the character once again and now sounds mysteriously frightening. Simultaneously, the right hand intones the same material in augmentation. As the left-hand motive climbs up in a pensive *ritardando*, everything seems to indicate the approaching cadence in G-sharp minor, a tritone away from the home key. True to the general tone of the work, it proves to be a misleading hint: the recapitulation, which starts in m. 205 (03:47), plunges back into D minor.

The first theme is presented in a truncated form and in a configuration different from that of the exposition: the melody is given to the left hand, while the right hand plays the accompaniment in sixteenth notes instead of triplets. The rest of the recapitulation, however, closely follows the way the themes were presented in the exposition, with appropriate changes in the tonalities. The bridge (m. 223, 04:05) is in A minor, the second theme (m. 255, 04:28) in F major, and the concluding section (m. 276, 05:04) in D minor. The harmonization of the second theme changes subtly, taking on a new color.

The music of the coda (m. 295, 05:30) is based on the first theme. It forges ahead with restless energy, growing in dynamics and covering an ever-increasing tonal range. The leaps, both in the second voice and in the left hand, contribute to a feeling of energetic decisiveness. The movement ends with an explosive succession of chords, with the pianist's hands playing at the extreme ends of the keyboard.

SECOND MOVEMENT: ALLEGRO MARCATO
(DISC I, TRACK 3)

This movement is one of Prokofiev's toccata-like scherzos. Its building blocks are a short ostinato motive and rhythmically uniform non legato chords, with continually moving middle voices. Prokofiev had used this type of writing to great effect in *Suggestion diabolique*, op. 4, no. 4 (Ex. 0.9) and Toccata op. 11 (Ex. 0.5b). The finale of Sonata No. 7 (Ex. 0.10), written much later, is based on the same principle. The technique of crossing hands, with the pianist's left hand jumping over the right, adds a visual component to the visceral excitement of the movement. The unchanged rhythm and short exclamations produced by leaps in the left hand create a feeling of primeval aggression.

The middle section (m. 27, 00:34) brings a great contrast. Delson describes it as a "childishly gracious episode in the sharp rhythm of a polka."[5] He fails to notice the mechanical, puppetlike quality in the regularity of the rhythm and the angularity of the texture. (I have mentioned earlier this episode's similarity to the bridge section of the first movement, m. 32, 00:34.) Let us not forget that Stravinsky's *Petrushka* had been written the previous year; there might be some indirect connection here. The melodic material is intentionally trivial, even silly, though there is something pitiful in the plaintive intonations of mm. 38–39 (00:50) and again in mm. 54–57 (01:13). The shifts in tonalities, from D to D-flat in m. 39 and from D-flat (enharmonically changed to C-sharp) to A in m. 47, are achieved in an intentionally obvious and angular way. A little slowing down of the tempo during each of these shifts enhances the feeling of "puppet music." At the same time, a fleeting reminiscence of the opening of the first movement in m. 46 (01:01) brings the tinge of a sad question.

The initial material returns in m. 58 (01:19) and is repeated in full. This time the theme begins in *piano* and in a low register. Its relentless growth ends abruptly and powerfully.

THIRD MOVEMENT: ANDANTE (DISC I, TRACK 4)

This movement is a *skazka* (Russian for fairy tale), a genre that Prokofiev turned to frequently. Its characteristic traits—monotonous, soothing harmonies; an unhurried unfolding of the melody; a mysterious ostinato; "frozen" sonorities, which descend chromatically; a weaving accompanying line that suggests the patina of a distant time—are all put to effective use here. It is written in the distant key of G-sharp minor. This tonality is a tritone away from the home key of D minor and a half step lower than the A minor of the preceding Scherzo; Prokofiev frequently employs the tonal relationships of the tritone and the minor second.

In my opinion, this movement shows the composer at both his strongest and his weakest. Prokofiev's striking ability to evoke a specific mood within a few initial measures of every new statement is strongly in evidence here. On the other hand, in this movement he refrains from giving the material any kind of thematic development, limiting himself to repeating themes within different textures. The movement consists of two episodes, each repeated with a different accompanying texture and with a slight change in the treatment of the second episode.

The first theme has three layers of sonority: a monotonous harmonic background in the bass; an ostinato in the middle voice with expressive, plaintive intonations; and a narrative, folklike melody in the top voice (starting in m. 5, 00:24). The unfolding storytelling becomes more impassioned in m. 15 (01:28) before calming down in m. 19 (01:51).

The contrasting episode starting in m. 23 (02:15) has an enchanted, haunted aura. There are three planes here, too: the bell tolling in the left hand, which alternates between the low tonic of G-sharp and chords in the tenor register; a weaving chromatic line in the middle voice; and a melody in the top voice that consists of a short motive repeated four times, each time a fourth lower than before. In m. 27 (02:37), another descending wave of the repeated melodic motive is initiated, with the bass moving to the new tonal center of C.*

As the descending line dissolves in the murky low register, the return of the first episode is prepared in m. 31 (03:00). We hear the ostinato again; this time it appears in a slightly altered fashion, with each note repeated twice. In addition, it is also intoned in augmentation in the bass. In m. 35 (03:22), the narrative melody reappears unchanged, while the left hand continues with the weaving line of sixteenths carried over from the previous episode.

The music of the second episode returns essentially unchanged in m. 53 (05:06). With the right hand playing an octave higher than before and the

*Ordzhonikidze interprets the tonality here as the extended modes of G and B presented against harmonic pedals in the bass on G-sharp and B, respectively. See Givi Ordzhonikidze, *Fortepiannye sonaty Prokofieva* [Piano Sonatas by Prokofiev] (Moscow: Muzgiz, 1962), 36.

bass remaining in the same register, the music embraces a broader range of sonorities. The melody descends to the low register, where it ends inconclusively, as if the narrator had gotten lost in his or her thoughts, forgetting to finish the tale.

FOURTH MOVEMENT: VIVACE (DISC I, TRACK 5)

The last movement is particularly striking in its range of contrast, verging on stylistic incongruity. The first theme is tarantella-like—a reference to such standard staples of the virtuoso repertoire as the finale of Saint-Saëns' Concerto No. 2, which Prokofiev would have heard at the conservatory. The movement's second theme sounds as if borrowed from the music hall. In the development, a lyrical theme from the first movement reappears nostalgically but is almost immediately turned into a cancan. Such abrupt contrasts are not typical for Prokofiev; they belong more to the aesthetics of Shostakovich. No wonder that contemporary listeners did not know what to make of this music. Prokofiev remembered that, after his recital in New York in 1918, "in appraising my music the critics wrote a good deal of nonsense; for example, the best of them maintained that the finale of Sonata No. 2 made him think of 'a herd of mammoths charging across an Asiatic plateau.'"[6] Ordzhonikidze rightly notes the carnival character of the movement.[7]

A brief introduction begins with the triplet pattern that later serves as an accompaniment to the first theme. There is a certain similarity between this element and the accompaniment to the opening theme of the first movement. The dynamics surge, and the hands of the pianist cover almost the entire range of the keyboard, leading to a brilliantly cascading arpeggio in m. 9 (00:07). The first theme (m. 18, 00:13) is a lighthearted melody marked *scherzando*. Its melody is interspersed by "asides" in the lower register. The bridge section (m. 34, 00:34) sounds like a light fanfare; it carries on the tarantella spirit.

A rude intrusion by a stomping motive (m. 50, 00:44) prepares the appearance of the second theme in m. 58 (00:50). The theme itself is of a completely different character; mockingly coy, it resembles cabaret music. This association is supported by the trite oompah accompaniment in the left hand. Unexpectedly, it grows into an assertive crescendo starting in m. 66 (00:56). The theme is repeated in a lower register, with textural fillers in the treble heard during the sustained notes in the melody.

The closing section, which starts in m. 97 (01:16), combines the fanfares of the bridge theme in the right hand with the accompaniment to the second theme in the left. It grinds to a halt in a markedly mechanical way (mm. 124–31, 01:34–01:40), clearly separating the exposition from the development.

The latter begins in m. 133 (01:41) with a nostalgic reminiscence of the first movement's second theme. It borrows the accompaniment from the first movement's development (m. 103, 01:59), but in a slower tempo; the overall impression is that of sad tenderness. An upbeat to m. 136 keeps repeating plaintively, reinforcing the feeling of sadness. The mood changes abruptly in m. 145 (02:03), when the intonations of the same theme are presented with a cancanlike accompaniment, as if the composer himself were making fun of the preceding lyrical passage. The pace accelerates and reaches *vivace*, the tempo of the opening, by m. 161 (02:18).

A development of individual themes or their fragments follows. The first theme is presented in an agitated mood, accompanied by nervous, rhythmically jarring chords; the character of this theme then suddenly switches to the familiar *scherzando* in m. 169 (02:24). In m. 177 (02:29), a sustained accompanying figure in the left hand is introduced; it derives from the accompaniment to the second theme. (The latter is based on the chords of C and F-sharp, just like a famous theme in Stravinsky's *Petrushka*.) The material of the first theme blends into the second theme in m. 193 (02:39). In m. 205 (02:47), the music of the bridge section is heard. All these themes mix and mingle in a kaleidoscopic succession.

Starting in m. 178 (02:30), a persistent single sound—C-sharp—intrudes repeatedly, bringing a disturbing note to this carnival-like section. Could it be a distant precursor of the ostinato three-note motive—with the same note of C-sharp at its center—in the finale of the Seventh Sonata?

In m. 209 (02:50), the accompanying triplets to the first theme appear in the home key of D minor, as if trying to usher in the recapitulation. (The left hand plays a non legato pattern deriving from the accompaniment to the second theme.) It is interrupted by a run employing a scale with two augmented seconds. The triplets reappear in a different key (C-sharp minor) in m. 217 (02:55), are interrupted again, and return to D minor in m. 225 (03:00). Throughout this passage, which echoes the brief introduction to the movement, the intruding C-sharps stubbornly persist until the proper recapitulation is reached in m. 238 (03:09). The themes then return in the order they appeared in the exposition; the first theme is heard in m. 242 (03:11), the bridge section in m. 258 (03:21), and the second theme in m. 282 (03:37). The latter now sounds in a minor key, mixing the cancan triviality with a hint of sadness.

In m. 305 (03:53), Prokofiev superimposes the first theme over the second. In m. 321 (04:04), the concluding section is presented in a texture that involves bold leaps, intermingling with the triplets of the first theme. A short coda (m. 337, 04:14) is based on the beginning element of the first theme, accompanied by nervously repeated chords. In a sudden loud outburst, the familiar cascading arpeggio (m. 345, 04:20) and a few decisive chords bring the sonata to a brilliant and charismatic end.

Master Class

FIRST MOVEMENT

While the top voice carries the main theme, both the middle voice and the bass line add tension to the character and must be clearly heard. The triplet motion should be unobtrusive and very steady. Starting in m. 8, play the bell-like notes in the middle voice from above, using the weight of your forearm. The diminuendo toward m. 9 should not cause a loss of clarity. In m. 24, distinguish between non legato in the right hand and staccato in the left hand. The chord in m. 31 should be resonant, like the stroke of a tam-tam.

Play the bridge section (m. 32) with clear and light fingers. In mm. 48, 50, and 54, make a little diminuendo toward the bar that follows each of them. This plaintive second E–D-sharp alternation should continue to be heard in mm. 56–57 and 58–59. In mm. 60–63, listen to the line of accented notes in the right hand (A–B-flat–B-natural–C), as well as to the sequence of quarters in the left hand (C–C-sharp–D–D-sharp.)

Give the second theme (m. 64) a light waltz lilt, but do not let it sound too lighthearted. Make sure that the long melodic line is not broken. In m. 72, the melody in the middle voice should be very expressive, a little gentler than before. (The dynamic is *pianissimo*, after *piano* in the first sentence.) The top voice should weave around it very delicately. After the diminuendo in mm. 79–81, start m. 82 slightly louder and make a second wave of diminuendo.

Return to the main tempo in m. 85. Hold the chords in both hands for their precise length with your fingers, not with the pedal. Observe the dynamics of this closing section scrupulously. Play the rhythm in mm. 96–102 precisely, and make almost no *ritenuto*.

In the beginning of the development (m. 103), do not play the repeated chords in the left hand too distinctly. The expressive phrasing of the four-note motive (starting in m. 105) should be the same every time the motive reappears. The sonority of the line of eighth notes in the top voice should be transparent but expressive.

In the following section, the mood should change abruptly. After the *scherzando* in m. 115, I suggest playing m. 117 decisively; m. 118 seriously; m. 121 lightly and in a visionary way, but with great clarity; m. 123 decisively and with agitation; and m. 124 stubbornly but expressively.

In the next section (m. 127), follow the ascending chromatic line in the top voice; make a slight diminuendo in each pair of descending seconds in the middle voice. The sixteenths in mm. 130 and 138 should sound extremely light and clear. Introduce breathing caesuras in the melody before mm. 135, 143, 159, and 175, as well as in the middle of m. 187. The second theme, which appears in augmentation in the top voice in m. 143, should have an expressive, singing sound; do not "poke" your fifth finger into the keys. To obtain a resonant sonority in the middle voice starting in m. 143, use the weight of the thumb of the right hand. The repeated chords in the middle voice, starting in m. 159, should be light but well articulated. The *fortissimo* in m. 187 should sound deeply resonant. After the *ritardando,* marked in mm. 189–92, come back to the tempo in m. 197 in order to have another wave of *ritardando* later. Follow the ascending chromatic line played by the thumb of the left hand.

In the recapitulation (m. 205), follow each of the three lines in the left hand, while giving preference to the main melody in the upper voice. The accompaniment in the right hand should be clear but not excessively articulated. Follow the melodic line in mm. 213–22 as indicated in Example 2.1.

Most of the earlier comments that pertain to the thematic material in the exposition are also valid for the corresponding part of the recapitulation. Feel the difference in the harmonization of the second theme (m. 255), in contrast to that of the exposition (m. 64). Bring out the left hand in m. 262; it is different from the analogous place in the exposition. Note that the *ritardando* in this measure is indicated later than in the similar place in the exposition. (It is impossible to say whether this change was intentional; it may have been an error or a misprint.)

In the coda (m. 295), mark the bass line slightly. Do not start the

Ex. 2.1 Sonata No. 2, mvt. 1

crescendo earlier than it is written. In mm. 309–11, the leaps in the secondary voice in the right hand should be played expressively, although they should not be confused with the main melody. Play the chords in the penultimate bar with strong fingers, but not too short; for reasons of clarity, play the chords in the left hand slightly shorter than those in the right. Try not to slow down at the end.

SECOND MOVEMENT

The key to the success of this movement lies in rhythmically steady playing. The tempo does not need to be very fast, but the pulsation of the eighth notes should remain unaffected by the difficult jumps in the left hand. The right-hand part must be played with well-articulating, strong fingers; the voice leading within the chords should be clearly followed through. The left-hand jumps need to be played courageously from above, without carefully preparing the note in advance. *Piano* in m. 5 should not bring any change to the quality of the staccato stroke. The last three chords of m. 16 are the only place in this section where you can stretch the tempo somewhat.

Play the middle section (m. 27) very evenly, both rhythmically and dynamically, in order to create the puppetlike character; this mood should be established as early as the transition (mm. 27–30). Here Prokofiev did not indicate a diminuendo, which would imply a gradual softening, but instead gave directions for terraced, angular changes of dynamics: *forte, mezzo piano, piano,* and *pianissimo.* Throughout the section, do not accent the first notes of the upbeats. The unexpected plaintive intonations in mm. 38–39 and 54–57 require a deeper tenuto touch. The *ritenutos* in mm. 39 and 47, which accompany the tonal shifts, should be quite small and executed in a slightly mechanical way.

The return of the initial material in m. 58 is marked *pianissimo,* but it should be played with utmost clarity. This section, like the opening one, must maintain extreme steadiness of tempo (with the possible exception of the last three chords in m. 73, where a small *allargando* is acceptable). No slowing down of the tempo at the end!

THIRD MOVEMENT

Throughout this movement, it is extremely important to bring out the melodic shape of the ostinato voice, which Prokofiev meticulously marked (Ex. 2.2). It remains valid in *forte* no less than in *piano*. The pacing needs to be steady, with the low bass notes resonant and the eighth notes in the left hand not too clearly articulated. The long melodic line starting in m. 5 should be played with a warm sound and must be well phrased.

Play the *forte* passage starting with the upbeat to m. 15 passionately, without any harshness in sound. Four accented eighth notes in the middle voice (upbeats to mm. 15 and 17) need to be played from above. Continue observing the phrasing carefully for the rest of the middle voice line. The left hand, by contrast, should not articulate too much, although the chromaticisms leading from m. 14 into 15, from m. 16 into 17, and in mm. 18 through 22 should be expressively meaningful. Listen through the long notes in the upper voice in mm. 19–20 and 21–22; feel the strangeness of the chromatically descending tritones in the left hand.

In the second episode (m. 23), I suggest feeling the $\frac{7}{8}$ time signature as $\frac{3}{4} + \frac{1}{8}$, with the last eighth note in the bar serving as an upbeat to the next. Put a clear stress on the second beat of each bar. Maintain *pianissimo* throughout the passage to create an impression of frozen stillness. The sixteenths in the

Ex. 2.2 Sonata No. 2, mvt. 3

middle voice should weave around the melody; play them with a light legato touch and without any articulation. The left hand should be gently resonant; use plenty of pedal here. Change the color in m. 27, as the tonal center shifts to C.

With the return of the initial material in m. 30, shape the ostinato line the same way as in the beginning—both in the right hand, where it is presented in repeated notes, and in the bass, where it is heard in augmentation. Play the sixteenths in the left hand (m. 35) without excessive articulation, but listen to every curve of the line, shaping it gently.

Expressive phrasing of the ostinato line should continue in *forte* (m. 44) as well. The loud dynamics in mm. 45–48 should sound dramatic but not harsh.

The return of the second episode in m. 53 is marked **ppp**. Play it in an even more delicate and visionary way than before, with a clear melodic line in the top voice. The dark ending should be played very softly, using a deep touch. The movement should end inconclusively.

FOURTH MOVEMENT

Steadiness of tempo is essential in the performance of this finale. Do not start it in a faster tempo than you can sustain in the technically challenging passages later. The tarantella-like first theme (m. 18) should sound light and crisp. Make the short "asides," shown in parentheses in Example 2.3, sound like a different instrument.

In the bridge section observe the dynamic markings with precision. Both the drop to *piano* in mm. 34, 38, 42, and 46 and the differences between *mezzo forte* (mm. 34 and 42) and *mezzo piano* (mm. 38 and 46) must be clearly audible.

The audaciously rude character in m. 50 requires a completely different sonority. Play the left hand with finger staccato and use strong fingers, while employing larger, "throwing" movements of the forearm in the right hand. Do not use pedal here. The big motion of the right hand should become progressively smaller in the course of the diminuendo in mm. 54–57. The

Ex. 2.3 Sonata No. 2, mvt. 4

crescendo starting in m. 66 should be played in a straightforward, even vulgar, way. It leads to a *forte*, which is delivered the same way as in m. 50.

In mm. 81 and 85, use the pedal to hold the long chords, but depress it
shallowly to preserve the dryness of the accompaniment in the left hand. In
the closing section that begins in m. 97, execute the dynamic differences as
precisely as possible. Between mm. 97 and 113, the left hand plays *piano* all
the time, while the dynamic indications to alternate abruptly between *piano*
and *forte* concern the right hand only.

In the diminuendo starting in m. 117, I suggest phrasing the right hand as
indicated in Example 2.4. The written-out *ritenuto* (mm. 124–32) should be
played with clockwork precision; the rests should be observed exactly, and
no slowing down of the tempo should take place.

Ex. 2.4 Sonata No. 2, mvt. 4

The reminiscence of the second theme from the first movement, which opens the development section in m. 133, is marked *Moderato* here (in contrast with the main tempo of the first movement, *Allegro ma non troppo*). This and the indication *dolcissimo e molto espressivo* require a greater delicacy of expression and a slower tempo than in the opening movement. When in m. 136 (and later, in m. 142) a weaving melodic line is added on top of the plaintive ostinato motive in the main voice, make these two voices sound distinctly different.

The mood and sonority should change drastically in m. 145. The dry staccato in the left hand should not be pedaled. Calculate the *accelerando* of this teasing passage to arrive precisely at the first tempo (*Vivace*) by m. 161. Play the *piano* "remarks" in mm. 151–52 and 159–60 as "asides," not as parts of the general line of *accelerando* and crescendo. Be rhythmically precise in the section starting in m. 161; while the character is constantly changing, the tempo must remain steady in order to create a dizzying carnival atmosphere.

The intruding C-sharp, first appearing in m. 178, should sound exactly the same every time it is played. In mm. 193, 197, and 201, hold the pedal just as long—and just as deep—as necessary in order to connect these long chords with the continuation of the melody, while preserving the clarity of the texture.

In m. 209, make a clear contrast between the legato triplets in the right hand and the non legato eighth notes in the left. Delay the crescendo in mm. 213–14 slightly for it to peak more effectively in m. 215. Play this run with finger legato, using the pedal minimally in order to make the non legato in the left hand clear. (Treat mm. 221–22 the same way.) Make a brief caesura before m. 225, and play the triplets clearly. The left hand is marked staccato here, in contrast with the non legato of the preceding passage. The crescendo in mm. 228–32 should sound like a single growing line. Prolong the lowest octave in m. 232 with the pedal, releasing it halfway through the brilliant descending arpeggio.

The remarks I have made regarding the opening of the movement are pertinent to the beginning of the recapitulation as well. In mm. 305, 309, 312, and 316, use a shallow pedal, just deep enough to hold the long chords, without blurring the rest of the texture. Play the leaps in the passage starting in m. 329 boldly, bringing out the melody in the top voice. The chords in the last five bars should be played from above, without any *ritenuto,* to produce a sound suited to the audacious, brilliant character of this ending.

Sonata No. 3 in A Minor, op. 28
(FROM THE OLD NOTEBOOKS)

Composed in 1917 (first version 1907). First performed by the composer on April 15, 1918, in Petrograd. Published by A. Gutheil in 1918. Dedicated to Boris Verin.[1]

The one-movement Third Sonata is the shortest of Prokofiev's sonatas. It is also the most carefully crafted of all his early works in this genre. Originating in an early sonata of his conservatory years (also no. 3), it must have been seriously reworked to arrive at its final shape. It possesses a remarkable energy that propels the work from beginning to end. The piece's general tone reflects a much more Romantic spirit than other works written by Prokofiev in this period. Sarcastic or ironic imagery, so conspicuous in many of his early compositions, is not part of this sonata's expressive vocabulary.

There is a sense of the young composer striving to prove his ability in composing a "real" sonata with a big Romantic climax (m. 146, 04:47), effective pianistic writing, and detailed motivic development. A closer look reveals that the sonata uses several short motives as its most important building blocks. Two of them (marked *a* and *b* in Ex. 3.1) appear in the first and second themes, respectively. These motives are based upon a mere three-note idea and are closely related: in both, the interval between the first and the last pitches is a third. Another pair of motives (*c* and *d*), which also play an important role in the composition, is shown in Example 3.2. The first is an ascending arpeggio; it is presented in the first theme. The second, introduced in the bridge section, is also built along the sound of a chord, but the direction of the arpeggiation has been reversed. The brevity of these impor-

Ex. 3.1 Sonata No. 3

Ex. 3.2 Sonata No. 3

tant motives allows them to be used in almost every episode; the fact that
they are related to one another creates a sense of compositional unity.

Another unifying aspect of the sonata is its rhythmic organization. Most
of it is built upon the incessant drive of triplets. Against their background,
two rhythmic formulas permeate the composition. One is the dotted rhythm

♩ ♪ ♩ ♪, another is its more placid version ♩ ♩ ♩, introduced first in the second theme.

Prokofiev regularly performed the Third Sonata in his recitals. He frequently opened his programs with it, following the advice of a friend. ("It was Souvchinsky[2] who once recommended me to begin all my concerts with it."[3])

Listening Closely

ALLEGRO TEMPESTOSO (DISC I, TRACK 6)

The sonata begins with an energetic, rhythmic reiteration of an E-major chord, the dominant of the composition's home key. A commanding fanfare statement follows. It is reminiscent of many themes of Scriabin, particularly those in his Third Symphony (*Divine Poem*).* The fanfare is accompanied by rapid chromatic runs in the left hand, another important binding element of the work. They bring in the tempestuous quality indicated in the tempo designation. This statement is so bold and imposing that one is tempted to take it for the main theme. In fact, this is an introduction, whose thematic material anticipates the first theme, which appears later. Compare the beginning of the introduction with m. 20 (00:31) (Ex. 3.3).

The whole introduction is based on the dominant harmony, which resolves to the tonic in m. 16 (00:25); this is where the main theme is fully introduced. It consists of two contrasting parts. The first one is light and lyrical; its upward melodic gesture has a flighty character (another quality typical of Scriabin's compositions). The theme's second half (m. 20, 00:31) is distinguished by its dry sonority and apprehensive yet determined charac-

---

*Prokofiev was fond of the latter work, as is evidenced in his 1910 letter to Vassily Morolyov: "I was very glad that you liked the *Divine Poem*, it is a truly wonderful piece of music. . . . I have been arranging it for two hands this winter and have already completed the whole first movement (and shown it to the author)." S. I. Shlifshtein, ed., *S. S. Prokofiev: Materialy, dokumenty, vospominaniya* [Materials, Documents, Reminiscences] (Moscow: Gosudarstvennoye muzykalnoye izdatelstvo, 1961), 391.

Ex. 3.3 Sonata No. 3

ter. Such abrupt changes in texture and character are recurrent features of the sonata.

The anxious and mysterious mood extends into the bridge section (m. 27, 00:42). It is based on an obsessive circling around the same intervals, interspersed with runs in both hands, the latter moving away from each other. (It is reminiscent of the bridge section in Sonata No. 1 [m. 26, 00:53, Disc 1, Track 1].) The episode gradually transforms from a soft sonority into dramatic octaves in the bass (m. 52, 01:19), which intone a fragment of the first theme.

A slow chromatic scale leads to the second theme (m. 58, 01:32), written in the style of a Russian song. Its simple melody vacillates between A minor and C major. Prokofiev also imitates a characteristic manner of folksinging in which a leader (*zapevala*) starts each phrase and a choir joins in. The chromatic line in the middle voice envelopes the melody, giving it the air of a fairy tale. The theme's second half (starting m. 78, 02:17) is more animated and expressive;* it moves to the high register before calming down in C major at the conclusion of the exposition.

The development starts with a fierce run in both hands (m. 94, 02:54),

*One can regard this latter half of the second theme as a closing theme.

which bears a strong resemblance, whether intentional or not, to the closing passage of "Gnomus" in Mussorgsky's *Pictures at an Exhibition*. It is followed by a compressed version of the beginning's fanfare (motive *c*). This time it sounds as if played by two trumpets in canon (mm. 96–98, 02:57–03:02).

A variant of motive *a* is introduced in m. 101 (03:05) by a stomping, loud bass, while the right hand presents motive *b* two bars later. The bass line moves chromatically in thirds, creating a sinister and threatening mood. In m. 111 (03:22), the music becomes somewhat plaintive; later (in m. 114, 03:28), it turns agitated and passionate. Here the right hand is developing the material of the second half of the second theme, while the left-hand part is based on the *b* motive from the same theme's first half. Incorporating huge leaps and spanning two and a half octaves, this material now assumes a commanding air. In m. 118 (03:35), fragments of the first theme are presented by the right hand with imitations in the left.

The mood abruptly changes in m. 123 (03:46), as a slower tempo is introduced. The second theme is accompanied by continual chromatic movement in the middle voices, which creates a feeling of uncertainty. Five bars later (m. 128, 04:01), the tempo is even slower, the sonority is softer, and the character becomes still more lyrical. It leads to a dreamy, visionary section (m. 132, 04:14), where the right hand intones the conclusion of the second theme while the octaves in the left hand glide through almost the entire span of the keyboard in a pattern deriving from the *b* motive.

The mood promptly changes again in m. 140 (04:31). The same pattern from the *b* motive is turned into a proud, bold declaration, as if played in canon by two trumpets. They climb higher in register, reaching the climax of the development in m. 146 (04:47). Huge waves of arpeggios rise toward the soaring melody in the right hand; the left hand supports it with mighty chords that sound as if played by low brass instruments. The development concludes with a crushing chord built on the dominant of A minor.

The chord is abruptly cut off (m. 154, 05:14) while one note continues to ring. Out of this single note a whirling new motive is born, hesitant at first but continually growing in energy and speed. Out of this motive, the bridge theme gradually takes its shape, and by m. 165 (05:37) it is fully formed. In fact, this theme is the only one that is fully restated in this highly compressed recapitulation. The second theme appears in augmentation in the middle voice in m. 189 (06:12), barely recognizable within the overall motion, while the first theme is omitted entirely.

The coda (m. 205, 06:37) brings both a faster tempo and a change in the prevailing rhythmic pulse: triplets give way to eighth notes. Motive *a* rises relentlessly from the low register to the high treble against the background of a galloping bass. Trumpet calls are heard in the middle voice in m. 213 (06:47). (In fact, Prokofiev's direction here reads *quasi tromba*—like a trumpet.) They continue while the latter part of the second theme triumphantly sounds in m. 217 (06:51). The precipitous motion of the bridge section returns in m. 221 (06:57). A sudden momentary lingering on a C-major chord in *pianissimo* (mm. 225–26, 07:02–07:05), surprisingly euphonious within this stormy and dissonant section, briefly interrupts the predominant energetic thrust. Decisive steps of the *b* motive (m. 229, 07:08) are followed by laconic repeated chords. The sonata concludes with great gusto in a slightly matter-of-fact way.

Master Class

To achieve a clean, powerful, brassy sound in the opening bars, I suggest using much pedal but changing it on every quarter beat. Take care that the pedal does not catch the initial grace notes. Make the top notes of the chords sound slightly more prominent than the rest of the texture. The opening statement (m. 3) must be played with a ringing, unforced tone, imitating the sound of a trumpet. Use a bigger forearm motion in an "out of the piano" stroke,* but avoid breaking the melodic line. Expressive playing of the chromatic passages in the left hand will enhance the drama of the introduction.

In the first theme (m. 16), let the initial musical gesture be weightless, as

---

*I discuss this kind of sound production in my book *Notes from the Pianist's Bench* (New Haven, Conn.: Yale University Press, 2000), 5–9.

if flying up. The harmonic accompaniment in the left hand should not be excessively articulated. Allow the chromatic line in the middle voice to be heard.

Start the bridge section (m. 27) mysteriously but with clarity, using almost no pedal. In contrast, the run that follows should be played legato, with a slightly blurred touch. The indications of *pianissimo* in mm. 30 and 32, as well as *piano* in mm. 39 and 41, suggest that Prokofiev expected a slight crescendo in each of the legato passages that precede them. Make these crescendos hardly noticeable the first two times, to leave room for growth. In mm. 34–35, use the pedal to connect the sounds in the left hand, which share the same harmony. In these two measures (and later in mm. 44–45), I suggest introducing a tiny caesura after each half bar. As you reach *forte* in m. 44, take care not to sound harsh. Here use the pedal every time the left hand moves along the chordal sounds, but release it for the chromatic fragments; the latter should be expressively enunciated. Make the swells in mm. 49–52 sound like gusts of wind. The octave passage in mm. 52–53 should be sonorous and imposing; take care that the melodic phrase comes across clearly.

The new tempo in m. 54 should not be too slow, and the following chromatic scale should not be articulated too clearly. In the second theme (m. 58), make every attempt to differentiate the sonority of the two voices in the right hand—a difficult task. Eighth notes in the left hand provide a slightly blurred background, while the bass gently indicates cadences, alternating between A minor and C major. The same challenge of differentiating between two voices—this time in the left hand—presents itself in m. 66. Observe the dynamic marking of *pianissimo* here, and make the character mysteriously evocative. The theme is repeated in m. 70 in a more outspoken way; the left hand now provides a richer harmonic accompaniment. Make the phrase that begins in m. 74 sound like woodwind instruments.

The melody becomes more animated in m. 78, helped by gentle syncopations in the left hand; do not let them sound too heavy or jazzy. Starting m. 82, when the melody climbs higher into the treble register, strive to produce a warm, singing tone. The accompaniment in the left hand should rock gently. In m. 86, listen both to the melody in the top voice and to the line of the tenor voice as they move in contrary motion.

Play the beginning of the development section (m. 94) with strong fingers non legato, and use no pedal. In m. 96, change the sound completely: make it very resonant and rich. Use an "out of the piano" stroke here, as in the fanfare theme at the beginning of the sonata. Make the passage sound like a dialogue between two trumpets.

In mm. 103–10, play the chromatic thirds in the left hand non legato. The ascending and descending wave of sixteenths in m. 105 should sound as one gesture, without being broken by changes in positions. In mm. 107–8, use half-pedaling to sustain the half notes in the right hand, but do not allow the low basses to become muddy.

Fast notes at the end of mm. 111, 112, and 113 should sound expressive, like a glissando of violins. The slurs in the left hand in mm. 112–13 need to be played expressively as well. In m. 114, play the melody with warmth; do not excessively articulate the sixteenths in the accompaniment. The bold statement in the left hand in mm. 115 and 117 should sound as an unbroken phrase, in spite of the big leaps. Take care that the soaring melody in octaves of the right hand (mm. 118–21) sounds uninterrupted by the imitations in the left.

Do not play the new section, beginning in m. 123, too slowly or too softly; leave room for the *dolcissimo* and further slowing down in m. 128, marked *Più lento*. Listen to the ever-changing harmonies. In the dreamy passage in m. 132, make the top voice clear, but the overall sonority should be very light; the left hand, especially, should sound as if it is gliding along the surface of the keys.

In m. 140, the imaginary trumpets have another dialogue. Play it boldly but without harshness, using the "out of the piano" stroke. The syncopated chords of the accompaniment should not be heavy. You may wish to make the climactic passage (starting in m. 146) a little easier by taking the first three notes of each group of grace notes with the left hand. The repeated notes in the right hand should not be heavy or percussive; their function is to create the illusion of a long-lasting sound in the soaring melody. The chords in the left hand should be resonant but not heavy. The low octaves in the bass should provide powerful support to the whole texture; sustain them with the pedal for as long as the texture does not become too muddy.

In the last chord of m. 153, bring out the highest note so that it can be clearly heard through the next bar. Start the transitional passage that follows with a blurred touch, gradually making it clearer as the tempo accelerates. By the time you reach *Allegro I* (m. 161), you need to recapture both the speed and the character of the bridge section in the exposition. In mm. 181–87, feel the harmonic content of the arpeggios in the left hand, while the fanfares at the ends of mm. 182, 184, and 186 should cut through the texture.

In the difficult passage starting with m. 189, try to preserve the difference between the triplets and the dotted rhythm. Bring out the second theme in the top voice of the left hand, but maintain the overall *pianissimo*. In m. 197, follow the ascending line in the treble voice while playing the descending scalar passages in the left hand expressively (consider making a slight diminuendo in each of them).

In the coda (m. 205), play the left hand with finger staccato, using no pedal. Make the chromatic line produced by the thumb of the left hand noticeable. In m. 212, the eighth notes in the right hand should sound lighter than the half notes. The sudden *pianissimo* in m. 213 should be played with light but well-articulated staccato. Play the trumpet calls, marked *quasi tromba,* by taking advantage of the free weight of the thumb. The melody in the fifth finger of the right hand in m. 217 should sing, and the left-hand accompaniment should be played expressively as well. In mm. 222 and 223, the second chord in each bar should not sound stronger than the first. The sudden C-major passage marked *pianissimo* in mm. 225–26 should be played very clearly with light fingers, while holding the pedal throughout. Play the last appearance of the *b* motive in mm. 229–30 with a free, trumpetlike sound.

Many pianists would be tempted to make a *ritenuto* in order to achieve an impressive ending to the sonata. In my opinion, this would ruin the energetic character of the ending; only a tiny slowing down is advisable. Strive to create a sense of conclusion by producing a full and unforced sound.

Sonata No. 4 in C Minor, op. 29
(FROM THE OLD NOTEBOOKS)

Composed in 1917 (first version 1908). First performed by the composer on April 17, 1918, in Petrograd. Published by A. Gutheil in 1918. Dedicated to Maximilian Schmidthof.[1]

This work concludes the series of sonatas written before Prokofiev left Russia. Like Sonata No. 2, the Fourth is dedicated to Prokofiev's close friend, Maximilian Schmidthof, who committed suicide in 1913. It was composed in 1917, although the material derives from Prokofiev's student years at the St. Petersburg Conservatory. In April 1917 Prokofiev made the following entry in his diary: "I was busy reworking a string suite into the Sonata No. 4. . . . I was looking for a new Andante for it: I used to have such an Andante among my works for the musical forms class, but could not find the lost manuscript. . . . I rejoiced when I remembered about the Andante from the E-Minor Symphony, which would work excellently on the piano as well; as for the Symphony, I doubt I would ever pull it out from under the dust which has covered it."[2] (In 1934 Prokofiev brought the Andante back to its symphonic origins by creating a version of it for a large orchestra.) In his autobiography, Prokofiev indicated a different, or additional, provenance for the sonata: the Conservatory-era Sonata No. 5.[3]

The character of the first movement is unique, the result of a curious combination of two radically different traits. On one hand, certain features make it sound neo-Baroque, in the vein of Prokofiev's stylization of Baroque dances, such as the Gavotte, Allemande, or Rigaudon in his op. 12. Among such features are strong rhythmic emphases, alluding to the bowing gestures in a minuet; short enunciated motives underlined by articulation

Ex. 4.1a Nikolai Medtner, Sonata–Fairy Tale, op. 25, no. 1, mvt. 1

Ex. 4.1b Sonata No. 4, mvt. 1

slurs; and occasional unexpectedly euphonious harmonies coupled with clear-cut cadences. One should also mention an extensive use of hemiolas favored by Baroque composers.* The neo-Baroque quality of the first movement is echoed by the neoclassic elements of the finale.

On the other hand, the movement's melodic and harmonic language, as well as its evocative usage of the piano's registers, connects the first movement with the Russian tradition of musical fairy tales, especially with the dark, spooky variety. Here the influence of Nikolai Medtner's piano works is particularly noticeable, including some striking similarities (compare mm. 21–23 of this movement [Ex. 4.1b] with the opening of Medtner's Sonata-Skazka [Sonata–Fairy Tale], op. 25, no. 1, composed in 1910–11 [Ex. 4.1a]). The mysterious fairy-tale traits of the opening movement, unusually earnest and concentrated for Prokofiev's early compositions, are carried over into the second movement.

*Another composer who used hemiolas extensively was Brahms. For this reason, certain passages in the Fourth Sonata's first movement (e.g., m. 107 in the development section) sound unexpectedly Brahmsian.

Listening Closely

FIRST MOVEMENT: ALLEGRO MOLTO SOSTENUTO
(DISC 1, TRACK 7)

The first theme, presented in a dark, low register, has a mysterious, lugubrious character. Its simple harmonies based on major or minor triads produce a peculiarly archaic effect, as do the ceremonial "bows" on emphasized chords. Many short motives are arranged as hemiolas, whose rhythmic ambiguity intensifies the feeling of uncertainty.

The more continuous melody of the bridge section (m. 17, 00:34) sounds somewhat disturbed and plaintive. The *sforzando* exclamations that punctuate the melody add dramatic tension. The structure of this theme is 4 + 2 bars. The group of four sixteenths (mm. 21 and 22, 00:41 and 00:44) recalls the opening figure of the movement.

In the second theme (m. 40, 01:15), the contrasting characters of the two preceding themes are melded. The darkly mysterious mood of the first theme is carried on by the slowly crawling low bass line, which is marked *il basso pesante* (the heavy bass). The melody in the right hand has a narrative character; its expressive octave leaps mirror the ascending exclamations of the preceding bridge section. The second theme takes shape gradually: first a long D-sharp appears, preceded by two grace notes (m. 37, 01:08); in the following bar the D-sharp changes to a D; in the succeeding bar the D, now an octave higher, is preceded by three grace notes. In the next bar a descending octave is added to this nucleus. The motive is repeated, followed by an additional bar that, in turn, develops into a four-bar phrase. Victor Delson hears in this restrained theme the influence of the stark landscape of northern Russia.[4]

The restatement of the second theme (m. 47, 01:27) is made more eloquent by extensions in the melodic line. In contrast, the closing theme of the exposition (m. 61, 01:53) is laconic, almost severe; the syncopated rhythm of the chords is decisive, and the melodic line climbs up stubbornly. The section ends abruptly with a matter-of-fact, unambiguous cadence in the parallel tonality of E-flat major, marking the end of the exposition.

The development section is built on a combination of various themes and elements from the exposition. A brief reminiscence of the first theme (m. 71, 02:10) is followed by music based on the closing material. As in the exposition, the section ends with a clear cadence, this time in C major (m. 78, 02:21). Here, however, the C-major tonic harmonies in the right hand are superimposed on the dominant fifth in the bass, which is intoned enigmatically in timpani-like strokes.

In m. 89 (02:41), the first theme in the left-hand part is juxtaposed against the second theme, played by the right hand. In m. 101 (03:03), the opening motive of the bridge theme is added. In m. 107 (03:13), both hands join in developing the first theme, adding to it a motive from the bridge section. The phrasing in the right hand creates hemiolas against the $\frac{3}{4}$ meter in the left hand. The reiteration of a short motive in the right hand in mm. 114–16 (03:25–03:30), played concurrently with its inversion in the left (Ex. 4.2a), creates the feeling of a rhetorical question.

A sudden drop in the dynamics in m. 117 (03:31) signals the beginning of a retransition and a new, final ascent toward the climax of the development section. Throughout the retransition (mm. 117–32, 03:31–04:01), the harmonic dominant pedal point is either reiterated or implied. The right hand

Ex. 4.2 Sonata No. 4, mvt. 1

plays the first three bars of the second theme, while the left hand plays the initial phrase of the first theme. After three bars, the hands exchange their material; they do so again after the next three bars. The ensuing passage (mm. 126–32, 03:48–04:01) develops the material of the bridge section. At the end, a variant of the previously heard rhetorical question is repeated with greater urgency (Ex. 4.2b). Having reached a peak in m. 132, the music is abruptly interrupted; the following four bars return to the mysterious character of the opening, its *pianissimo* sonority, and its dark low register.

The recapitulation, beginning in m. 137 (04:10), closely follows the general outline of the exposition. Both the first theme and the bridge are truncated. A colorful harmonic shift in m. 159 (04:52) precedes the second theme, which appears in m. 162 (05:00) without the gradual evolution that we witnessed in the exposition. The closing theme (m. 183, 05:39) is expanded; it consists of three four-bar phrases, not two. A long crescendo, together with the intensified chromatic climb to a higher register, amplifies its assertive character. The movement concludes severely, with stark repeated chords.

SECOND MOVEMENT: ANDANTE ASSAI (DISC I, TRACK 8)

This movement must have been Prokofiev's favorite. In addition to orchestrating it, he included it in the group of works he recorded for HMV in 1935. It is built on a dramatic conflict between the somber, chromatic first theme and the lyrical, diatonic second theme, which uses only the white keys of the piano. (Prokofiev wrote these kinds of melodies throughout his life; one can recall the opening of the Third Piano Concerto or the first theme of the Ninth Sonata.) The structure of the movement is a complex one. It combines aspects of variations with a ternary (ABA) form and the sonata form without a development.

A gloomy, severe mood is set by the repeated thirds in the low register that accompany the main theme. This melody consists of an ascending chromatic scale, followed by an ascending minor triad and a concluding descending chromatic line. It lends itself well to polyphonic treatment, which

Prokofiev uses extensively. In m. 5 (00:22), before the melody is completed, it is imitated in a new voice. Another imitation in m. 8 (00:38) increases the feeling of a pent-up tension. This phrase is interrupted by an explosion in m. 10 (00:48), repeated later in m. 12 (01:00).

The presentation of the first theme is followed by two variations. In the first (m. 13, 01:07), the melody is enveloped by a weaving line of sixteenth notes in the middle register. New voices take over the theme. While the texture of the accompanying sixteenths is idiomatically pianistic, the orchestral colors of the imitations of the theme are clearly felt. The explosions of mm. 10 and 12 are repeated in a more elaborated form in mm. 22–23 (01:45–01:55).

In the second variation (m. 25, 02:03), the tonality shifts to G-sharp minor, a half step from the original A minor, and the melody is heard simultaneously with its inversion. The voices move toward each other and, having reached a common tone in m. 29 (02:11), continue moving, now away from each other.

Measure 33 introduces new material, anguished and tormented. Strong exclamations punctuate the melody, which covers an astonishingly wide range; the chords in the left hand are repeated mercilessly. Tonally, this passage is very unstable. Suddenly, in m. 36 (02:47) a great change occurs. The loud sonority is replaced by a calm *pianissimo* and a gentle pendulum of soothing chords and rocking accompaniment. In m. 39 (03:05), a beautiful Russian-style melody is heard. It is reminiscent of the second theme of the Third Sonata in its simplicity and lyrical, fairy-tale character. Both are also "white-keys" themes; the tonalities of both are ambiguous, vacillating between C major and A minor.

The lyrical melody fades away almost hypnotically, the shifting harmonies settling on the C-major chord at the end of m. 53 (04:36). In the following bar, the first theme reappears in G-sharp minor (the key of the second variation) and in a similar texture, albeit with a faster tempo and in a light *pianissimo*. Here, too, the theme is heard concurrently with its inversion, enveloped by arpeggios in both hands. Its initial intense darkness gives way to a dreamy, visionary mood.

In m. 62 (05:08), the transitional dramatic material is heard again, even more tormented than before, with an angular melodic line and jarringly stumbling repeated chords. (Actually, the precursors of these nervous chords were the repeated notes in m. 24, 01:54.) The tension is brought to a peak before being interrupted by an abrupt dissonant chord.

The ensuing section (m. 71, 05:36) (see Ex. 0.15b) combines the two principal themes in a masterful way. Once again the mood changes dramatically: a monotonously repeating accompaniment in both the bass and treble registers creates a magical, spellbound feeling. In m. 77 (06:06), the second theme is strangely chromaticized, bringing a disturbing note to this enchanted picture.

The coda, starting in m. 81 (06:27), restores the initial key of A minor, as well as the bleak and stark atmosphere of the beginning. The repeated chords become progressively sparse. Three bars before the end (06:53), the pitch of C-sharp hints at the possibility of A major. The somber minor key returns, however, and the music fades away in the distance.

THIRD MOVEMENT: ALLEGRO CON BRIO,
MA NON LEGGIERO (DISC I, TRACK 9)

This movement is a brilliant tongue-in-cheek imitation of the Classical style similar to that of the Classical Symphony, op. 25. Prokofiev wrote the symphony at the same time as the Fourth Sonata and conducted its premiere in St. Petersburg just four days after the sonata's premiere. If in the symphony Prokofiev is concerned with imitating the orchestral style of the Viennese composers of the eighteenth century, here he is mimicking the conventions of the Classical piano style. Thus, the Alberti bass accompaniment typical of Mozart's piano textures is recalled in the left-hand accompaniment of the opening theme. Delicate and transparent in Mozart, it is much thicker and more audacious in Prokofiev's rendering, peppered with leaps and dissonances. The form of this movement is sonata-rondo, one much favored by the composers of the Classical era.

After his first performance of the sonata in St. Petersburg in April 1918,

Prokofiev remarked in the diary, "Until now, I have been afraid that my finale had a chopped-off tail. Now it is clear to me that it is good, that the last buildup, if it is played properly, fully reveals the climax [the last appearance of the first theme] that concludes the Sonata and after which the end should come immediately."[5]

The movement begins with a brilliant run across almost three octaves, certainly not a feature of the Classical period. The first theme is in "almost pure" C major, with the occasional "wrong" notes revealing its twentieth-century provenance. By contrast, the bridge section (m. 25, 00:25) contains many chromaticisms that create a somewhat apprehensive mood. The second theme (m. 43, 00:42) is also chromatic and possesses a mysteriously disturbing character. The melody alternates between uncertainly stuttering initial measures and bold exclamations that follow them. In m. 67 (01:08), the first theme reappears, represented by its concluding part; the latter is repeated in m. 75 (01:15) in a more embellished and brilliant manner.

The contrasting middle section (m. 84, 01:25) introduces a lyrical theme of a completely different nature, with a texture highly suggestive of orchestral sonorities. This is a precursor to Prokofiev's lyrical ballet music, such as found in *The Prodigal Son* or *Romeo and Juliet*. The recapitulation begins in m. 134 (02:17) with the reappearance of the first theme, represented by its concluding part. First it is heard in *pianissimo,* as if from far away, with a light, intricate ornamentation. This strain is then repeated more loudly, within a more brilliant virtuoso setting.

The return of the bridge section (m. 153, 02:36) carries the same apprehensive tension as it did in the exposition. It is interrupted by a brief reminiscence of the melody from the movement's middle section (m. 162, 02:44). This theme sounds simultaneously in the original form and in its mirrored inversion. The bridge music resumes and leads to the second theme (m. 178, 03:00), which is presented in fiercely brilliant *fortissimo.* The sonority drops to *piano* in m. 194 (03:17), before a preparation for the last appearance of the main theme begins. First we hear no less than four "false starts" of the initial scalar run (beginning in m. 201, 03:25), each one climbing higher than its predecessor. The final run, the longest of them all (m.

207, 03:32), brings in the first theme in its most audacious form, with hands playing at opposite ends of the keyboard. The ebullient energy continues un-abated—the left hand jumps fearlessly above the right, and the sonata ends triumphantly, with outrageous dissonances spicing up the conventional final cadence.

Master Class

FIRST MOVEMENT

It is not easy to capture the character of this movement. Its minuet aspect presupposes a certain ceremonial formality. To convey this feeling, I suggest gently marking the cadences in the upbeats to mm. 4, 7, 12, and 17. How-ever, this should not make the music sound dry or rigid; it has to coexist with the fairy-tale narrative atmosphere. To bring out the minuet character, the short articulation slurs should be clearly separated, without breaking the continuity of the melodic line. Gently voice the chords so as to highlight the fifths in the left hand; this will help to create a somber sonority. In con-trast, starting with m. 7, bring out more of the melody in the right hand.

The grace notes starting in m. 17 should sound melodic. Beginning with m. 29, pay attention to the difference in the slurs between the right and the left hands. Treat mm. 32–37 as a long, sweeping musical gesture. In the sec-ond theme (m. 40), make sure that the bass line sounds legato. The octave "dives" in the right hand should sound expressive in a vocal way. Unlike the phrases in the first theme, those in the second are long. Play the imitations in mm. 50, 52, and 54 expressively, but do not allow them to detract from the melody in the right hand. Let the canon between the soprano and the tenor voices in mm. 55–58 be heard. In the closing section (m. 61), observe the ar-ticulation markings. Follow the top line, while giving an energetic character to the leaps in the bass.

The development section is full of mood changes, stemming from the quick succession (or simultaneous appearance) of different thematic frag-ments from the exposition as well as register changes. The pianist must ac-knowledge them fully. Play mm. 71–73 using full, dark sound. The subsequent phrase should have a lighter, *dolente* character. In the material of the decisive closing section that follows, clearly articulate the sixteenths in the left hand. The group of grace notes in m. 78 should sound like the glissando of a brass instrument; the following chords in the right hand should sound like the pizzicato of strings (play them with finger staccato), while the left hand resembles timpani. Pedal through the grace notes in m. 78, then use no pedal until m. 81.

The octaves in m. 88 should be played non legato (but not staccato) and *pesante*. In the section beginning in m. 89, give each hand its own expression and articulation. Do not begin this section too loudly: it is marked *forte,* as opposed to *fortissimo* later on. The elements of the bridge theme appearing in m. 101 (and later, in m. 105 and m. 109) should be brought out in an emphatically expressive way. Toward the end of the section in m. 116, the phrases become shorter and the mood more dramatic. In mm. 114–16, the melodic phrases in both hands are inversions of each other; play them equally expressively (the same applies to mm. 129–32).

A sudden drop in dynamics in m. 117 starts a new buildup. It is more compressed and covers a large dynamic range, from *piano* to *fortissimo,* in ten bars. The phrases are shorter: three-bar phrases beginning in mm. 117, 120, and 123, compared to four-bar phrases in mm. 99, 103, and 106. In m. 126, juxtapose the expressive two-note motives stemming from the bridge theme against the insistent, chromatically ascending motion in the left hand. After a rhetorical interruption in m. 132, the bass voice intones the same motive that we have just heard in mm. 131–32, albeit slightly altered; make these four bars (132–36) meaningful in a darkly mysterious way.

The recapitulation in this movement closely follows the structure of the exposition, but the themes are shortened. Lev Oborin recommended playing it "gentler, calmer, more peaceful than the exposition."[6] The first theme begins exactly as in the exposition except for a $\frac{4}{4}$ bar (m. 148) replacing the *ritardando* of m. 11. In the bridge section, some editions substitute accents for *sforzandos* (which are present in the exposition) in mm. 151–52. The chromaticisms in the tenor voice that envelop the melody should not be too clearly articulated. Play the F-sharp-minor chords in mm. 159–60 *pianis-*

simo subito, giving them a special new color. For clarity, it may be useful to separate this harmony slightly from the preceding music, especially in a resonant hall.

The second theme (m. 162) is marked here **ppp**, as opposed to **pp** in the exposition. Oborin recommended playing it as tenderly as possible.[7] As in the exposition, play the bass line *molto legato.* The imitations in the left hand in mm. 172, 174, and 176, as well as the canon between the soprano and the tenor starting in m. 177, must be clearly heard.

In the extended closing theme (m. 183), listen to the ascending top line. Observe the articulation markings and do not let your tone get harsh in crescendo. The severe chords of the last two bars should be played with the utmost authority and without any *ritenuto.*

SECOND MOVEMENT

The dark, narrative character of this movement should have a stark, austere hue. Much depends on the sonority of the opening bars, where most pianists pedal through the repeated thirds of the accompaniment. Listen to Prokofiev's own recording, however, and you will notice that in his performance these thirds are detached. Similarly, in the orchestral version of the movement, they sound separate. The orchestration of this accompaniment calls for a bassoon, a contrabassoon, a bass drum, and pizzicato double basses (see Fig. 3). In my view, pedaling through the opening makes the sonority too lush and contradicts the movement's general mood; I use a short and shallow pedal, just enough to make this accompaniment richer in overtones, but maintaining the separation of each third from each other.

In his recording, Prokofiev plays this movement at an unexpectedly fast tempo ($\flat$ = 114). The reason for this may have been the desire to fit an uninterrupted passage onto the four-minute side of a 78 rpm record. (In this recording, the four minutes are reached by the end of m. 53, which concludes with a long fermata chord. The break at this juncture is justified.)

The main theme requires carefully shaped dynamic phrasing, as shown in Example 4.3. Throughout the movement, the imitations and simultane-

Fig. 3 First page of the Andante from Sonata No. 4, op. 29bis, orchestrated by the composer.

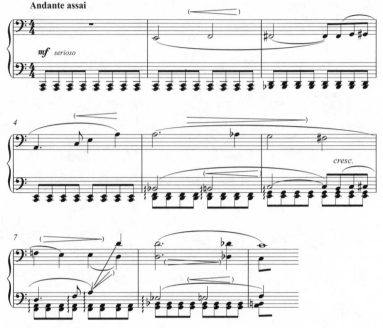

Ex. 4.3 Sonata No. 4, mvt. 2

ous appearance of the theme and its inversion require the pianist to be able
to suggest different orchestral sonorities by varying the touch. I strongly recommend listening to Prokofiev's orchestration of this movement to get an
idea of the colors he envisioned for this music. Make the crescendos in mm.
9 and 11 sound dramatic. Make sure that the bass part in m. 10 and the tenor
in m. 12 are expressively brought out. The staccato eighth notes in the left
hand in m. 13 should sound light, like pizzicato. The melody in the left hand
in m. 18 needs to cut through the texture with a brassy trombone sound.
Make the repeated notes in m. 24 sound clearly.

In the section starting at m. 25, both the theme in the tenor voice and its
inversion in the soprano need to be played with a long-lasting tone, while the
accompanying sixteenths in both hands should be light and even, but nevertheless shaped expressively.

In m. 33 a dramatic transitional episode begins. The angular melodic line covers a vast register range, with octave exclamations and repeated brassy triads in the accompaniment enhancing the drama. The tempo relationship between this bar and the preceding one should be ♩ = ♩.. This is how it is marked in the orchestral score of the movement, and this is also how it sounds the second time this episode is heard, in m. 62. However, Prokofiev himself plays the new episode slower than that, regaining the ratio of ♩ = ♩. not sooner than m. 36. In the latter bar a great change occurs, and a profound calmness follows the anguished, zigzagging melody.

The new theme in m. 39 has a naive purity; in the orchestral version it is given to a flute. Play it with a gentle, warm expression. Prokofiev plays it very evenly and without rubato, but his phrasing is exquisitely shaped. The accompaniment should be played with an enveloping legato, not excessively articulated, while the responding secondary voices should be subdued but expressive. In the second half of m. 52, make a gradual change in the way you play the chords: from legato, through tenuto separato, to staccato.

The indications of *pianissimo*, as well as a faster tempo, necessitate playing the return of the main theme in m. 54 in a light, airy way. As before, the pianist should shape both melodic lines well while keeping the accompanying sixteenths even and unobtrusive.

The reappearance of the transitional episode in m. 62 should sound more tortured and anguished than earlier, having acquired a jagged rhythm in both the melody and the accompaniment. The crescendo in m. 69 will sound more impressive if delayed until the second half of the bar. Play the chord in the middle of m. 70 without the pedal, but not too short.

In the beginning of the *Poco meno mosso* episode in m. 71 (see Ex. 0.15b), the abbreviation *Ped.* is printed in most editions. I interpret this as an indication for ample, rather than continuous, pedaling; the latter may make the sonority too thick or boomy. Playing the triplets in the right hand evenly is quite difficult and requires considerable practice. Give each of the two themes a character of its own. It is important to shape the top melody well rather than just to poke at the high notes.

Playing the coda (m. 81), Prokofiev brings out the top notes of the chords in the left hand and adds a G in m. 84, as shown in Ex. 4.4. This note is miss-

Ex. 4.4 Sonata No. 4, mvt. 2

ing in the piano score, although it appears in the orchestral version. In addition, Prokofiev plays the sixteenth notes in the left hand in mm. 82 and 84 as
thirty-seconds.

In the last four bars, bring back the stark, concentrated mood. Observe
the indications of dynamics and articulation precisely.

THIRD MOVEMENT

This movement must be played with youthful ebullience and vigor. Though
the initial run and all similar ones should be played evenly and strictly in
tempo, they should not sound careful or pedantic.

Avoid accenting the first notes in the arpeggio-like passages in mm. 6 and
8 (and later in mm. 17, 74, 141, 212, and 214). This will help give them a
sweeping character. In m. 10 do not let the loud dynamics and the rests
break the line; think in two-bar phrases. Do not make a diminuendo in m.
17, and let the *piano* in the following bar appear suddenly; play it lightly but
brilliantly, not lyrically. As you descend into the lower register (mm. 15–17
and 23–25), the sonority may become indistinct. Prevent this by using less
pedal or by playing with less legato.

The bridge theme (m. 25) should have a sense of propulsive motion. I suggest playing the tenor voice with sharp finger staccato and phrasing it as indicated in Example 4.5. When this theme appears in the recapitulation, the
composer's markings are *precipitato* and *senza pedale*. I would adopt these
indications for the exposition as well.

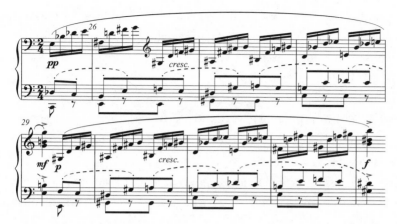

Ex. 4.5 Sonata No. 4, mvt. 3

The second theme (m. 43) has a spooky, slightly frightening character. Play the top voice distinctly staccato, but maintain the two-bar phrasing. The first chord in each phrase should always be unstressed. The left hand's chromaticisms contribute to the uneasy character. Play them with light legato. Work toward being rhythmically precise in mm. 52 and 54 and similar passages, in spite of the technical difficulty of the jumps.

Play the return of the first theme (m. 67) *forte leggiero*. Avoid accenting every quarter note in the left hand, something that tends to happen because of the difficult leaps. The ornamented version in m. 75 should be played with active, brilliant fingers. Prokofiev's markings here make it evident that he regards the second bar of these two-bar phrases (mm. 76 and 78) as stronger than the first. (We see the same indication in the recapitulation starting in m. 134.) You may decide either to apply the same phrasing to the earlier appearances of the same material (mm. 10, 18, and so on) or to play them in a different way. Finish the section with matter-of-fact brusqueness. Play the accented notes non legato and use no *ritenuto*.

In the middle section (m. 84), change the sonority completely. The long melody should sound lyrical and naive. Make the color of the two melodic lines distinctly different, as if played by different wind instruments. The repeated thirds in the left hand should be played gently non legato, although not too short. The long phrase starting in m. 100 should sound with gentle warmth; strive for a good legato and never let the top line be overpowered. The accompaniment in m. 118 should not be too jumpy; play it as if violins and violas were taking turns.

The beginning of the recapitulation (m. 134) should sound as if from far away, but with utmost clarity (play it with distinctly enunciating fingers). In mm. 146–48, use a good legato touch in the left hand to contrast it with the articulation of the right hand.

Stay in *pianissimo* in the bridge theme for as long as marked; do not start the crescendos (mm. 158 and 172) too early. Make the contrasting reminiscence of the melody from the middle section and its inversion in mm. 163–66 recognizable. Place the accents in the run in 176–77 precisely as indicated (Ex. 4.6a; not as shown in Ex. 4.6b).

The reappearance of the second theme in m. 178 should have a powerful, ebullient character. Bring out the melody played by the thumb of the left hand, and do not accent the first chord in these two-bar phrases. Make the *piano* in m. 194 sound unexpected. Starting in m. 201, each of the scalar runs should sound more exciting than the previous one, reaching the level of *fff* in m. 208. There should be no accent on the first note of each of these runs.

Ex. 4.6 Sonata No. 4, mvt. 3

Playing the first theme for the last time, you may allow yourself to sound quite wild, with the low bass notes thundering in the left hand. Prokofiev judiciously recommends pulling the loudness level back to *fortissimo* and, later, in m. 216, to just *forte*. However, the indication *con effetto* (with effect) in m. 216 directs us to play this phrase in a particularly brilliant and engaging way. Make sure that the leaps in the left hand in mm. 220–21 do not cover the melody in the right hand. Play the last chords brightly, courageously, and without any *ritenuto*.

Sonata No. 5 in C Major, op. 38 (First Version), op. 135 (Second Version)

Composed in 1923 (second version in 1953). First performed by the composer on March 9, 1924, in Paris. Published by A. Gutheil in 1925 (first version) and by Muzgiz in 1955 (second version). The original version is dedicated to Piotr Petrovich (Pierre) Souvchinsky; the dedication has been removed from the second version.

Between the Fourth Sonata, completed in 1917, and the group of War Sonatas (Nos. 6, 7, and 8), all started in 1939, Prokofiev composed only one piano work in this genre. (He did write three sonatinas, though: Two Sonatinas op. 54 and Sonatina pastorale, op. 59, no. 3.) The Fifth Sonata, written in Paris, differs significantly from both the early sonatas and the later ones. Its musical language shows Prokofiev in his more experimental phase, as do his many other works of this period.

On December 10, 1923, Prokofiev wrote to Souvchinsky, the sonata's dedicatee, that "the sonata as a whole seems to be successful, the finale unquestionably so."[1] The composer premiered the new work on March 9, 1924, in Paris. In his diary he recorded that there were few people in the audience and that "the response was good but restrained."[2] A lukewarm reception seems to have accompanied this work's many performances by Prokofiev during the following few years, including those given during his tour of the Soviet Union in 1927, his first visit after leaving Russia in 1918. What was the reason for this relative lack of enthusiasm? Prokofiev blamed the sonata's adventurous, dissonant language: "The Fifth Sonata, the Quintet and the Second Symphony, continuing from the *Sarcasms* through the *Scythian Suite* and *Seven, They Are Seven,* were the most chromatic of all my compositions. This was the effect of the Parisian atmosphere where complex patterns and dissonances were the accepted thing, and which fostered my predilection for complex thinking."[3] The sonata, however, lacks the brutal force of the *Scythian Suite* or the energy of the Second Symphony. Its dissonant harmonies and zigzagging melodies are more akin to the expressionistic language of Prokofiev's opera *The Fiery Angel* (which bears the opus number 37, close to that of the sonata, although the opera was not completed until 1927). The sonata's modernistic features blend, perhaps not fully organically, with the neoclassic simplicity of its stylized cadences and mock Alberti basses.

The lower level of energy in the Fifth Sonata, compared with its predecessors, could not go unnoticed by contemporary audiences, especially since Prokofiev tended to program the new composition with Sonatas No. 2, 3, or 4. In a letter to Myaskovsky dated July 15, 1924, Prokofiev attributed the sonata's calmer outlook to "my poor state of health . . . when I was planning out the sonata; my heart was in poor condition as a result of the scarlet fever I [had] contracted five years ago."[4]

Mira Mendelson-Prokofieva wrote that "In 1944 to [Prokofiev's] great joy the pianist Maria Grinberg gave a performance in the Small Hall of the Moscow Conservatoire of his long-neglected Fifth Sonata for piano. After the recital he asked Myaskovsky, who sat next to him, whether there were many 'false notes' in the sonata. Myaskovsky replied that 'all traces of the scarlet fever had disappeared.' Nevertheless in 1952 before the publication of a new edition of the sonata Sergei Sergeyevich decided to revise it and wrote a new version. He often told me how pleased he was that he had rewritten that sonata."[5]

Prokofiev believed that the changes warranted a new opus number, 135. If one compares both versions closely, however, one can discern few radical differences between the two. Most of the changes are minute and seem to be aimed at making the texture clearer and the angular melodic language more eloquently expressive. The largest number of changes happen to be in the finale, the very movement with which Prokofiev was especially satisfied when he first completed the work in 1923 (see the quotation from his letter to Souvchinsky above). In the new version, the composer tightened the development section of the finale and significantly expanded its coda. In the first movement, he made significant changes to the second theme in all the sections—the exposition, the development, and the recapitulation. The coda of this movement in the new version sounds more transparent, as Prokofiev eliminated some of the original contrapuntal complexity. The second movement underwent numerous small changes, but its substance remained unaltered. Table 5.1 summarizes the significant differences between the two versions.

The second version of the Fifth Sonata was published by Muzgiz for the

Table 5.1   Significant Differences between Op. 38 and Op. 135

	Original Version (op. 38)		Revised Version (op. 135)
First Movement	mm. 46–56 (01:26–01:47)	. . . are replaced by . . .	mm. 46–57 (01:27–01:49)
	mm. 113–20 (03:19–03:32)	. . . are replaced by . . .	mm. 114–22 (03:17–03:33)
	mm. 178–86 (05:16–05:33)	. . . are replaced by . . .	mm. 180–87 (05:14–05:31)
Coda	mm. 191–200 (05:46–06:00)	. . . are replaced by . . .	mm. 192–202 (05:44–06:00)
Third Movement	mm. 33–39 (00:59–01:14)	. . . are replaced by . . .	mm. 33–39 (00:57–01:12)
	mm. 58–30 (01:47–04:10)	. . . are replaced by . . .	mm. 59–103 (01:43–03:06)
Coda	mm. 143–54 (04:41–05:05)	. . . are replaced by . . .	mm. 116–40 (03:42–04:35)

first time in its 1955 complete collection of Prokofiev's piano sonatas (volume 2 of the composer's complete works). This edition does not contain the first version of the work. Since many later publications of the complete sonatas are reprints of this Muzgiz edition, most of them contain only the second version of the Fifth Sonata. As a result, the score of the op. 38 version is not easily available and is less known than op. 135. This is unfortunate, because the first version has much to offer and some performers may prefer it.

The customary "Listening Closely" and "Master Class" sections follow, covering each version separately. When the discussion concerns passages that are identical in both versions, the corresponding sections of the text are repeated.

Listening Closely (original version)

FIRST MOVEMENT: ALLEGRO TRANQUILLO
(DISC I, TRACK IO)

This movement has an idyllic outlook, more introverted than most of the opening movements of Prokofiev's sonatas. In its objective lyricism one may hear the influence of French music contemporary to the sonata. Another noticeable influence here is Stravinsky; in addition to his neo-Baroque style, Stravinsky's polytonal writing may have given Prokofiev the idea of concurrently using different tonalities in the development section (see mm. 77–87, 02:19–02:36).

Each of the three principal themes—which are labeled here as the first, the bridge, and the second themes—plays an equally important role. The first theme is a simple melody of conventional Classical proportions. The accompaniment is reminiscent of Alberti bass, even though it is presented in a high register. Prokofiev uses this staple of Mozart's keyboard texture as an obvious allusion to the Classical style. Another nod to Classicism is the period-like phrase structure. The harmonies are markedly simple, though Prokofiev occasionally uses chords that do not belong in C major, giving the music an unmistakably twentieth-century sound.

A slightly mysterious connecting passage (m. 20, 00:35), especially its hesitantly ascending part, will recur throughout the movement. It leads into the fairy tale–like bridge theme (m. 26, 00:48). Prokofiev's marking for this section is *narrante* (narrating). Unfolding without haste and punctuated by rests, the melody contrasts with the monotonous, chromatic accompaniment that adds dreaminess to the character. The tonality of this theme is ambiguous, although the chromatic figuration in the left hand centers on E. The connecting "refrain" reappears in m. 34 (01:03). The melody is repeated, this time with more dissonant harmonies. It climbs up and grows to a *forte* before coming back to both the register and the dynamics of the initial connecting section.

The second theme (m. 46, 01:26) is short and anxious. After a chromatic climb, a recurring pleading motive is introduced. The previously heard "refrain" returns in m. 53 (01:39). Its ascending line is extended; it reaches close to the keyboard's highest limit. This gently disappearing passage concludes the exposition; after the tonal ambiguity, the key of A major is crystallized.

Following a brief pause, the development commences in m. 62 (01:55) with the opening motive of the first theme. Presented in augmentation, it has a fanfarelike, decisive character. Most of the development is based on material from this theme. The harmonies in the two hands are often unrelated, including a passage in mm. 77–87 (02:19–02:36) when each of the hands explores two different tonalities (E major and B-flat major), swapping them along the way. (As has been frequently observed, Prokofiev liked juxtaposing tonalities a tritone apart.) The right hand plays the songful first theme, while a galloping dotted rhythm in the left hand creates a nervous, agitated mood.

A dramatic buildup starts in m. 91 (02:42), with rising triplets originating in the second theme. Against their background, the material of the bridge section appears in m. 95 (02:50). Now its sonority is dissonant, angular, and tense. It is interspersed with brusque chords in the bass (m. 103, 03:01), which derive from the questioning intonations of the second theme. The emotional intensity increases even further. The second theme (m. 113, 03:19) appears in the most dissonant and dramatic of its incarnations, featuring bold leaps in the melody and chromaticisms in all voices. The climax of the development is reached in m. 125 (03:38), when the first theme is heralded in a triumphant and sonorous B-flat major. Prokofiev's piano writing is unusual here, bringing the pianist's left hand high above the right to play the jubilant accompaniment.

A calming transition leads to the recapitulation in m. 140 (04:03). The first theme starts as in the beginning, but a descending line in the left hand is added to the subsequent phrase (m. 148, 04:18). The bridge theme in m. 161 (04:44) uses mostly the same pitches as in the exposition, but the accompaniment is different: now it circles around C, creating the feeling of a new tonal center. In addition, sustained chords in the middle register, tonally unrelated to the rest of the material, create a mysterious, fairy tale–like mood.

The return of the emotionally volatile second theme (m. 178, 05:17) covers a broad dynamic spectrum, with markings ranging from *forte* to *pianissimo*. It concludes with the transitional material we heard first in the exposition (see m. 20, 00:35). Enigmatic trills in the low register confirm the home key of C major.

The brief coda (m. 190, 05:46) introduces a faster tempo; it expounds upon the first theme and is surrounded by busy chromatic movement. The initial anacrustic motive of the first theme is imitated repeatedly in various registers. Starting in the high register and descending to the low bass, it flies by us as yet another of Prokofiev's fugitive visions.

SECOND MOVEMENT: ANDANTINO (DISC I, TRACK II)

This movement is a peculiar amalgamation of different characters and images typical for Prokofiev. The $\frac{3}{8}$ meter suggests a waltz; the mechanistically unchanging accompaniment and angular melodic lines give it an ironic slant. Furthermore, certain sonorities, especially in the middle section, represent Prokofiev's spooky kind of fairy-tale imagery. They also cast their shadow on the character of the waltz, lending it a frozen, spellbound quality.

Prokofiev chose G-flat major as the home key for this movement, explor-

Ex. 5.1 Vision fugitive, *op. 22, no. 10*

ing once again tritone tonal relationships with the sonata's outer movements. This tonality is quickly abandoned, however, and various distant keys
are hinted at in the course of the movement. The initial key and the general
ironic tone, as well as certain melodic turns, recall the tenth piece of the set
Visions fugitives, op. 22, marked *Ridicolosamente* (ridiculously) (Ex. 5.1).

The movement begins with four bars of a dry, waltzlike accompaniment.
It hardly changes during the course of the movement's first third, creating
the monotony of a mechanistic puppet dance. Against this background the
main theme presents itself. It has several important components: a chromatically descending three-note motive (first heard in m. 5, 00:09), an angular motive of a conversing or complaining character (first heard in m. 8,
00:15), a fanfare that sounds as if played by a toy trumpet (m. 12, 00:22), and

a mocking response consisting of dissonant repetitions and a trill-like succession of notes (m. 13, 00:26). All these elements are constantly developed through ever-changing dynamics and varying registers, using a highly chromatic language. The musical character is continually transformed—from naive to plaintive to desperate.

The middle section (m. 59, 01:55) brings the new key of E minor, as well as different, contrasting imagery. Gone are the waltz character and the dissonant sonorities. The harmonic language becomes markedly consonant, while the low register creates a dark, fairy tale–like atmosphere. Several intruding "barking," dissonant chords (mm. 65, 02:09; 73, 02:26; 82, 02:45) strengthen the frightening, spooky feeling. A sudden *forte* (m. 75, 02:29) brings back the chromaticisms and angular melodic lines. This expressionistic cry of pain soon subsides, sinking back into the mysterious darkness.

The waltz returns with the upbeat to m. 84 (02:47). The mocking character is enhanced by an ironic quasi glissando that precedes every downbeat. Repeated without any changes, these slides have a frightful, chilling effect. Most of this section retains the stylized mood of the beginning. Starting with m. 106 (03:30), however, a nostalgic feeling creeps into the music.

The coda (m. 116, 03:50) brings back the material of the middle section. Though its melody is the same, the harmonies are far less euphonious than before. The music sinks into a very low register, where a G-flat-major sixth chord is established (m. 123, 04:08). For the first time in the movement, Prokofiev instructs the pianist to sustain the pedal, creating a feeling of magical suspense. The dry waltz is recalled for the last time in the lugubrious low register in m. 129 (04:20), before signing off with a low G-flat-major triad, preceded by another rumbling quasi glissando.

THIRD MOVEMENT: UN POCO ALLEGRETTO
(DISC I, TRACK 12)

In the third movement, neoclassical stylization can be heard on various levels. These include the use of the sonata-rondo form favored by the Viennese masters in their finales; the accompaniment to the first theme, presented in a modified Alberti bass formula; and various melodic turns of phrase. At the same time, this movement is the most "modernistic" in the sonata, bearing the unmistakable signs of Prokofiev's more radical language during the 1920s. As in the first movement, the neoclassical traits are primarily associated with the first theme and the expressionistic elements with the second. However, the contrast between the two styles is much greater in the finale; this stylistic dichotomy fuels the dramatic collisions within the movement.

The first theme is a combination of various motives and phrases, most of which are developed extensively later in the movement: a monotonous repetition of the same tone a (mm. 1–2); a chromatic and angular ascending line b, followed by a tumbling descent (mm. 3–4, 00:05–00:08); a ceremonious reiteration of the tonic harmony c (upbeat to m. 5, 00:08); a "toy trumpet" fanfare and its immediate imitation in the middle voice d (upbeat to m. 6–m. 8, 00:10–00:14); a trill-like passage followed by chromatic runs e (mm. 9–10, 00:15–00:19); a repetition of two hopping chords that differ by a single note f (mm. 11–12, 00:19–00:22) (Ex. 5.2a); and a succession of chromatically descending pairs of falling thirds g (m. 17, 00:29) (Ex. 5.2b). Together this assortment of disparate characters creates a peculiar and humorous emotional quilt. The polytonal writing of the first movement is recalled in mm. 9–10 (00:15–00:19), where the right-hand part, with its tonality centered on B, is superimposed on the left-hand part, centered on F. This procedure is used frequently throughout the movement.

The laconic bridge section (m. 19, 00:33) continues the driven motion of chromatically running sixteenths and accompanying eighth notes; the latter are based on the tonic of C major. The second theme is a passionate melody full of wide intervals (m. 25, 00:44), covering an ever-increasing melodic range. A short concluding section, filled with chromatic motion (mm. 36–39, 01:06–01:14), is based on the bridge material. It brings us to the return of the initial eight bars of the first theme (m. 40, 01:14). They are repeated virtually verbatim, with the exception of the dronelike tonic fifth in the bass, which has been replaced by the subdominant. There is a clear formal caesura at the end of the exposition, typical of many of Prokofiev's movements in sonata form.

Ex. 5.2a Sonata No. 5, mvt. 3

The development is introduced in m. 52 (01:35) by a somber, somewhat spooky unison passage in the bass, built on the motive *b* in augmentation. This motive continues in various registers, tonalities, and voices and is interspersed with repeated chords derived from element *a* of the first theme. The second theme makes its appearance in the upbeat to m. 63 (01:56). Pre-

Ex. 5.2b Sonata No. 5, mvt. 3

sented in augmentation, it is densely surrounded by other voices before leaping to the top in the middle of m. 67 (02:05), where it is boldly intoned with a trumpetlike sonority, reminiscent of certain moments in the Third Sonata. The dissonant chromatic background enhances the development's expressionistic drama, which recalls the complex musical world of the opera *The Fiery Angel*. The tension subsides by m. 74 (02:17), where the two initial elements of the first theme are developed. Another dramatic explosion in m. 82 (02:33) is based on the material of the bridge section, as well as on additional segments from the first theme. The new *piano* passage (m. 90, 02:48), deriving from element *e* of the first theme, evokes a fairy-tale character with its monotonous repetitions and gentle dissonances; it ushers in the recapitulation in m. 95 (03:00). The beginning of the first theme is omitted here, and the composer goes directly to element *e,* the basis of the previous passage.

The development's dramatic tension, caused by the intensely chromatic language and tonal instability, spills into the recapitulation. At its start, all the elements of the first theme are presented—except for the opening one—but their order and tonalities are different from the exposition, as if the composer still feels the need to sort out and complete the unfinished processes of the development. Only by the bridge section in m. 108 (03:23) do we sense some stability.

The dramatic intensification of the second theme in the development section continues in the recapitulation (m. 113, 03:33). Its setting is complex, chromatic, dissonantly polyphonic, and even more tonally ambiguous than before. The movement reaches its climax in m. 131 (04:11), where the beginning of the first theme is hammered out *fortissimo*. The composer's use of "barbaric" dissonances to accompany every note of the melody is clearly calculated to produce a shocking effect. The following mysterious *pianissimo* passage in m. 139 (04:30), echoing the same intonations, is no less effective; it almost negates the dramatic impact of the preceding *fortissimo*.

A short coda (m. 143, 04:41) is almost exclusively based on the element *b* of the first theme. Its intonations weave continually and are imitated in different voices, in an intensely chromatic setting. The general dynamics of the coda are hushed, except for a brief crescendo in mm. 149–50 (04:52–04:55). At the end, element *a* of the first theme appears, concluding the work in an enigmatic *piano*. Could this hushed ending be partly responsible for the tepid reception of this version? The second version ends in a much more brilliant and assured way.

Master Class (original version)

FIRST MOVEMENT

Play the opening theme with simplicity, but be sensitive to every fresh, unexpected harmony. In m. 9, make sure that the top line is not overpowered by the busy texture. Play the upbeats to mm. 17 and 19 expressively. In m. 20, make the color darker. The tempo in mm. 24–25 can be stretched a little, in response to the remark *un poco penseroso* as well as to the tenuto dashes. (The same applies to mm. 35–36.) In m. 26, carry the melody over the rests, and then play the thirds in m. 29 shorter and lighter than the preceding part of the melody. The chromatic accompaniment in quintuplets should sound slightly blurred. A good legato in all voices is required in mm. 31–33. In mm. 42–44, do not let the crescendo sound shrill.

The ascending eighth notes in the second theme (mm. 46 and 50) should be played with agitation, while the short motives in both hands in mm. 47–48 have a plaintive, pleading expression. In your voicing of the unisons in mm. 53–56, give preference to the left hand in order to achieve a dark sonority. The ascending passage in mm. 57–60 should be played lightly and evenly.

Play the first theme in the left hand at the beginning of the development (m. 62) with a clear, trumpetlike sound. In m. 65, let the top line in the right hand take over the role of the main melody. The first theme in the treble register in m. 69 should possess a singing quality. Play the *piano* in m. 73 in a slightly jocular mood; change the color in the following bar, as if a new instrument were answering. In the polytonal passage in m. 77, let the top melody sing; use very little pedal, in order to maintain the transparency of the texture.

The dramatic episode starting in m. 91 should be played expressively, but I still recommend using the pedal sparingly. The rests in the bridge theme in m. 95 should not interrupt the long line.

The big leaps in the melodic line of the second theme (m. 113) should sound expressively. In m. 117, follow both lines in the right hand. In the climax of the development section (an upbeat to m. 125), play the melody in the right hand with a singing tone and avoid letting the accompaniment in the same hand sound heavy. Play the figurations in the left hand with a light and ringing tone. I use a lot of pedal here, but I try to avoid blurring the sonorities.

In the second phrase of the recapitulation's first theme (m. 148), play the new descending line in the left hand with a smooth legato. The *piano* in m. 156 and the subsequent *calando* should prepare the mysteriously enchanted mood of the bridge section in m. 160. Here each of the three elements—the *narrante* melody, the murmuring quintuplets in the bass, and the harplike chords in the left hand—should have its own tone color. You probably will need to use half-pedal in mm. 162–64 to keep the chords ringing without losing overall clarity.

The second theme in m. 178 has the same combination of nervous urgency (ascending eighth notes) and pleading *piano* intonation as in the exposition. In the following passage (mm. 187–90), use a deep legato touch in the left hand and a light legato in the right.

The coda (m. 190) should have an eerie character. Let the melodic line be clearly heard, but play the accompanying voices, including the imitations of the opening figure, very lightly, like a fleeting vision. There should be hardly any crescendo or *ritenuto* at the end.

SECOND MOVEMENT

Throughout the waltzlike sections of the movement, I advocate very sparing use of the pedal. This restraint will make the passage at the end (mm. 123–28), where the pedal is marked by the composer, sound absolutely magical. At the same time, you should strive to provide a great contrast in the touch between the short and dry staccato of the accompaniment and the expressive legato of the melodic material. When necessary, a discreet use of the pedal will help to connect notes in the melody.

Make the fanfare motive in m. 12 sound like a toy trumpet. It is answered by the repeated seconds in *piano;* they should be played portamento, not staccato. In mm. 21–23, as well as 28–30, catch the grace notes with the pedal, but release it by the second eighth note of each of these bars. The wide melodic leaps from the upbeat to the downbeat of mm. 24 and 25 should be played *legato espressivo*. The sixteenths in the right hand starting in m. 30 need to sound very expressively, as do all three voices in mm. 35–36.

The general dynamic in mm. 55 and 56 is *piano;* the crescendos toward the end of each of these bars help reinforce the mysterious mood. The new theme of the middle section (m. 59) should be played darkly and with a good legato, but without much pressure in the touch. Here I would use the pedal liberally, with the exceptions of mm. 65–66, 73–74, and 82–83; the staccato chords in those bars should sound quite dry, short, and frightening. Measures 75–78 contain the most expressive and personal music of this movement. Play them with a warm touch.

In the return of the initial material (an upbeat to m. 84), hold the pedal through the entire run at the end of each bar to imitate the effect of a glissando. Make sure that each group of sextuplets ends with a diminuendo; release the pedal precisely on the downbeat.

In the passage starting in m. 106, play the right hand expressively and observe the indications of the dynamics. For the *piano* in m. 110, change the color completely to make it sound pale and ghostly. In m. 123, hold the pedal for six bars. The chords in the left hand should sound enigmatic, while the remnants of the melody in the higher voices should be light and airy. In m. 129, bring back the dryness of the beginning. The last two bars need to be played in a matter-of-fact way, without any *ritenuto*.

THIRD MOVEMENT

Each of the short motives that form the first theme should have its own special character: still and monotonous in mm. 1–2; expressive in m. 3; nervous in m. 4; mockingly important in the upbeat to m. 5; teasing in the upbeat to m. 6, and so on. Different voices in the right hand in mm. 6–8 should sound like different instruments. The *pianissimo* in m. 9 must be extremely clear and light. Play the melody in the right hand of mm. 13–14 *poco espressivo*. Throughout the first theme, I use very little pedal except where indicated by the composer. I recommend playing the pairs of eighth notes in m. 17 *pesante espressivo*.

The second theme in m. 25 needs to sound warm and expressive, with good legato in the right hand and without excessive articulation in the accompaniment of the left hand. Here I use the pedal generously but change it frequently. Use a light touch in the short and densely chromatic closing section (m. 36). Gently stress the subdominant fifth in the bass in mm. 40 and 44.

The beginning of the development (m. 53) should sound as if played by low orchestral strings. Measures 59–62 require attentive polyphonic listening and sensitive shaping of the lines in different voices. When the second theme appears in augmentation (an upbeat to m. 63), make sure that it cuts through the surrounding texture and is shaped as a long melodic line. When it moves to the treble register in the middle of m. 67 and is imitated in the middle of m. 69, I hear the sonority of two trumpets. Throughout this section, you need to use the pedal to bridge the wide leaps and to reduce the harshness of the sound, but do it discreetly, in order not to lose the clarity of the texture. In the following soft section, melodic phrases in the right hand are imitated by other voices (mm. 74, 76, 78, 80). Make them sound as if played by different instruments. The left-hand accompaniment should not be excessively articulated. I choose to interpret the chromatic passage afterward (mm. 82–87) in a *scherzando* vein, although other approaches are possible as well. Treat the last section of the development (mm. 90–94) as a soothing transition to the recapitulation, which starts in m. 95. The initial material should be played here with the same energy and clarity as in the beginning of the movement.

The extensive recapitulation of the second theme (mm. 113–27) requires a singing tone, free of excessive pressure. With each appearance of the melody, restated in different registers and dynamics, the character changes. In the exuberant climax of the movement in mm. 131–37, play the right hand expressively, without forcing the sound. Hold the pedal for the entire seven bars; the eighth notes in the left hand should resonate like jubilant bell chimes. Release the pedal at once in m. 138. The following *pianissimo* should sound enigmatic and dry, using almost no pedal.

The same mood is preserved in the short coda (m. 143). Shape all these melodic phrases well, gently separating them from one another, but stay in *piano* except for the crescendo in mm. 149–50. Play the concluding statement (m. 151 to the end) without any pedal or *ritenuto*, in a *scherzando misterioso* character, and without losing clarity of articulation.

Listening Closely (second version)

FIRST MOVEMENT: ALLEGRO TRANQUILLO
(DISC 2, TRACK 1)

This movement has an idyllic outlook, more introverted than most of the opening movements of Prokofiev's sonatas. In its objective lyricism one may hear the influence of French music contemporary to the sonata. Another noticeable influence here is Stravinsky; in addition to his neo-Baroque style, Stravinsky's polytonal writing may have given Prokofiev the idea of concurrently using different tonalities in the development section (see mm. 78–88, 02:19–02:37).

Each of the three principal themes—which are labeled here as the first, the bridge, and the second themes—plays an equally important role. The first theme is a simple melody of conventional Classical proportions. The accompaniment is reminiscent of Alberti bass, even though it is presented in a high register. Prokofiev uses this staple of Mozart's keyboard texture as an obvious allusion to the Classical style. Another nod to Classicism is the period-like phrase structure. The harmonies are markedly simple, though Prokofiev occasionally uses chords that do not belong in C major, giving the music an unmistakably twentieth-century sound.

A slightly mysterious connecting passage (m. 20, 00:35), especially its hesitantly ascending part, will recur throughout the movement. It leads into the fairy tale–like bridge theme (m. 26, 00:48). Prokofiev's marking for this section is *narrante* (narrating). Unfolding without haste and punctuated by rests, the melody contrasts with the monotonous, chromatic accompaniment that adds dreaminess to the character. The tonality of this theme is ambiguous, although the chromatic figuration in the left hand centers on E. The connecting "refrain" reappears in m. 34 (01:03). The melody is repeated, this time with more dissonant harmonies. It climbs up and grows to a *forte* before coming back to both the register and the dynamics of the initial connecting section.

The second theme (m. 46, 01:27) is different in the new version from that of op. 38. In op. 135, it has two contrasting parts: a bold, unaccompanied trumpetlike statement and a pleading short intonation, which is reiterated against a chromatically shifting background. This change gives the second theme a more decisive character, making the contrast with the preceding material greater than in the first version.

The ascending line of the previously heard material (m. 58, 01:49) is extended; it brings the pianist close to the keyboard's highest limit. This gently disappearing passage concludes the exposition in the key of A major.

Following a brief pause, the development commences in m. 63 (01:56) with the opening motive of the first theme. Presented in augmentation, it has a fanfarelike, decisive character. The initial section of the development is based on the material from the first theme. The harmonies in the two hands are often unrelated, including a passage in mm. 78–88 (02:19–02:37) when each of the hands explores two different tonalities (E major and B-flat major), swapping them along the way. (As has been frequently observed, Prokofiev liked juxtaposing tonalities a tritone apart.) The right hand plays the songful first theme, while a galloping dotted rhythm in the left hand creates a nervous, agitated mood.

A dramatic buildup starts in m. 92 (02:41) with rising triplets originating in the second theme. Against their background, the material of the bridge section appears in m. 96 (02:49). Now its sonority is dissonant, angular, and tense. It is interspersed with brusque chords in the bass (m. 104, 03:05), which derive from the questioning intonations of the second theme. The emotional intensity increases even further. The second theme (m. 114, 03:17) appears in the most dramatic of its incarnations, featuring bold leaps in the melody and chromaticisms in all voices. (The melody is more clearly and boldly etched than the corresponding passage in the original version.) The climax of the development is reached in m. 127 (03:40), when the first theme is heralded in a triumphant and sonorous B-flat major. Prokofiev's piano writing is unusual here, bringing the pianist's left hand high above the right to play the jubilant accompaniment.

A calming transition leads to the recapitulation in m. 142 (04:05). The first theme starts as in the beginning, but a descending line in the left hand is added to the subsequent phrase (m. 150, 04:19). The bridge theme in m. 163 (04:44) uses mostly the same pitches as in the exposition, but the accompaniment is different: now it circles around C, creating the feeling of a new tonal center. In addition, sustained chords in the middle register, tonally unrelated to the rest of the material, create a mysterious, fairy tale–like mood.

The decisive second theme (m. 180, 05:15) concludes with the transitional material we heard first in the exposition (see m. 20, 00:35). Enigmatic trills in the low register confirm the home key of C major.

A brief coda (m. 192, 05:44) in a suddenly faster tempo expounds upon the first theme and is surrounded by a busy chromatic movement. Starting in the high register and passing to the low bass, it ends with two chords affirming the key of C major.

SECOND MOVEMENT: ANDANTINO (DISC 2, TRACK 2)

In the second version of the Andantino, Prokofiev made a number of minute changes but no significant revisions on the scale of the finale or even of the first movement. These small alterations in melodic turns or harmony are not important enough to draw the listener's attention. For this reason, the description of this movement is left unchanged from that of the original version above. It is repeated here for the sake of providing accurate recording timings.

The movement is a peculiar amalgamation of different characters and images typical for Prokofiev. The $\frac{3}{8}$ meter suggests a waltz; the mechanistically unchanging accompaniment and angular melodic lines give it an ironic slant. Furthermore, certain sonorities, especially in the middle section, represent Prokofiev's spooky kind of fairy-tale imagery. They also cast their shadow on the character of the waltz, lending it a frozen, spellbound quality.

Prokofiev chose G-flat major as the home key for this movement, exploring once again tritone tonal relationships with the sonata's outer movements. This tonality is quickly abandoned, however, and various distant keys are hinted at in the course of the movement. The initial key and the general ironic tone, as well as certain melodic turns, recall the tenth piece of the set Visions fugitives, op. 22, marked Ridicolosamente (ridiculously) (Ex. 5.1).

The movement begins with four bars of a dry, waltzlike accompaniment. It hardly changes during the course of the movement's first third, creating the monotony of a mechanistic puppet dance. Against this background the main theme presents itself. It has several important components: a chromatically descending three-note motive (first heard in m. 5, 00:10), an angular motive of a conversing or complaining character (first heard in m. 8, 00:17), a fanfare that sounds as if played by a toy trumpet (m. 12, 00:24), and a mocking response consisting of dissonant repetitions and a trill-like succession of notes (m. 13, 00:28). All these elements are constantly developed through ever-changing dynamics and varying registers, using a highly chromatic language. The musical character is continually transformed—from naive to plaintive to desperate.

The middle section (m. 59, 02:03) brings the new key of E minor, as well as different, contrasting imagery. Gone are the waltz character and the dissonant sonorities. The harmonic language becomes markedly consonant, while the low register creates a dark, fairy tale–like atmosphere. Several intruding "barking," dissonant chords (mm. 65, 02:17; 73, 02:35; 82, 02:55) strengthen the frightening, spooky feeling. A sudden *forte* (m. 75, 02:39) brings back the chromaticisms and angular melodic lines. This expressionistic cry of pain soon subsides, sinking back into the mysterious darkness.

The waltz returns with the upbeat to m. 84 (02:59). The mocking character is enhanced by an ironic quasi glissando that precedes every downbeat. Repeated without any changes, these slides have a frightful, chilling effect. Most of this section retains the stylized mood of the beginning. Starting with m. 106 (03:45), however, a nostalgic feeling creeps into the music.

The coda (m. 116, 04:07) brings back the material of the middle section. Though its melody is the same, the harmonies are far less euphonious than before. The music sinks into a very low register, where a G-flat-major sixth chord is established (m. 123, 04:23). For the first time in the movement, Prokofiev instructs the pianist to sustain the pedal, creating a feeling of magical suspense. The dry waltz is recalled for the last time in the lugubrious low register in m. 129 (04:38), before signing off with a low G-flat-major triad, preceded by another rumbling quasi glissando.

THIRD MOVEMENT: UN POCO ALLEGRETTO
(DISC 2, TRACK 3)

Of the sonata's three movements, the third movement underwent the most extensive revision. The new version is significantly clearer and less dissonant. As a result, the movement's neoclassic qualities are highlighted. The stylization can be heard on various levels. These include the use of the sonata-rondo form favored by the Viennese masters in their finales; the accompaniment to the first theme, presented in a modified Alberti bass formula; and various melodic turns of phrase. The expressionistic qualities of the movement, which originally served as a dramatic counterbalance to the slightly objective stylizations, have been significantly toned down. Although the second theme—the main proponent of the modernistic qualities—remained unchanged, much of the dissonant angularity attached to it in the development and recapitulation has been purged. In the new version, the development section is also significantly shorter, and the number of contrasting episodes in it is reduced.

The first theme, whose revision was minimal, consists of various motives and phrases, most of which are developed extensively later in the movement. Here we encounter a monotonous repetition of the same tone *a* (mm. 1–2); a chromatic and angular ascending line *b* followed by a tumbling descent (mm. 3–4, 00:05–00:07); a ceremonious reiteration of the tonic harmony *c* (upbeat to m. 5, 00:07); a "toy trumpet" fanfare and its immediate imitation in the middle voice *d* (upbeat to m. 6–m. 8, 00:09–00:14); a trill-like passage followed by chromatic runs *e* (mm. 9–10, 00:15–00:18); a repetition of two hopping chords that differ by a single one note *f* (mm. 11–12, 00:18–00:21) (Ex. 5.2a); and a succession of chromatically descending pairs of falling thirds *g* (m. 17, 00:28) (Ex.5.2b). Together this assortment of disparate characters creates a peculiar and humorous emotional quilt. The polytonal writing of the first movement is recalled in mm. 9–10 (00:15–00:18), where the right-hand part, with its tonality centered on B, is superimposed on the left-hand part, centered on F. This procedure is used frequently throughout the movement.

The laconic bridge section (m. 19, 00:31) continues the driven motion of chromatically running sixteenths and accompanying eighth notes; the latter are based on the tonic of C major. The second theme is a passionate melody full of wide intervals (m. 25, 00:42), covering an ever-increasing melodic range. The concluding section (starting in m. 37, 01:04) has been rewritten. Now it consists of a trilling bass and a short recurring melodic pattern that lead seamlessly into the return of the first theme's initial material (m. 41, 01:12). This is repeated virtually verbatim, with the exception of the drone-like tonic fifth in the bass, which has been replaced by a subdominant one. There is a clear formal caesura at the end of the exposition, typical of many of Prokofiev's movements in sonata form.

The development is introduced in m. 53 (01:32) by a somber, somewhat spooky unison passage in the bass, based on the motive *b* in augmentation. This motive is repeated two more times in its original form and is interspersed with repeated octaves derived from element *a* of the first theme. The second theme reappears in the upbeat to m. 60 (01:44). Its first half, presented in augmentation, is boldly intoned with a trumpetlike sonority, reminiscent of certain moments in the Third Sonata. Heavily stomping basses in m. 69 (02:01) accompany the marchlike variation of element *a* interspersed with element *b*. A decrease in tension brings us to a calm *piano* section (m. 76, 02:14), based on element *e* of the first theme. The monotonously repeated bass and suspended chords are familiar devices used by Prokofiev to evoke an enchanted, fairy-tale character. This episode connects smoothly with the recapitulation in m. 80 (02:22); the beginning of the first theme is omitted here, and the composer goes directly to element *e*, the basis of the previous passage.

After the bridge section in m. 86 (02:32), a short connecting passage establishes the key of C major in m. 95 (02:49). The second theme now reappears in significantly different surroundings. The texture is idiomatically orchestral, recalling Prokofiev's instrumentation in some of his late works (let us not forget that the sonata's revision was undertaken in 1953). Tonally, this passage is unambiguously rooted in C major. An additional novelty is the unexpected lightening of the mood in m. 98 (02:53), where repeated chords in *piano* create a playful character. A broad crescendo leads to the movement's climax in m. 104 (03:06), when the beginning of the first theme is hammered out *fortissimo*. The composer's use of "barbaric" dissonances to accompany every note of the melody is clearly calculated to produce a shocking effect. (Without the original version's dramatic intensity to precede it, however, this passage sounds somewhat incongruous here.) The following mysterious *pianissimo* passage in m. 112 (03:30), echoing the same intonations, reestablishes the fairy-tale character.

While the development section of the movement has been significantly shortened for the new version, its coda has been expanded. In the process, its character has altered: instead of the murky, chromatic imitative section leading to a hushed, mysterious ending, it sounds now energetic and brilliant, echoing the ending of the Fourth Sonata in the same key of C major. The coda starts in m. 116 (03:42) with a fanfare in the low register; it cannot fail to remind us of the famous Petrushka motive in Stravinsky's ballet. The fanfare is based on the pitches of element *b* of the first theme. It continues with running sixteenths in unison, deriving from the same material. Some of the fast notes deviate from the home key, but the latter returns with marked decisiveness. The rudely stomping music in m. 125 (03:59) is based on elements *a* and *b*. Following a determined crescendo, the passage is repeated *fortissimo* with audacious octaves and leaps in both hands. A sudden *piano* in m. 135 (04:20) gives impetus to another ascending run before the sonata ends on a firmly placed C-major chord.

Master Class (second version)

FIRST MOVEMENT

Play the opening theme with simplicity, but be sensitive to every fresh, unexpected harmony. In m. 9, make sure that the top line is not overpowered by the busy texture. Play the upbeats to mm. 17 and 19 expressively. In m. 20, make the color darker. The tempo in mm. 24–25 can be stretched a little, in response to the remark *un poco penseroso* as well as to the tenuto dashes. (The same applies to mm. 35–36.) In m. 26, carry the melody over the rests, and then play the thirds in m. 29 shorter and lighter than the preceding part of the melody. The chromatic accompaniment in quintuplets should sound slightly blurred. A good legato in all voices is required in mm. 31–33. In mm. 42–44, do not let the crescendo sound shrill.

The opening phrase of the second theme (m. 46) should be presented with declarative authority, as if played by a trumpet. The second half of the theme, in contrast (mm. 48–50), has a plaintive or pleading expression. The ascending passage in mm. 58–61 should be played lightly and evenly.

Play the first theme in the left hand at the beginning of the development (m. 63) with a clear, trumpetlike sound. In m. 66, let the top line in the right hand take over the role of the main melody. The first theme in the treble register in m. 70 should possess a singing quality. Play the *piano* in m. 74 in a slightly jocular mood; change the color in the following bar, as if a new instrument were answering. In the polytonal passage in m. 78, let the top melody sing; use very little pedal in order to maintain the transparency of the texture.

The dramatic episode starting in m. 92 should be played expressively, but I still recommend using the pedal sparingly. The rests in the bridge theme in m. 96 should not interrupt the long line.

The big leaps in the melodic line of the second theme (starting in m. 114) should sound with bold expressivity. In mm. 119–20, follow both lines in the right hand. In the climax of the development section (an upbeat to m. 127), play the melody in the right hand with a singing tone and avoid letting the accompaniment in the same hand sound heavy. Play the figurations in the left hand with a light and ringing tone. I use a lot of pedal here, but I try to avoid blurring of the sonorities.

In the second phrase of the recapitulation's first theme (m. 150), play the new descending line in the left hand with a smooth legato. The *piano* in m. 158 and the subsequent *calando* should prepare the mysteriously enchanted mood of the bridge section in m. 162. Here each of the three elements—the *narrante* melody, the murmuring quintuplets in the bass, and the harplike chords in the left hand—should have its own tone color. You probably will need to use half-pedal in mm. 164–66 to keep the chords ringing without losing overall clarity.

In the second theme (m. 180), the left hand intones a declarative first phrase while the right hand provides an agitated accompaniment. When the texture changes to legato in m. 185, play the melodic lines in both hands very expressively. In the following passage (mm. 188–91), use a deep legato touch in the left hand and a light legato in the right.

In the coda (m. 191), let the melody be clearly heard; play the accompanying voices lightly. Change the color starting with the upbeat to m. 196, using a warm touch to evoke the sound of strings. The concluding passage (m. 199) should fly by, like a vision. Do not start the crescendo earlier than it is written, and use no *ritenuto* at the end.

SECOND MOVEMENT

Please refer to the preceding remarks about the original version of this movement.

THIRD MOVEMENT

Each of the short motives that form the first theme should have its own special character: still and monotonous in mm. 1–2; expressive in m. 3; nervous in m. 4; mockingly important in the upbeat to m. 5; teasing in the upbeat to m. 6, and so on. Different voices in the right hand in mm. 6–8 should sound like different instruments. The *pianissimo* in m. 9 must sound extremely clear and light. Throughout the first theme I use very little pedal except where indicated by the composer. I recommend playing the pairs of eighth notes in m. 17 *pesante espressivo*.

The second theme in m. 25 needs to sound warm and expressive, with good legato in the right hand and without excessive articulation in the ac-. companiment of the left hand. Here I use the pedal generously but change it frequently. In m. 37, achieve a mysterious legato sonority in the left hand; different sections of the melody in the right hand, separated by a leap in register, should differ in sound. Gently stress the subdominant fifth in the bass in mm. 41 and 45.

The beginning of the development (m. 53) should sound as if played by low orchestral strings. When the second theme appears in the upbeat to m. 60, I hear it as a trumpet solo. Create a long melodic line by playing non legato and using the weight of your arm. In the middle of m. 66, a second trumpet joins in.

In m. 71, play the octaves in the left hand with heavy non legato and the dotted rhythms in the right hand tenuto non legato, not staccato. In contrast with these bars, the legato phrases in mm. 70, 72, 74, and 75 should sound highly expressive. In the passage beginning in m. 76, give different colors to the different registers.

When the second theme reappears in the recapitulation (at the upbeat to m. 96), make both melodic lines sound warm. The unexpected *piano* (at the upbeat to m. 98) brings in a new character; play it *poco scherzando,* without making these chords too short. The expressive melodic lines in both hands in mm. 102–3 lead to the exuberant climax of the movement in mm. 104–10. Play the right hand expressively, without forcing the sound. Hold the pedal for the whole bar in each of these measures; the eighth notes in the left hand should resonate like jubilant bell chimes. Release the pedal at once in m. 111. The following *pianissimo* should sound enigmatic and dry, and should be played with almost no pedal.

After a heavy and sonorous fanfare in mm. 116–18, drop to *mezzo piano* in m. 119; play the unison sixteenths with well-articulating fingers and with good legato, using no pedal throughout—including the chords at the end of m. 120. I feel that mm. 123–24 need a crescendo to lead into the *forte* in m. 125. In mm. 125–29, use little pedal unless your hands are too small to hold the long notes in the right hand with your fingers. Differentiate the sound in the right hand between the fanfare melody and the dry accompanying chords. My suggested fingering for this passage is shown in Example 5.3. When the same passage returns in *fortissimo* (mm. 132–34), I use plenty of pedal. Make sure that the melody here is not overpowered by the accompaniment.

Ex. 5.3 Sonata No. 5 (second version), mvt. 3

The following *piano* (m. 135) needs to sound very distinct, without using the pedal. The ascending spirited run of sixteenths in mm. 137–38 should be played melodically, but again with almost no pedal. The last chord should last exactly a quarter beat.

Sonata No. 6 in A Major, op. 82

Composed in 1939–40. First performed by the composer on April 8, 1940, in Moscow (studio broadcast) and by Sviatoslav Richter on November 26, 1940, in Moscow. Published by Muzgiz in 1941.

The Sixth Sonata was the first of Prokofiev's three most significant works in this genre. It was written during his most productive period, when his style reached the peak of maturity.

In the West, Sonatas Nos. 6, 7, and 8 are often referred to as the "War Sonatas"; Russian musicology does not use this term. Considering them as a group, however, is justified both by their musical properties and by the circumstances of their composition. According to Mira Mendelson-Prokofieva, "in 1939 [Prokofiev] began to write three piano sonatas, [the] Sixth, Seventh and Eighth, working on all the ten movements at once, and only later did he lay aside the Seventh and Eighth and concentrated on the Sixth."[1]

The Sixth Sonata was completed in 1940, before the Second World War came to the USSR in 1941. It is difficult to tell whether it was the events in western Europe, Prokofiev's home during 1922–35, or the increasingly repressive climate in the Soviet Union that influenced the composer's mood, but this sonata definitely has turbulent energy and an anxiety concordant with the political tensions of the time.

Prokofiev himself premiered the Sixth Sonata in a radio broadcast in Moscow, as well as in a public concert in Leningrad. This was the last time he himself presented a new piano work in public. The sonata's lasting success on the concert stage was assured by Sviatoslav Richter, who gave its first public performance in Moscow. The pianist later described his first impressions of the work after hearing it played by the composer in a private home: "The remarkable stylistic clarity and the structural perfection of the music amazed me. I had never heard anything like it. With wild audacity the composer broke with the ideals of Romanticism and introduced into his music the terrifying pulse of twentieth-century music. Classically well-balanced in spite of all its asperities, the Sixth Sonata is an utterly magnificent work."[2]

Richter's feeling that, in the Sixth, Prokofiev turns away from Romanticism can be understood: in 1940 the pianist probably had not heard anything as modern as this. In the context of Prokofiev's other piano sonatas, however, this is a much more emotionally engaged work than its predecessors. In fact, one could argue that in the Sixth Prokofiev turned *toward* the Romantic concept of the sonata, with its traditional exploration of the conflict between the individual and fate or other impersonal forces beyond one's control. The mechanistic qualities of Prokofiev's music, familiar to us from his earlier works, play the crucial role in this drama; they collide with the warmly human thematic material, suppressing and brutalizing it. The carnival atmosphere or the "masques" of the early sonatas and the objective neoclassicism of the Fifth are abandoned, never to return in Prokofiev's subsequent works in this genre.

It is telling that Dmitri Shostakovich, a composer of great dramatic intensity, held the Sixth Sonata in particular esteem. After the first performance, he wrote to Prokofiev, "The Sixth Sonata is magnificent. From beginning to end. I am very happy that I had the opportunity to hear it two times, and regret that it was only two times."[3]

Prokofiev's new dramatic approach to the sonata form is evident in all three of the "War Sonatas." In the Sixth, however, it is mostly confined to the first and the last movements. The second movement, a lighthearted scherzo, and the third, a warm waltz, serve as counterbalancing components, while remaining deeply connected with the outer movements. In addition, the middle movements reveal many stylistic similarities with two of Prokofiev's major ballets: *Romeo and Juliet* and *Cinderella*. This is not surprising, as Prokofiev was working on both ballets while composing the Sixth Sonata. *Romeo and Juliet,* written in 1935–36, was staged in Leningrad in

January 1940. On the occasion of this production, Prokofiev made some revisions to his score and composed additional numbers. Later in 1940, he
started working on *Cinderella*, although because of the war this ballet was
not completed until 1944 and was first staged in November 1945. Among
other things, the connection with these two orchestral works may explain
why the writing in the sonata is strongly suggestive of various instrumental
colors.

Listening Closely

FIRST MOVEMENT: ALLEGRO MODERATO
(DISC 2, TRACK 4)

There is something frightening in the way the sonata opens. A restless and
agitated short motive in thirds in the right hand is hammered multiple
times; it is destined to play the role of a motto throughout the entire work.
This motive is accompanied here by bell-like octaves in the left hand, oscillating between the pitches of A and D-sharp, a tritone apart. The bell sonority immediately lends an epic character to the music, in line with the Russian musical tradition of the nineteenth century. These are just two of
several "bricks" from which the first theme is built. Another is a short,
dancelike Russian tune (mm. 5–6, 00:14–00:18), presented in a rhythmically displaced way and sounding strangely out of place in this context. It is
followed by a precipitous arpeggio in the right hand (m. 7, 00:19), which
shoots across the whole range of the keyboard like an arrow, being chased by
the left hand. The way these disparate elements are violently juxtaposed sets
a disturbingly aggressive mood for the whole movement. In m. 12 (00:25),
another subject of the first theme is heard in the middle voice. This brassy,
commanding statement is not given any further attention in the movement
until it reappears in the recapitulation, significantly transformed.

The bridge theme (m. 24, 00:50) brings a softer sonority for the first time,
but the dramatic tension does not diminish. The chromatically crawling, oscillating melody in the middle voice has a searching, apprehensive charac-

ter. It is taken over by other voices as if different groups of instruments were joining in. Reaching the high register and a loud dynamic level in m. 31 (01:05), the melody acquires a passionate quality, leading to an outburst of bell tolling in m. 33 (01:10).

The second theme (m. 40, 01:28) creates a lyrical contrast (see Ex. 0.13a) to the violence that has reigned until now. A long melodic line with intonations of a Russian song unfolds against the sustained bass. This theme is reminiscent of the music associated with Juliet or Cinderella, the female protagonists of Prokofiev's most famous ballets. In m. 60 (02:11), what was a melody becomes harmonic texture: the enveloping line of eighth notes is built on the intonations of the second theme. It serves as a background for a restatement of this theme, slightly varied rhythmically, in m. 64 (02:19). Losing its original tranquility, it is then drawn into a quickening stream of running notes.

In m. 70 (02:29), a short motive of four descending notes is introduced; it becomes the basis for the exposition's concluding section. Mercilessly obstinate, the motive is coupled with bell chimes in m. 77 (02:41) to convey the feeling of a tragedy. Eventually the motion slows down, limping and stumbling. In m. 88 (03:06), lugubrious triplets appear in the bass; they decelerate mechanically, as if a heavy machine were grinding to a halt. (The last bar of this section [m. 91, 03:16] was different in Prokofiev's first version of the movement. According to Richter, the composer added the triplet figure after Neuhaus's comment "that the A in the bass could not be sustained for five bars."[4])

The melodic material of the second theme plays a leading role in the development, which commences in m. 92 (03:22). Most of it is based on the incessant motion of eighth notes. Within this stream of sound, the first three notes of the second theme stand out. The initial calm of this theme gives way to an anxiously nervous atmosphere of relentless rhythmic pulsation. The staccato arpeggios zigzagging up and down also derive from the second theme, like the arpeggios heard earlier (m. 60, 02:11). A full rendition of the theme is heard for the first time in the development in m. 112 (03:48), where it assumes a stern and commanding tone. The shards of the "motto" from the first theme turn up randomly. This motive makes its more complete appearance in m. 116 (03:54), permeating the rest of the development.

Starting with m. 129 (04:10), the second theme, presented in augmentation, takes center stage. Its original lyrical character is replaced by an outspoken passion. (Similar significant transformations occur in the development of the Seventh Sonata as well.) Fragments of the two major themes surround the melody in a chaotic frenzy of incessantly pulsating eighth notes. By m. 141 (04:26), the music encompasses a greater range of the keyboard. The second theme is restated in the middle register with a trombone-like sonority. It is accompanied by sporadic, brutal clusters of bass notes (the first occurs in m. 142, 04:28). Prokofiev indicated that these should be played *col pugno* (with the fist). Boris Volsky[5] remembered that when he learned the Sixth Sonata and played it for the composer, he "did not know what *col pugno* means and played these chords with fingers. Sergei Sergeyevich explained that it meant 'to play with the fist' and he wrote it 'to intimidate grandmothers.'"[6] This visually aggressive gesture magnifies the violent atmosphere.

After a sudden dramatic caesura, a new phase of the development begins in m. 157 (04:50). The driving pulsation of eighth notes ceases, quarter notes become the prevailing rhythmic unit, and the music sounds less anguished and more deliberate. The disjointed intonations of the second theme are interspersed with those of the bridge theme. Later, starting with m. 169 (05:07), attention focuses on the development of three short, interrelated motives. Motive *a* derives from the beginning of the bridge section; motive *b* comes from the latter half of the second theme; and motive *c* is a four-note succession of pitches taken from the concluding section. Later (m. 176, 05:19), these elements are set against each other, as shown in Example 6.1, creating a feeling of sparks flying as they collide. In m. 185 (05:36), frenzied, almost hysterical trills that sound like violins in a high register are added to the mix.

The impassioned music in m. 188 (05:40) is based on the bridge theme. The short "motto" reappears randomly in different registers. It leads to a dramatic bell-tolling passage in m. 196 (05:48). Against this background of

Ex. 6.1 Sonata No. 6, mvt. 1

chimes, the movement's opening motive is heard again. At the end of the development, dark, menacing triplets return (m. 212, 06:20); they were first
heard in the conclusion of the exposition. As before, they slow down and
come to a halt in an ominously mechanical fashion.

The recapitulation (m. 218, 06:36) is greatly condensed. After the initial
material is presented, the second subject of the first theme (see m. 12,
00:25), which has not been heard since the beginning of the movement, assumes an unexpected prominence. Appearing in augmentation and in the
treble register (m. 229, 07:01), it exchanges its commanding tone for an outspoken passion. It is accompanied by rising waves of eighth notes, in which
we can detect the second theme's opening intonation, and by occasional
tam-tam-like strokes. The second theme returns in m. 242 (07:26), also in
augmentation; it now uses increasingly wide intervals, as does the accompaniment in the left hand (see Ex. 0.11b). Nothing is left of its original lyrical
character. As observed by Ordzhonikidze, "the second theme makes a
switch into the mode of the first."[7] The emotional tension rises, exploding in
a final episode of bell tolling in m. 253 (07:46), which quotes the similar passage from the development (see m. 196, 05:48). Above the mighty bells motive *b* is heard (see Ex. 6.1). Its intonations, compressed within a narrow

chromatic succession of pitches, sound like a cry of pain. While the volume of the "chimes" subsides during the course of this episode, the *c* motive always sounds in *fortissimo*, as if any restatement brings back painful memories of an undiminished, hardly bearable intensity. The initial "motto" is heard for the last time in m. 270 (08:23), followed by a crushing stroke in the bass.

SECOND MOVEMENT: ALLEGRETTO (DISC 2, TRACK 5)

This movement is a prickly scherzo in E major with a familiar Prokofievian kaleidoscope of moods. Angularity, dance features, and spicy harmonies mix within a generally stable tonal framework. Orchestral allusions are strongly felt throughout. The movement's main tone is ironic mockery. This is one of very few examples among Prokofiev's last works of irony playing an important role; we know well that in Stalinist Russia this was not an encouraged form of artistic expression.

The first theme has a somewhat mechanistic character, generated by the clockwork pacing of even quarter notes. A simple diatonic melody is accompanied by dissonant harmonies, creating a peculiar combination of steadiness and instability. This feeling is enhanced by the nature of the voice leading in these chords: it alternates between moving fairly actively and being "stuck" on the same pitch. The bass line, for instance, remains largely immobile in the first four bars but becomes quite active from m. 5 on (00:06). In turn, the top line trades its melodic design for a strange, "catatonic" moment of repeated notes in mm. 14–16 (00:19–00:24). The poker-faced impassiveness of the chords is combined with unexpected accents on the last note of each phrase, as if the composer were suddenly sticking out his tongue at the audience. A warm, lyrical phrase with wide interval leaps in m. 21 (00:30) contrasts with the preceding material.

An unexpected crescendo and modulation into C major bring a new theme in the bass, characterized by a rude and slightly vulgar assuredness (m. 30, 00:43). It is restated again in m. 44 (01:03), alternating with mocking *pianissimo* renditions of the first theme in the high register (m. 36,

00:52; m. 50, 01:12). Both times it is accompanied by seemingly innocuous but fiendishly difficult arpeggios in the left hand.

In m. 57 (01:22), the assertive theme develops into an expressive dialogue between two voices. The theme's last two notes give birth to a new melodic idea in m. 63 (01:31): a somewhat agitated reiteration of a chromatic motive consisting of four pitches. Here one can hear distant echoes of the first movement's bell chimes. In m. 79 (01:56), the first theme returns, accompanied by a mockingly serious counterpoint in the left hand.

The middle section begins in m. 93 (02:18). Its warm, lyrical character contrasts greatly with the wry tone of the preceding section. Tonally, it vacillates between B-flat minor and B minor. The beautiful theme, played by both hands in unison, recalls the musical world of *Cinderella*. It comes as a shock to realize that this melody is, in fact, related to the previously heard awkwardly vulgar statement (compare m. 94, 02:19, and mm. 30–31, 00:43). In m. 96 (02:24), the plaintive chromatic motive (see m. 63, 01:31) returns in the bass to support the sweeping waves of the melody with a lyrical lilt. The theme transforms into a warmer and more passionate statement as it travels through different tonalities and registers. After the key of B-flat minor has been reestablished, four bars of repeated quarter notes (m. 127, 03:28) prepare the mood and pacing of the return of the opening section.

The reprise of the initial material (m. 131, 03:36) brings back the key of E major. In comparison with the exposition, it is shorter, and the sequence of the elements is different. After the first theme is restated, accompanied by fleeting arpeggios in the left hand, the "rude" theme attempts twice to make its presence known in the bass (in mm. 141, 03:51, and 145, 03:57), but both times it does not extend beyond the initial two measures. Later, in m. 147 (04:00), the lyrical melody in the treble is all lightness and grace. In a short coda (m. 151, 04:07), the chords of the first theme rise to the high register, their persistent repetition conveying an air of warning. Nevertheless, the movement concludes in a mood of smiling wonderment.

THIRD MOVEMENT: TEMPO DI VALZER LENTISSIMO
(DISC 2, TRACK 6)

The third movement is a lush, slow waltz in C major, composed in ABA form. Each section is based on a single melody; the themes are presented in varying keys, registers, and textures. The quasi-orchestral writing recalls the sonority of the *Cinderella* waltzes, with their corresponding warm, amorous emotion. Yet in several subtle ways, this movement is connected to the dramatic first movement. To begin with, the opening statement (see Ex. 0.14) derives from the b motive (see Ex. 6.1), which plays such an important role in the first movement's development. This intonation permeates the third movement. The expansive first theme contains some oscillating, bell-like intonations, such as heard in m. 7 (00:26), which are also reminiscent of the first movement. These connections add sinister undertones to the third movement's prevailing warm lyricism.

The first theme is a long, beautiful melody, supported by lilting chords. It flows freely, passing through varying registers and modulating to different keys. In m. 21 (01:25), the theme starts again in the new key of A-flat major. It undergoes various small changes that create an atmosphere of improvisatory freedom. Toward the end of the section, in m. 38 (02:34), the theme is played *pianissimo*. Having just begun, it fizzles away as if falling into slumber. This feeling is enhanced by the soothing, rocking rhythm in mm. 39 and 41 (02:39 and 02:49).

The middle section follows seamlessly in m. 42 (02:54) with a dreamily repetitive motive that is heard in various registers and rhythmic guises, accompanied by a monotonous motion of octaves in the left hand. It is not entirely innocuous, as becomes clear when one realizes that this oscillation bears a strong resemblance to the scene of Prince Bolkonsky's delirium in *War and Peace* (Ex. 6.2). (Prokofiev composed this opera during the three years following the completion of the Sixth Sonata.) In m. 45 (03:01), a simple lyrical melody emerges in the upper voice. It is repeated in m. 57 (03:32), split between different registers as if played by different instruments in an

Ex. 6.2 War and Peace, *scene 12*

orchestra. The imitations in m. 61 (03:42) are also orchestral in nature. In m. 67 (03:57), the soothing murmuring comes back, tapering away in m. 70 (04:04).

A sudden change in both tonality and overall texture occurs in m. 71 (04:07). Having modulated a half step up to A major, the music acquires a flighty and elusive quality. The mood changes again in m. 76 (04:17), when the carefree atmosphere gives way to a much more agitated, even cross, character. The familiar theme of the B section appears in a high, piercing register, interrupted by "barking" staccato chords reminiscent of French horns. All this happens against a persistent, agitated accompaniment. The

last appearance of this material is in m. 83 (04:30), where it sounds dissonant and disturbing.

Unexpectedly, the music plunges into a full-voiced, passionate rendition
of the opening theme in m. 88 (04:41), starting in the middle of the sentence. Later it calms down and, having begun in B major, modulates into the
home key of C major to prepare for a proper recapitulation of the A section
in m. 97 (05:13). Here, once again, Prokofiev ingeniously imitates the juxtaposition of different orchestral groups. The upper, more important voice is
marked *piano* while the imitating voice in the tenor range bears the indication *mezzo forte,* as if the soft sonority of a string group were juxtaposed with
the sound of a single brass instrument. In m. 101 (05:30), the writing suggests the singing sound of violins in *forte,* with accompanying chords of
brass instruments in the left hand. Measures 105–12 (05:47–06:21) repeat
the preceding statement one tone lower, in B-flat major. Measures 113–16
(06:21–06:42) are a repetition of mm. 38–41 (02:34–02:54), with the
melody succumbing to slumber. Measures 117–19 (06:42–06:51) are similar to mm. 42–44 (02:54–03:02), which led into the middle section. Here
they are followed by a brief phrase resembling a bird call (m. 120, 06:51).
The ensuing cadence lacks in finality; it requires two additional bars to conclude the movement.

FOURTH MOVEMENT: VIVACE (DISC 2, TRACK 7)

Describing the finale, Harlow Robinson writes: "*Vivace* starts out like another one of Prokofiev's naughty, toccata-like exhibitionistic displays, but
takes an unexpectedly serious turn in the middle."[8] While some of the
themes can be described as "naughty," I find nothing exhibitionistic in this
movement. From the very beginning, it is imbued with a turbulent inner
drama. The direct quotations from the first movement enhance the sonata's
dramatic unity. (Prokofiev had used this device only once before, in the Second Sonata. He does so again later in the Ninth Sonata.)

The fourth movement's sonata-rondo form is rather complex. The exposition is rich in melodic material and contains three main themes; the development includes an episode based on material from the first movement; and the recapitulation presents the themes in an inverted order, followed by an extensive and highly dramatic coda.

The first theme or refrain (see Ex.0.17) creates an atmosphere of relentless energy, with its continual motion of sixteenths and an insistent repetition of certain patterns. It begins in A minor but shifts unexpectedly a half step down to G-sharp minor in m. 21 (00:16). The sunny, naive quality of the lyrical second theme, in C major (m. 29, 00:22), evokes the music depicting Juliet or Cinderella. This theme, whose structure is ABA, has a contrasting middle section presented in m. 45 (00:35). Its angular, wide leaps are bold and slightly sarcastic. The C-major tune reappears in m. 61 (00:47) and is juxtaposed against humorously awkward material characterized by abrupt staccatos, starting in m. 68 (00:52).

The music of the refrain returns in m. 85 (01:05), first in B-flat minor and then a half step lower in the home key of A minor. Here it functions as a bridge and contains a new statement: a strikingly bold melody with huge leaps set against hopping staccatos in the accompaniment (m. 100, 01:16). The refrain's melodic pattern comes back and seems ready to bring the section to a close, but a third important theme bursts in at m. 127 (01:36), violently changing the tonality to G-sharp minor, half a step down from the home key. Its audaciously insistent and confident character recalls one of the themes from "The Battle on Ice" in *Alexander Nevsky* (1938–39) (Ex. 6.3).

Ex. 6.3 Alexander Nevsky, *"The Battle on Ice"*

The refrain returns again in m. 158 (02:01) but is interrupted twice (in m. 161, 02:03, and m. 168, 02:08) by stubborn repeated notes in the bass, before closing the exposition in m. 184 (02:20). These interruptions are particularly significant because they juxtapose a sustained A against repeated D-sharps, the same pitches that were used in the bell-tolling octaves in the left hand in the first movement's opening.

The following *Andante* episode is based on two themes from the first movement. It starts with that movement's "motto," which here sheds its original aggressive character and sounds strangely questioning; it is answered in m. 189 (02:30) with a meditative, recitative-like phrase. In m. 204 (03:00), the modified bridge theme from the first movement (see m. 24, 00:50 in the first movement) makes an appearance. This hesitant, searching chromatic phrase is repeated three times, each repetition bringing changes in the accompanying voices. In m. 210 (03:15), the melody passes to the bass, while the right hand plays the "motto" motive followed by the recitative-like melodic line. The pianist's hands move away from each other, reaching the extreme ends of the keyboard. The episode concludes with insistent, questioning repetitions of the "motto" motive.

The opening melodic pattern of the last movement, heard in the bass in m. 229 (03:56), heralds the beginning of the development proper. Hesitant at first, it quickly grows into an unstoppable torrent of sixteenth notes, involving different tonalities and various registers of the piano. In the upbeat to m. 257 (04:19), a new, markedly aggressive element is introduced: three consecutive diminished thirds. This pattern is elaborated upon in mm. 279–90 (04:35–04:43), where it starts sounding very much like the beginning of the third theme of the finale. The latter reappears in m. 290 (04:44) in the home key of A minor, thus launching the movement's recapitulation section. The rude, commanding theme that had been presented in the exposition in m. 100 (01:16) immediately follows in m. 304 (04:56). Starting with m. 320 (05:08), this galloping theme gradually becomes calmer, preparing for the emergence of the lyrical second theme in m. 341 (05:25). The latter is presented here in a slower tempo and in augmentation, enveloped by the accompaniment's waves and projecting a dreamy mood.

The perpetual-motion theme reenters in m. 370 (05:52), interspersed with the "motto" motive from the first movement. Starting in *piano* and in a slower tempo, it grows steadily, as if readying itself for a final battle. It reaches a fervent *forte* in m. 380 (06:00); from there the dramatic intensity does not diminish through the end of the movement.

With the beginning of the coda in m. 399 (06:16) (see Ex. 0.6a), all hell breaks loose. The feeling of tonality is gone; alarming repeated notes echo one another in all registers in a desperate frenzy. The chaos stops abruptly in m. 420 (06:34), where the pattern of repeated notes sounds in a much slower and determined way, as if asserting control over the proceedings. The willful repetitions of the "motto" motive that opened the sonata bring the work to a violently assertive close.

Master Class

FIRST MOVEMENT

The character of the opening statement is powerful and determined. To avoid dryness, I recommend using the pedal generously, changing it with each new octave in the left hand. In m. 5, pay attention to the dynamic change from *fortissimo* to *forte*. Here the repeated chords should be played non legato, but not staccato. In the run in m. 7, use almost no pedal. In m. 12, carry the melodic line in the octaves of the middle voice, making them sound as if played by brass instruments.

In the bridge theme (m. 24), soft but full of tension, the melody in the middle voice needs to be played tenuto and with a certain heaviness. Observe the dynamic indications scrupulously; each new dynamic level should resemble the entry of a new group of instruments. The forte melody in m. 31 needs to be highly expressive. To achieve a bell-like sonority in m. 33, I recommend playing from a certain distance above the keyboard.

The second theme (m. 40) has a simple, lyrical long line. The imitation in m. 48 should sound as if played by a different instrument. In m. 52, play the quarter notes in the left hand lightly, in order not to impede the flow of the melody. The dotted rhythm in mm. 56–57 should not destroy the lyrical character. Play the running eighth notes (m. 60) in a gently melodic way. The restatement of the second theme in m. 64 should have, again, a long melodic line.

In m. 68, use a *martellato* stroke, but do not lose the feeling of melodic direction. Play the motive of four accented notes in m. 70 with gravity. The left-hand bell chimes in m. 77 should sound richly resonant. Bring out the four-note motive played by the thumb of the right hand in m. 81, as well as in the bass line of the left hand in mm. 83–84. The accents in mm. 88–90 should be very much alike. The *ritenuto* should not start earlier than written; it must proceed with a mechanical determination.

Throughout the development section, which starts in m. 92, carefully observe the dynamic indications. Play the running eighth notes with finger staccato and use almost no pedal, holding the long chords in the left hand with your fingers. Notes marked with accents should be clearly differentiated from the rest of the eighth notes. Do not make a crescendo in m. 94, and do not anticipate the crescendo in m. 101. In m. 111, shape the melody in the left hand, but do not play it with a touch that is too thick.

When the initial motive in thirds reappears (first in m. 117), play it dryly, with clearly articulating fingers. Hold the half notes in mm. 118–19 for their full value with your finger, not with the pedal.

In m. 124, shape the melody expressively, but do not use much pedal. Differentiate the sound of the various elements: the melodic line, the initial motive in thirds, the three-note motive of the accented eighth notes (the opening of the second theme), and the rest of the pulsating eighth notes. Play the theme in m. 140 using an "out of the piano" stroke to imitate the full and airy sound of trombones, and shape it as a long, melodic line. The clusters of notes in mm. 142, 146, and 149 have the composer's indication *col pugno* (with the fist). (This instruction was omitted in the first complete edition of Prokofiev's works: it must have been judged too radical by the Soviet editors. This omission has been carried over into many later reprints.)

Clear the air at the end of m. 156 by making a clean pause, as written. In m. 157, differentiate among the various elements of the texture by varying the touch: weighty accents in the right hand, somewhat lighter eighth notes in the left hand, and tenuto in the bridge theme in the middle voice played by both hands. In m. 165, make sure that the bridge theme is heard in the left hand as well as the right.

The sonority should change drastically in the upbeat to m. 177; it must be dry, bright, but not too heavy; the *b* motive (see Ex. 6.1) needs to stand out and sound brilliant. In m. 185, take care not to slow down, even if it means executing fewer thirty-second notes than written; play them very close to the keys as imitations of violin trills. In m. 188, make the melody sound very intense, while the motive in thirds should be played with a lighter stroke.

The chimes of m. 196 should have a lot of resonance; use the pedal generously. Play the first theme that comes on top of it with an "out of the piano" stroke. The triplets of m. 212 should have a dark sonority and a mechanical character; the *ritenuto* should convey the feeling of a machine gradually running out of steam.

Make the beginning of the recapitulation, marked *forte* (m. 218), sound different from m. 225, marked *fortissimo*. In mm. 229 and 235, play the right hand with a singing tone. The left-hand line should envelop the melody. To prevent dryness, use the pedal generously but change it frequently. The right-hand chords in mm. 233 and 239 should sound like a big bell or a tam-tam; the eighth notes in mm. 233–34, and later in mm. 239–42, should emerge as if out of a shadow cast by the preceding chord. The drop in dynamics to *mezzo piano* in m. 242 should not diminish the intensity of feeling. The difficult leaps in the left hand starting in m. 248 should not sound too dry. Make the chimes in m. 253 resonant and atmospheric; the triplets in the high register, starting m. 254, should be bright and sonorous, not dry. Following the example of Richter, I interpret the indication *fortissimo* in mm. 254, 259, and 266 as referring solely to the right hand, while the chiming chords make a terraced diminuendo. Even when the chords reach *pianissimo* in the upbeat to m. 268, they should continue sounding resonant, to contrast with the dry matter-of-factness of the concluding statement.

SECOND MOVEMENT

Play the chords with finger staccato, staying close to the keys. Bring out the upper voice lightly, as well as the other voices whenever they move. Make the phrasing clear, but do not make an obvious crescendo toward the last note, which should sound unexpected and teasing. In m. 21, make the melody sound like woodwinds; the accompanying chords should continue to be played staccato. In mm. 26–27, do not let the accompanying chords cause accents in the eighth notes of the outer voices. In m. 30, play the melody in the bass with a full sound; the character should be assertive but not dry. In the *subito pianissimo* in m. 36, keep the volume down while bringing out the top melody. Play the runs in the left hand very close to the keys, and use no pedal. The tumultuous *forte* in m. 43 should not be anticipated. At the end of m. 48, the top voice should take over the melody of the bass. Mm. 50–56 should sound similar to mm. 36–42.

In the passage beginning with m. 57, make the melodic lines in the top and bottom voices answer each other. Separate the accompanying chords from one another with firmness, but do not play them too heavily. In m. 63, play the narrow half-tone intervals in the melody *poco dolente*, but stay in a sonorous *forte* until m. 73. Play the transition mm. 77–78 tenuto, imitating the sound of a bassoon. In m. 79, the right hand should play the same way it did in the opening of the movement, while the left hand spins out a mockingly serious chromatic line of its own. I hear the left-hand part here as played by a bassoon, with comic commentaries from a contrabassoon in the low register in mm. 81–82, 87, and 91–92.

The opening melody of the middle section (starting in m. 93) should have lyrical simplicity, and the tempo must not be too slow. Play the dotted rhythm in the left hand starting in m. 96 with a lilt. In mm. 104–26, give the melody orchestral colors as it appears in different registers and keys. Treat the ascending and descending melodic waves in mm. 112–13, 114–15, 123–24, and 125–26 as two-bar gestures.

Make no *accelerando* in the bars leading to the return of *Tempo I* in m. 131, which should have the lightness of the similar passage in mm. 36–43. Do not overdo the *pochissimo crescendo* in m. 134. When the fast notes move into the right hand in m. 140, do not let them be too bright. While the principal melodic line in m. 151 is in the left hand, pay attention as well to the top line of ascending chords in the right hand. Play the repeated chords in mm. 155–58 very similar to each other (non legato, not staccato). The chromatic line in the inner voices should sound as if played by different instruments. Make almost no *ritardando* at the end.

THIRD MOVEMENT

This movement requires a lush, warm sonority that is not easy to achieve, especially in the sections where the melody climbs into the high treble register. Much depends on the tempo, which, while being slow, should still possess the rocking lilt of a waltz. The pianist's ability to shape a long melodic line is crucial as well. Although in the score all chords in the left hand are separated from each other by rests, I recommend extending those on downbeats with the pedal. This will help to treat the three beats in the bars differently: the first as a longer one, the second as a light one, and the third as leading into the next bar. In this movement, even more than in the others, I think about orchestral colors, often in a very concrete way.

In m. 5, if you need to break the wide chord in the left hand, I suggest beginning it together with the grace notes in the right hand. The top note in m. 7 is unlikely to last as long as it is written. However, imagining it sounding will help you find the right sonority for the other voices. The octaves in the left hand at the end of m. 16 should sound light and should lead into the next downbeat. The same is true of the octaves leading into mm. 18, 19, and 21. The new key in m. 21 should be introduced with a new sonority. Strive to achieve a different sound for each of the voices. Starting with m. 25, make every triplet lead into the following long note. The *fortissimo* in m. 30 should sound like a full orchestral tutti. The octaves in the right hand in mm. 32–33 should have a singing tone, without any hardness. I hear the upbeat to m. 34 as the beginning of a trombone solo. This phrase is imitated in the top voice in m. 35. Play the theme in m. 38 with a warm *pianissimo* touch. The pairs of thirds in mm. 39 and 41 should have a slight diminuendo in each of them.

In the first three bars of the middle section (mm. 42–44), the imitations in the right hand should each have a different color, while the left hand plays with a light legato touch. In mm. 50 and 52, place the phrasing commas before the last eighth note of these bars, as well as after the last note of m. 56. (In the latter bar, such phrasing is indicated in some editions.) In the repetition of this theme that begins in m. 57, make the melodic line clear while it travels through different registers, as if passed from one instrument to another. The other voices should be played with a lighter touch. In m. 61, shape the melodic lines of the two upper voices to highlight the imitations, while the bass line should sound lighter and softer. In m. 67, play the oscillations in the bass with a good, though light, legato touch.

In m. 71, keep the sonority of the left hand light and transparent. In the right hand, each figure of ♩ ♩ 𝄾 should be played with a light diminuendo. Here again, the melody should sound as if it is passing from one group of instruments to another. Do not make the crescendo earlier than it is written in m. 72. The touch has to become more direct and persistent during the crescendo at the end of m. 74. Play the melody in m. 76 with fairly strong fingers and make it non legato, not staccato. In contrast, the eighth notes in m. 78 should sound resonant; play them with weighty staccato. Play the passage starting in m. 83 with a heavy tenuto non legato touch; to assure clarity, do not use much pedal.

In m. 88, come back to the lush sound of a full orchestra, bringing out the melodic line in the upper voice. Make the return of C major in m. 97 sound like a homecoming. I suggest playing the top voice here warmly and expressively, imagining the full string section of an orchestra, while making the imitation in the tenor voice expressive but thinner, like a solo brass instrument. I use the same approach in the phrase starting in m. 105. In m. 101, make sure that the brassy chords in the left hand do not overpower the melody in the upper voice (the same applies for m. 109). Play the *mezzo forte* in m. 115 more warmly than the *pianissimo* in m. 113, but without any agitation.

For the return of the dreamy music (m. 117) that originally led to the middle section, I favor taking a slightly faster tempo, that of *Poco più animato* of the B section (m. 42), coming back to the main tempo during the *un poco crescendo* in m. 119. Treat the imitations in mm. 120–21 orchestrally. The bass octave in m. 123 should sound like a light pizzicato. Play the last two bars calmly and conclusively, with a warmly singing bass line.

FOURTH MOVEMENT

In this movement, as in the first, it is essential to be precise in observing the composer's dynamic indications, especially in all passages connected with the material of the first theme. Avoid adding accents to the running sixteenths as, for instance, in mm. 17–20; such stresses will destroy the effect of perpetual motion. Play the first theme with active, precise fingers and use very little pedal. The *mezzo piano* indication in m. 9 is for the left hand only; the right hand joins in the new dynamic in the next bar. The crescendo in mm. 15–20 should not be big; the unexpected diminuendo should be delayed until the very end of m. 20. Let the new key of G-sharp minor in m. 21 have a different color; do not prepare the *sforzandos* in mm. 25–27 with crescendos.

Give the new theme in m. 29 a completely different character, naive and carefree. The right hand should produce a sonority suggestive of a flute, and the left-hand triplets should be even and transparent; do not use much pedal. Change the color in m. 36 in response to the slight darkening of the mood. In mm. 43–44, feel the conclusiveness of the cadence in C major. In mm. 48–49, try to achieve as much legato as possible with the fingers, rather than smudging the texture with the pedal. In mm. 53–60, the continuity of the running sixteenth notes is essential; do not introduce any accents. Achieve good legato in both hands in the fade-out in m. 60. The pedal marked by Prokofiev in mm. 61 and 71 should not be held for longer than 1½–2 bars. Use a short finger staccato in mm. 68–71 to contrast with the subsequent light, flutelike melody.

Return to clear, even, well-articulated finger playing in m. 85; use no crescendo or accents in mm. 91–94. Modify the color at the key change in m. 95. In m. 100, play the right hand with a very good finger legato, using the pedal only sparingly. Do not lose clarity in the diminuendo, which starts in m. 122.

In the bold new theme in m. 127, execute the marked accents assertively, and do not let the left hand get heavy. Make a clear caesura before each new phrase, that is, before the upbeats to mm. 134, 141, and 148.

The *mezzo forte* in m. 161 should sound like an unexpected intrusion. When it appears for the second time in m. 168, the dynamics should remain unchanged for four bars until the diminuendo in m. 172. The energy of this section should not drop until the very end, nor should there be any *rallentando*.

In m. 185, play the opening thirds with a good legato touch. I suggest that the new melody in m. 189 should sound somewhat freer in tempo; I imagine the sound of a saxophone here. (Prokofiev liked the timbre of this instrument and used it effectively in his orchestral scores.) When this melody returns in m. 199, let it be simple in expression and suggestive of the sound of a flute and a bassoon.

In m. 204, create a light, airy legato sound. Play the octaves of the left hand in m. 212 *legato espressivo*, juxtaposing them with the light thirds in the right hand. As your hands start moving away from each other in m. 214, the growing gap between them suggests a mysterious feeling. Pay attention to the difficult-to-execute contrast in the dynamics, playing *piano* in the left hand and *mezzo forte* in the right. After holding the fermata in m. 228, I recommend feeling the last eighth note of the bar in the tempo of the next section.

In m. 229, the sixteenths in *pianissimo* should be clearly articulated. Play mm. 240–42 mysteriously. In the passage that follows, the indications of dynamics, as well as the infrequent accents, must be observed precisely. The diminished thirds in the left hand in the upbeat to m. 257 should be played with a straightforward, matter-of-fact sound.

Play the theme in m. 290 with ferocious energy, but with a ringing rather than percussive sound. The left hand should not be too heavy. Do not play the eighth notes in m. 320 too short; those in the left hand should be slightly longer and more melodic than in the right. In the passage that begins in m. 332, the right hand remains in *piano* all the time, while the left makes a crescendo to *mezzo forte* before coming back to *piano*.

The light, dreamy melody in m. 341 is surrounded by airy figurations in the left hand, which should be played without any accents. When the left hand takes over the melody in m. 349, it should have a warm, cello-like sonority. The melody in m. 354 is marked *pianissimo*, as opposed to the *piano* in m. 341; make the difference audible. You can take a bit of extra time for the run in m. 354. Feel the modulation leading to m. 362.

Increase the speed gradually, starting with m. 370. I recommend reaching *Tempo I* by m. 380 and not accelerating any further. Make the fanfares of re-peated notes, which appear first in the left hand in m. 401, cut through the general turmoil. When they sound for the last time in a varied form in mm. 420–21, play the repeated notes tenuto. The ending of the movement, start-ing with m. 425, can be played either strictly in tempo, slowing down only in the last two bars, or with an *allargando* in mm. 425–28, returning to the pre-vious tempo in m. 429 without any further *ritenuto*.

Sonata No. 7 in B-flat Major, op. 83

Composed in 1939–42. First performed by Sviatoslav Richter on January 18, 1943. Published by Muzgiz in 1943.

This sonata is the second of the so-called "War Sonatas." Prokofiev began composing it in 1939, simultaneously with the Sixth and the Eighth Sonatas, and completed it in 1942. While the Sixth Sonata reflects the nervous anticipation of World War II and the Eighth looks back to those terrible events retrospectively, the Seventh Sonata projects the anguish and the struggle of the war years as they were experienced in real time. This is one of the most successful of Prokofiev's works, distinguished by its tight structure and careful, complex development of material.

Sviatoslav Richter, the first performer of the work, wrote: "Early in 1943, I received the score of the Seventh Sonata, which I found fascinating and which I learned in just four days. . . . The work was a huge success. The audience clearly grasped the spirit of the work, which reflected their innermost feelings and concerns. (This was also felt to be the case with Shostakovich's Seventh Symphony, which dates from more or less the same period.)"[1]

Richter clearly had strong feelings for the sonata. It moved him to the following eloquent description: "With this work we are brutally plunged into the anxiously threatening atmosphere of a world that has lost its balance. Chaos and uncertainty reign. We see murderous forces ahead. But this does not mean that what we lived by before thereby ceases to exist. We continue to feel and love. Now the full range of human emotions bursts forth. Together with our fellow men and women, we raise a voice in protest and share the common grief. We sweep everything before us, borne along by the will for victory. In the tremendous struggle that this involves, we find the strength to affirm the irrepressible life-force."[2]

Analyzing the special qualities of this sonata, Ordzhonikidze writes: "One dramatic idea permeates the whole sonata. It seems that contradictory tendencies in the musical style of Prokofiev are exposed and lead to a greater synthesis. Romantic exaggeration of feelings in this sonata sharply contradicts the ironclad logic of the classical sonata-allegro. This bipolarity is reflected in the combination of the essentially two-part, Scarlatti-like piano writing with harsh chords of complex harmonic nature, in the complex modal structure of the sonata-allegro, and, most importantly, in the character of musical images."[3] Ordzhonikidze also observed that "this sonata has none of [Prokofiev's] beloved masques, nor has it the polypersonalia of early sonatas. The Seventh Sonata has one protagonist and one purpose. In this sense, it is a monodrama."[4]

Listening Closely

FIRST MOVEMENT: ALLEGRO INQUIETO (DISC 2, TRACK 8)

The first movement is the most complex of the three in this sonata. Its tonality is not always clearly defined; indeed, in terms of tonal ambiguity, this may be the most extreme of Prokofiev's sonata movements. Ultimately, however, a general gravitation toward B-flat major becomes apparent. For the most part, the musical texture remains dry, transparent, even austere; the pianist's hands frequently explore the opposite ends of the keyboard.

The thematic material is rich and diverse: short melodic and rhythmic statements composing the first group of themes evolve into each other, while the second theme consists of a single long, unfolding melody. In contrast with Prokofiev's other sonata-allegro movements, this opening movement blurs the delineations both between the exposition and the development and between the development and the recapitulation.

The movement starts with an angular and energetic principal theme presented in unison (see Ex. 0.4c), which I will designate as *1a*. It is immediately followed by a "drumbeat" rhythmic pattern A (♩♩♩♩.♪♪♪♪♪♪), which will permeate the entire movement (mm. 5–6, 00:05–00:06). In m. 20 (00:16), another important new rhythm, a "galloping" pattern B (♪♪♪♪♪♪♪♪♪♪♪♪) is introduced.* Stubbornly repeated, it leads to the first of many *fortissimos*.

The *1a* theme reappears in the high register, like a zigzag of lightning (m. 28, 00:22). The dynamic level drops to *piano* as rhythm A restores the apprehensive atmosphere. In m. 36 (00:29), the initial theme is combined with the galloping rhythm B. This rhythmic pattern, in turn, shapes the new statement *1b*, a heavy, threatening, chromatically ascending melodic line; it appears in octaves in the low bass register (m. 45, 00:36). The second phrase of this theme sees the iambic† pattern of weak-strong beats of rhythm B transformed into a trochaic‡ accompaniment in the right hand (Ex. 7.2, m. 53, 00:42). Once again, the *1a* theme blazes in the treble register, with the left hand stomping far below (m. 61, 00:49). This time the theme has an added fanfare motive of a descending major triad, which will also play an important role throughout the movement. It gives birth to another theme (*1c*) in which wide leaps and narrow chromatic motion are combined with fanfares of descending triads, accompanied by unexpectedly euphonious sustained chords (m. 65, 00:52). While this theme evolves, we observe that the order of the two bars making up drumbeat pattern A has reversed (Ex. 7.3, m. 75, 01:00). The further development of this material creates an urgent, insisting atmosphere and leads to another statement (*1d*) that combines chromatic motion with the fanfares in a different way (m. 89, 01:12).

---

*These rhythmic patterns A and B generate additional rhythmic combinations that appear throughout the movement, as outlined in Example 7.1.

†Iambus: in verse, a meter characterized by a succession of unstressed-stressed syllables.

‡Trochaeus: in verse, a meter characterized by a succession of stressed-unstressed syllables.

Ex. 7.1 Sonata No. 7, mvt. 1

The chordal accompaniment of this theme gives it a decisively marching character; the final section establishes the key of A minor.

The bridge section (m. 119, 01:38) is extremely short, consisting of only a few chords. It seems to have no function other than to modulate into the key in which the second theme begins. The manuscript, currently in the Russian State Archive of Literature and Art (RGALI), shows that Prokofiev had doubts about this passage. It has a marking of *GP* (general pause) and a footnote in Prokofiev's handwriting: "here to bring back the theme that is in the copy from which the engraving has been made." The same footnote appears in the corresponding place in the recapitulation (m. 333, 06:06). However, no traces of this variant of the bridge section have been found, and it is not mentioned in any other source.

Ex. 7.2 Sonata No. 7, mvt. 1

Ex. 7.3 Sonata No. 7, mvt. 1

The second theme begins in A-flat in m. 124 (01:47, Ex. 0.12), although by the very next bar gravitation to this key is no longer perceptible. The expansive, eloquent melody presents a striking contrast to the preceding music. Strongly reminiscent of many lyrical pages from Prokofiev's ballets, its sinuous beauty recalls the expressive movements of Galina Ulanova, the first Juliet, as captured in the 1954 film version of *Romeo and Juliet*.[5] The piano texture is polyphonic: the main melody is supported by two lower voices.

Although it presents an opposing mode to the opening group of themes, the second theme is intrinsically connected with them. Its very first motive—four repeated notes—recalls the rhythmic formula A from m. 5. In general, the contour of this theme is related to that of the theme *1a*, as shown in Ex. 7.4.

Ex. 7.4 Sonata No. 7, mvt. 1

In m. 153 (03:26), repeated notes in the bass bring an apprehensively dark feeling. They serve as the background for the concluding theme, which appears two bars later; it derives from the second theme's final phrase. In a deviation from his usual practice, Prokofiev does not clearly separate the exposition from the development; instead, the ever-quickening pulsation of eighth notes leads directly into it. A sudden *forte* (m. 168, 03:49) crushes any vestige of the second theme's lyrical atmosphere as the *accelerando* continues.

The main tempo is restored in m. 182 (04:02), signifying the beginning of the development. Relentless energy is unleashed by the familiar rhythmic formula B. In a dramatic battlefield frenzy of mighty, dissonant chords, different themes from the exposition are churned together. Theme *1a* is heard in m. 186 (04:05). The restatement of the rhythm B in m. 207 (04:23) is followed by material that derives from theme *1a*, played by both hands in unison. Rhythm A thunders in the low bass register in m. 215 (04:29). Theme *1b* is developed in m. 218 (04:31), and the development of theme *1d* follows in m. 234 (04:44). In m. 252 (05:00), everything gives way to the obsessive rhythmic formula B, later joined by its trochaic inversion. Against this background we hear a menacing statement in the bass (m. 269, 05:13). This is the beginning of the second theme in augmentation, stripped of its lyrical qualities and assuming an outspokenly dramatic tone.* In m. 286 (05:26), the treble voice takes over this melody, which adopts the energetic rhythm of the first theme and becomes almost unrecognizable.

Later (m. 293, 05:31), the insistent repetition of the same note appears in

---

*A similar complete transformation of the second theme occurs in the development of the Sixth Sonata's opening movement.

the melody. It happens again in m. 298 (05:37), but only in m. 303 (06:06) are we able to identify this event as the beginning of theme 1d, which sounds in its entirety in B minor. By now we realize that we have entered the recapitulation, which drastically reorders the exposition's thematic narrative. Theme 1d is the first to return; then, after a short modulating bridge section (m. 333, 06:06), the second theme appears (m. 338, 06:16). It starts in B-flat major but soon abandons this key.

Finally, in m. 359 (07:32) we hear the initial 1a theme. Resuming the first tempo at once, this section has the character of a brisk march. It begins in *pianissimo* and is constructed in three waves of surging crescendos. The last one reaches its peak in m. 397 (08:01), when rhythm A is hammered in the treble register like a frenetic Morse code. After the last appearance of the principal theme (m. 401, 08:04), the tide recedes and the movement ends in hushed tones. The rhythmic energy, however, continues undiminished until the very end.

SECOND MOVEMENT: ANDANTE CALOROSO
(DISC 2, TRACK 9)

The second movement presents an entirely different emotional picture. Its deeply felt expressivity projects the grandeur of a national tragedy, extending beyond any single person's drama. It is conceived as a monumental symphonic movement, with many allusions to orchestral sonorities.

Harlow Robinson remarks that this movement, "like the third movement of the Sixth Sonata, . . . is in a waltz time."[6] Personally, I find no similarity in atmosphere between the lush waltz of the Sixth and the movement in question, even though the $\frac{3}{4}$ time signature does contribute a flexible lilt to the pacing. The movement is in E major, a tritone away from the key of two outer movements. As has been observed before, this is a tonal relationship much favored by Prokofiev.

Written in a modified ABA form, the movement reveals deep connections on various levels between the sections. To begin with, the first three notes of the initial statement, which rise chromatically, permeate the entire fabric of the movement. They can be heard in the tenor voice in mm. 14 (00:57) and 16 (01:04), in the alto and the bass leading into m. 21 (01:25), in the tenor again in m. 23 (01:35), and so on. In the second section, they generate intensified chromatic activity in the left hand in mm. 35–38 (02:23–02:34), in m. 44 (02:48), in m. 50 (03:06), and elsewhere.

The broad first theme unfolds unhurriedly, like the flow of a mighty river, setting the tone of an epic narrative. Starting in a reserved and noble way, it soars, encompassing an ever-greater range, before calming down in m. 24 (01:40). In m. 33 (02:12), the clouds gather, and a new theme starts ominously in the low register. In m. 41 (02:38), a phrase begins as the embellishment of the preceding theme before starting a torturous, stubborn ascent (m. 44, 02:48). Two chromatic lines crawl upward, while a third line counterbalances them, descending chromatically. The full orchestral sonority in m. 46 (02:55) breaks into a passionate lament. This material is taken from mm. 13–16 (00:52–01:07) of the A section (compare excerpts a and b in Ex. 7.5.) Another chromatic climb brings even greater emotional intensity before a ringing E-major chord erupts as an announcement of a stunning discovery. Sonorities imitating bells, a traditional Russian musical symbol of a national tragedy, make their appearance in m. 56 (03:31) (see Ex. 0.16). With the pianist's hands playing in nonsynchronized rhythms, the texture communicates a feeling of great turmoil. The whole emotional and dynamic ascent of mm. 32–56 is revisited in compressed form in mm. 60–61 (03:42–03:50).

The dark, subdued theme from m. 32 now laments outspokenly in the top voice (m. 65, 03:59). A new set of bells rings out in m. 69 (04:13) (see Ex. 0.6b), dying away and introducing the most mesmerizing passage of the whole sonata (starting with m. 79, 04:36). For me, this music paints a picture of complete devastation. The continually repeated two notes of the ringing bell conjure up a lone belfry in a burned-out village.

The first theme returns in m. 98 (05:36) but is soon abandoned, as if the peaceful mood of the beginning is out of place after the tragedy we have just witnessed. Additional brief chimes close this extraordinary movement.

Ex. 7.5 Sonata No. 7, mvt. 2

THIRD MOVEMENT: PRECIPITATO (DISC 2, TRACK 10)

The finale is a toccata, harking back to the famous Toccata op. 11 (see Ex. 0.5b) and other works in a similar vein, such as *Suggestion diabolique*, op. 4, no. 4 (see Ex. 0.9), or the second movement of the Second Sonata. Like the earlier pieces, the movement is based on perpetual motion and a constantly repeated short motive (see Ex. 0.10). It is sometimes described as jazzy, and its ostinato three-note motive has been said to reflect the influence of American blues. I believe these comparisons miss the point entirely. Whatever the superficial resemblances may be, the muscular, unyielding force of this music is miles away from the casual ease associated with the blues. The overall defiant energy of the movement is without parallel in Prokofiev's sonatas. Unlike the first movement, the finale is grounded in a firm sense of tonality, established by the very first chord, the tonic of B-flat major. In fact, the tonally ambiguous passages here seem intended to recall the chaotic turbulence of the first movement. The two movements thus represent the polarities of an unfolding conflict.

The time signature of this movement is an unusual $\frac{7}{8}$. As previously mentioned, such asymmetrical meters, often encountered in Russian folk songs, were used by Russian composers of the nineteenth century in music with a national flavor. (Prokofiev's use of such meters in Violin Sonata No. 1 is illustrated in Ex. 0.2.)

The combination of asymmetrical meter and predictably regular phrasing works very successfully in this finale. Most of the phrases are two bars long; in addition, the ostinato motive in the bass appears with inevitable regularity, often every other bar. The crawling chromatic movement in the inner chordal voices and the overall tonal stability constitute another dichotomy.

The movement's steely, determined pace is occasionally interrupted by zigzagging angular phrases in mm. 27 (00:32–00:34), 30 (00:36–00:39), and 35 (00:42–00:44)—all with preceding upbeats—as well as in m. 38 (00:47). Their texture, which resembles that of a two-part invention, is a clear reminder of the first movement's chaos and turmoil. These passages create a strong contrast with the surrounding massive chords.

The transitional section, starting in m. 50 (01:01), also employs short motives reminiscent of the beginning of the first movement. Compare the succession of the fanfarelike motive and chromatic motion of mm. 52–57 (01:04–01:11), shown in Example 7.6b, with the similar combination, albeit in a reverse order, of mm. 92–93 (01:14–01:16, Track 8) of the first movement (Ex. 7.6a).

The drum roll of mm. 74–76 (01:31–01:35) ushers in a more melodious and slightly calmer middle section (m. 79, 01:37). Its tonality (E minor) is a tritone away from the movement's home key (B-flat major.) This relationship mirrors that between the outer sections of the sonata as a whole (B-flat major) and its second movement (E major.) The new thematic material

Ex. 7.6a Sonata No. 7, mvt. 1

Ex. 7.6b Sonata No. 7, mvt. 3

bears similarities with the transitional section (mm. 50–78, 01:01–01:37) and, therefore, with the first movement.

The transitional material returns in m. 105 (02:09), abruptly ending the short respite and throwing us again into the combative atmosphere that dominates the movement. Another drum roll, similar to the one we heard earlier, degenerates into an almost intolerable hammering of the note A, the leading tone of B-flat major (mm. 125–26, 02:34–02:36), before returning to the first theme. Thus, the overall structure is revealed as palindromic (ABCBA). The first statement of the main theme is repeated without changes. Later (from m. 145, 02:59), it grows in scope and dynamics, covering an ever greater registral range. The hammering on one note, heard earlier, turns into a fierce repetition of entire chords (mm. 163–70, 03:21–03:31), before resolving into the tonic of B-flat major (m. 171, 03:31). Initially marred by occasional dissonances, the chord and the B-flat major scale clean themselves of extraneous notes in the final bars of this most rousing of Prokofiev's endings.

Master Class

FIRST MOVEMENT

The beginning needs to be played with finger non legato in order to create the restless (*inquieto*) character: playing it legato will make the sonority too sweet, while the fast tempo makes using the wrist for playing non legato impractical. Observe the dynamic markings on the first page precisely. The crescendo from mm. 12 to 23 is better achieved if each of the accents on the downbeats of mm. 14, 16, 18, 20, 21, 22, and 23 is progressively louder, and if the dynamics recede somewhat with the notes immediately following these accents.

In mm. 36–40, the right hand plays *forte* portato (but not staccato), while the left hand continues playing *piano*. Most editions indicate the rhythmic values in m. 44 erroneously, making the bar consist of three eighth notes only; the scalar run of triplets should be notated in eighth notes, not in sixteenths. (Richter played it this way, maintaining the same bar length.)

Pay attention to the differences in dynamics between the phrases beginning in mm. 45 and 53, respectively. The former starts with *mezzo forte* in the left hand and *piano* in the right hand; the latter with *forte* in the left hand and *mezzo forte* in the right hand. Make the four-bar phrasing in the left hand apparent, carrying the melodic line across the rests (see Ex. 7.2).

In m. 65, the left hand plays *mezzo forte* tenuto after the preceding *fortissimo*. Try to achieve a sonority that imitates French horns. I feel the need to introduce a phrasing comma before m. 95. Do not play m. 119 (*Poco meno mosso*) too slowly, just a bit slower than the main tempo.

The second theme (m. 124) must have lyrical expressivity and a balletic plasticity. I suggest holding the long bass notes in mm. 124–25, 129–30, 131–32, and so forth with the right pedal, rather than using the sostenuto (middle) pedal; this is perfectly attainable if your left-hand touch remains delicate when playing in the middle register. In mm. 137–39, I take the upper B of the arpeggio in the left-hand part with the right hand: first with the thumb, then changing it to the second finger. Later, I also press down the low B-flat bass note silently: this allows me to release the pedal without losing the bass. I do the same in the recapitulation in mm. 353–55.

The long *accelerando,* starting in m. 151 and extending through m. 181, must be well calculated so that the pianist will reach exactly the right tempo in m. 182. Prokofiev did not indicate a crescendo to go along with this *accelerando.* For this reason, I insist on sustaining a piano dynamic until the crushing *forte* arrives in m. 168. Make the intonation of the descending tritone (across the octave) clear and meaningful in the top of the right-hand chords in mm. 168 and 170 (Ex. 7.7). It will be repeated later in mm. 175 and 177, 195 and 197, and 201 and 203.

The development section starting in m. 183 ushers in a long passage of loud playing. To give some relief to the listeners' ears (and to your right hand), observe the differences between *fortissimo, forte,* and *mezzo forte.*

In the phrase that begins in m. 218, bring out the ascending chromatic melody in the outer voices; it is repeated in the low bass (starting m. 226) and again in the outer voices (starting m. 230). I suggest phrasing the passage starting in m. 240 as indicated in Ex. 7.8.

In mm. 260, 262, and 263, I hold the pedal for the whole bar to create a quasi-glissando effect, highlighting the contrast with the dry sonority of the preceding and following bars. Starting m. 269, phrase the bass line so that

Ex. 7.7 Sonata No. 7, mvt. 1

Ex. 7.8 Sonata No. 7, mvt. 1

the second theme in augmentation comes out dramatically expressive, but keep the rhythm of the eighth notes steady.

In mm. 306 and 310, show the difference in dynamics in the bass (*forte* after *mezzo forte*). In m. 308, I suggest inserting a phrasing comma before the last eighth note, similar to the one recommended between mm. 94 and 95.

Hold the last chord of m. 358 for as long as you feel is right. The release of the untied notes and of the pedal in m. 359, however, should signify the beginning of a new tempo; allow no delay or hesitation there. The ensuing passage is the recapitulation of the opening theme, as previously mentioned. It should be played with all the dramatic intensity of the beginning rather than being treated as a fleeting coda. These last two pages should be played using finger non legato; painstakingly observe the dynamic indications, just as in the beginning of the movement.

Another misprint appears in most editions: the last note of m. 372 (D) should read D-flat, to match the interval relationship of the opening statement. Richter recorded it this way.

SECOND MOVEMENT

The rare indication *Andante caloroso* (warm) requires that the pianist produce a full, singing tone in the melody. Throughout, Prokofiev meticulously specifies different dynamics for varying sound layers. These indications, as well as the gaps between the bass and the leading middle voice, recall the composer's frequently idiosyncratic orchestrations. I imagine cellos and violas playing the main melody in unison, accompanied by a bassoon and double basses in the bass, with French horn chords at the top. The instrumentation clearly changes in mm. 7 and 8.

The pianist should strive to create a long melodic line; I suggest phrasing it as indicated in Example 7.9. Your playing should have an evolving quality here, with one short phrase flowing into the next one. Beware of making the second quarter notes too prominent in mm. 1, 3, 9, 11, and so on. In mm. 13–16, play the moving inner voices expressively but lighter than the main melody in the top voice. Its curvaceous line has a plasticity akin to the second theme of the first movement.

Ex. 7.9 Sonata No. 7, mvt. 2

The *Poco più animato* section (m. 32) must have an ominous, foreboding character. In the first two bars, I slightly emphasize the left hand. Later (mm. 36–39), let the melody weave uninterruptedly for four bars, while paying attention to the bass line and playing the moving voices in the middle register expressively but lightly. Treat the phrase that begins with the upbeat to m. 40 as an ornamentation of the new theme that was presented in m. 32. Give dramatic intensity to the three simultaneously unfolding chromatic lines in m. 44 (and later in m. 50), while avoiding harshness in sound.

The *Più largamente* in m. 46 should sound like a natural "opening up" of the phrase, with the scalar run in the right hand imitating the sliding shift of violins. (The same effect occurs later in the run at the end of m. 61.) After this highly chromatic passage, the E-major chord in m. 53 should sound like a ray of light. Create a resonant, brassy sonority, full of air. In mm. 53–54, treat the texture as consisting of two parallel lines: one of chords and another of low octaves. Measure 56 introduces mighty bell chimes based on two alternating chords. I suggest playing m. 65 *espressivo dolente*. In the section beginning in m. 69, the bell tolling alternates with an expressive melodic line in the left hand.

I feel the necessity to slow the tempo slightly in the two bars leading to the haunting passage beginning in m. 79. The A-flat–G ostinato, introduced in m. 81, should be played in an uncompromisingly even way, without a hint of diminuendo between the two notes, which would turn this powerfully devastating passage into sentimental wailing. This motive should sound totally independent of the chordal progression in other voices, creating a polytonal effect.

It is difficult to decide whether to interpret the final section as a severely truncated recapitulation or as a coda. I lean toward the former and try to give it as much weight as possible, in order to counterbalance the first section after such an extensive and eventful middle section. Here the meticulous observation of all dynamic indications is essential for highlighting the harmonic changes in the last reminiscence of the bell chimes, which starts with the upbeat to m. 103.

THIRD MOVEMENT

There are three conditions that I find crucial for unleashing the full power of this movement: (1) Do not play it too fast; the prescribed *Precipitato* should be created by a relentlessly steady rhythm, rather than through sheer speed. (2) Make sure that the three-note ostinato figure in the bass is played exactly the same way wherever it appears, without varying its inflection. (3) Play the chords in the right hand with a keen sense of voice leading in all three voices of the chords, rather than paying attention only to the upper line.

Observe the dynamic indications and do not get too loud too soon. Be prudent and save the imposing crescendos and crushing *fortissimo* sound for those few spots thus specified, such as mm. 43–45, 122–127, and 168 to the end. In the beginning, the chords should be played with a thick tenuto non legato touch, not staccato. The angular passages, as in mm. 27, 30, 35 (all with preceding upbeats), and 38, should have a lighter, piercing sound, reminiscent of the shrieking sound of flutes in a high register.

The passage starting with m. 50 (01:01) should bring a change in the sonority. Lessen the weight of the chords in the right hand, but let them continue to sound *forte*. Every new phrase in the left hand should suggest the entry of a different instrument.

The E-minor section, starting with m. 79, should sound more melodic than everything that preceded it, but certainly not lyrical. The *détaché* chords in m. 105 should bring back the sonority of m. 50. Make the transition from this texture to the chords played by the right hand in m. 108 absolutely seamless.

The three accents on the downbeats of mm. 122, 123, and 124 should have the direct and brutal sound of trombones and tuba. When the opening material returns, dropping to *mezzo piano* in m. 128 gives you a chance to catch your breath and to relax a little, in anticipation of the movement's taxing conclusion. (The audience, however, should not be aware of your "taking it easy.") When the texture becomes thicker in m. 145, the three-note ostinato figure must continue to stand apart from the chords. The voice leading within the chords needs to be clear in spite of the jumps between registers. In the passage starting m. 165, mark every change of the harmony that occurs on the downbeats of mm. 165 and 171, as well as on the second beats of mm. 166 and 168. Make the melodic line in the last seven bars clearly audible.

Sonata No. 8 in B-flat Major, op. 84

Composed in 1939–44. First performed by Emil Gilels on December 30, 1944, in Moscow. Published in 1943 by Muzgiz. Dedicated to Mira Mendelson-Prokofieva.

This is the last of the "War Sonatas," written between 1939 and 1944, although some of its material was conceived earlier. By the time it was completed, the outcome of the war had become clear. This may explain both the victorious coda of the finale and the general reflective mood of the first movement.

The Eighth is the most expansive of Prokofiev's sonatas; the first movement in particular unfolds in an unhurried fashion. The composer initially intended the sonata to consist of four movements, not three.

Some of the Eighth Sonata's material was taken from earlier unfinished incidental music for projects connected with works by Alexander Pushkin: a theater production of *Eugene Onegin* (op. 71) and a film version of *The Queen of Spades* (op. 70). They were undertaken on the occasion of the centenary of the great Russian poet's death, which was commemorated extensively in the Soviet Union in 1937. Unfortunately, neither of these projects was realized, nor was a theater production of *Boris Godunov,* for which Prokofiev wrote music listed in his catalogue as op. 70bis. As Prokofiev observed, "None of my Pushkin pieces was ever produced. The music lay for a long time on the shelf and was gradually incorporated into other compositions."[1] The Eighth Sonata absorbed some of this Pushkin material; the first movement's initial theme derives from music for *The Queen of Spades,* and the second movement is based on music for *Eugene Onegin.**

The sonata is dedicated to Mira Mendelson-Prokofieva, the composer's partner since 1939, the year the work was conceived. Their new relationship may be responsible, at least in part, for the music's introspective, lyrical character. It seems that Prokofiev's personal feelings, the country's momentous present, and the material from unrealized works all combined to create a unified work of epic proportions and tone.

Emil Gilels premiered the sonata on December 30, 1944. He later recalled: "I studied the sonata from the manuscript, and at that time I frequently visited S[ergei] S[ergeyevich] at home. . . . I played for him the work I had just learned very tentatively. S. S., while checking certain passages, made corrections in the score. Sometimes he would sit at the keyboard and, without playing every note, indicate what he would like to hear from the performer above all."[2] Gilels recorded the sonata in 1974.

Sviatoslav Richter started playing the Eighth Sonata soon after Gilels's premiere performance. Richter played it in the All-Union Piano Competition in 1945 and recorded it in 1962. He also wrote about hearing the work for the first time in 1944:

Prokofiev himself played it at the Composers' Union but it was Gilels who gave the first public performance.

Prokofiev played it twice. Even after a single hearing, it was clear that this was a remarkable work, but when I was asked whether I planned to play it myself, I was at a loss for an answer.

S. S. now had difficulty playing. He no longer had his former confidence, and his hands fluttered helplessly over the keys.

After the second hearing, I was firmly resolved to learn the piece. Someone began to snigger: "It's completely outdated! You don't really want to play it?!"

*Subsequently, conductor Gennady Rozhdestvensky compiled a suite he called *Pushkiniana* (published by Sovetskiy kompozitor in 1962). It is based on the music for all three Pushkin projects and includes both fragments used in the Eighth Sonata.

Of all Prokofiev's sonatas, this is the richest. It has a complex inner life, profound and full of contrasts. At times it seems to grow numb, as if abandoning itself to the relentless march of time. If it is sometimes inaccessible, this is because of its richness, like a tree that is heavy with fruit.

It remains one of my three favorite works, alongside the Fourth and Ninth Sonatas. Gilels played it magnificently at his recital in the Grand Hall.[3]

Listening Closely

FIRST MOVEMENT: ANDANTE DOLCE (DISC 3, TRACK 1)

This movement, which alone lasts almost a quarter of an hour, is expansive in a way unusual for Prokofiev. The only first movement in his sonatas written in a slow tempo (the Ninth Sonata's opening Allegretto is a close second), it anticipates the epic narratives of the opening movements of the Fifth Symphony, op. 100, written in 1944, and of the Seventh Symphony (op. 131, 1951–52). It conveys both tenderness and a nostalgic regret, as if the composer has allowed himself to look back to the war's tragic events and to the happiness that preceded them and was shattered. Hearing this movement, I cannot help thinking about Schubert's great sonata in the same key (D. 960), although I doubt that this work was ever on Prokofiev's mind. Even the structure of the opening statement is reminiscent of Schubert's approach: instead of consisting of 4 + 4 bars, as dictated by the convention, it is built of 5 + 4 bars or, more precisely, (4 + 1) + 4. This statement, one of the three that compose the first theme, is based on the film music for *The Queen of Spades*, where it depicted Lisa, one of the leading characters. Comparing the film music with the beginning of the sonata allows us a glimpse into Prokofiev's creative workshop. The order of two period-like phrases (*c* and *b* in Exx. 8.1a and 8.1b) is reversed in the sonata. In addition, they are preceded by another melodic statement (*a*) that resembles a loose inversion of the phrase *c*.

Each of the three statements will later play its own role and be developed

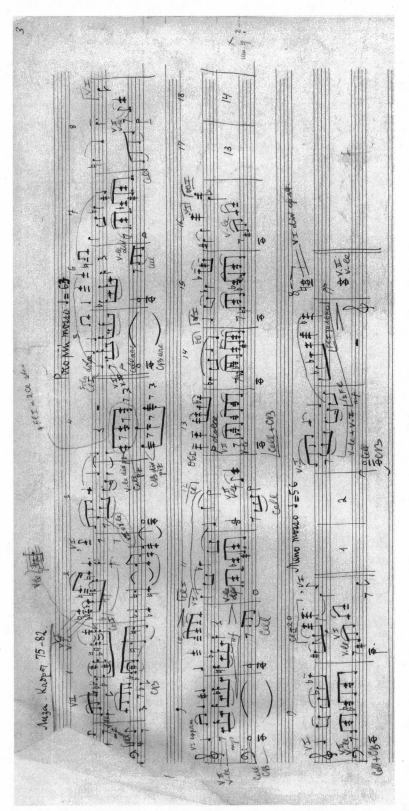

Fig. 4 Music for the projected film of The Queen of Spades, op. 70 (manuscript). Russian State Archive for Literature and Art (RGALI). Reproduced by permission of the Estate of Sergei Prokofiev.

Ex. 8.1a The Queen of Spades, *film music for "Lisa" episode*

Ex. 8.1b Sonata No. 8, mvt. 1

separately. Even at their first appearance, however, each has its own character. The first is warm and noble, with a wide-ranging melody. The bass line
moves slowly, giving the music a stately air; the interweaving middle voices
envelop the melody. The second big phrase (m. 10, 00:39) is more poignant.
It starts with a plaintive chromatic intonation; the first four bars are repeated
immediately in a varied form. The third statement (m. 18, 01:10), closer in
character to the first, is in the subdominant key of E-flat major. After the
third of these period-like phrases, the first is restated (m. 26, 01:44).

The material of the bridge section (m. 35, 02:21) plays a particularly
significant role in the movement. Against a background of sustained basses,
slow arpeggios in the right hand descend gently, as if a tree were shedding
its leaves. In m. 42 (02:46), the movement quickens; the same arpeggios
now cascade quickly, interchanging with fragments of the first theme's initial phrase. For a short time the music becomes more intense but later calms
down, leading to the concluding part of the bridge theme (middle of m. 54,
03:19). In contrast with the eloquence, variety, and freedom of the preceding
material, this part is based on a short, four-note phrase, set in a four-part
polyphonic texture, which is imitated, inverted, and varied in all voices before arriving at the new key of D major. After the note D is heard in a descending succession of five octaves, the second theme starts with the same
pitch (m. 61, 03:47).

This theme (in G minor, a relative minor to the home key) consists of an
enigmatic recurring short phrase and an answering plaintive melody in the
treble. Sustained bass chords contribute to the haunting atmosphere, which
may be connected to the scene in *The Queen of Spades* in which Gherman,
the protagonist, stealthily enters the house of the old Countess.

The concluding part of the bridge theme, first heard in m. 54 (03:19), returns in a higher register (upbeat to m. 79, 04:58). A somewhat strained
sonority adds bitterness to the familiar music. The exposition ends with yet
another short recurring motive, reminiscent of a distant cuckoo call (m. 84,
05:19), as if reminding the listener of the passage of time.

The development section (m. 90, 05:43) starts with the restless motion of
sixteenths drawn from the bridge section (see m. 42, 02:46). The cascading

arpeggios return in m. 94 (05:50); now they have an apprehensive, troubled character. In m. 100 (06:01) in the bass voice, we hear the melody of the first theme's third big phrase in augmentation. Amid the general agitation, the running arpeggios suddenly slow down to half their former speed (m. 111, 06:21). Sounding pensive and sad, they lead to a two-bar reminiscence of the beginning of the movement (m. 114, 06:27). Sviatoslav Richter's previously quoted description of the music as "grow[ing] numb, as if abandoning itself to the relentless march of time" seems particularly apt here.

The motion resumes, becoming increasingly determined and leading to another appearance of the bridge section's concluding phrase (m. 133, 07:05). Now presented twice as slowly and *fortissimo,* it sounds like a desperate scream. From here through to the end of the development, every theme from the exposition appears in augmentation, adding a quality of epic monumentality. First, the second phrase of the first theme is resolutely hammered out (m. 141, 07:24). In m. 149 (07:44), it climbs into a higher register, while the left hand plays it in a doubly augmented and dissonant version. In contrast, the first theme's initial statement is presented legato (m. 155, 07:59). The same succession of augmented fragments of the theme reappears ever higher and more dramatic until it reaches the second theme, also in augmentation (m. 169, 08:36). The haunted three-note motive now sounds like a tragic bell toll, while the lyrical melody is transformed into a passionate cry.

The climax of the movement is reached in m. 183 (09:15). This section, not carrying any previously heard thematic material, is composed as an imposing and dramatic evocation of chimes, with a mighty bell swinging like a gigantic pendulum. Starting with m. 190 (09:52), the tension recedes, bringing us to a mysterious repetition of the preceding rhythmic formula, marked in the score as *quasi Timpani* (like kettledrums). To conclude the development section, the "cuckoo call" motive of the closing theme is heard again (m. 196, 10:26). Presented more slowly and in a more extended way than before, it sounds like a hypnotic mantra.

The recapitulation, beginning in m. 206 (11:31), restates the first theme as in the beginning, except that its ABCA structure is now abbreviated to ABC.

The bridge theme (m. 231, 13:08) is likewise truncated. Presented in augmentation, it conveys the frozen or numb quality that we have already experienced in this movement. The second theme, now reappearing in B-flat minor (m. 245, 14:02), is also abbreviated, like a question left hanging in the
air.

The coda section (m. 261, 15:14) begins as the development did, with a
driving torrent of sixteenths growing to an alarming bell ringing in the high
register in m. 275 (15:37.) The stream of notes is interrupted dramatically by
a tumbling melodic gesture in m. 286 (15:57) and then rolls down and stops
two more times. Rude upward runs (m. 290, 16:05), like trombone glissandos, fill in the interval of a ninth. This intonation is familiar to us as the inversion of the second theme's opening (see m. 61, 03:47). A peaceful conclusion ends this richly sprawling movement.

SECOND MOVEMENT: ANDANTE SOGNANDO
(DISC 3, TRACK 2)

The sonata's second movement is much shorter and less substantial than
the other two. It can be conceived as a brief relief or a nostalgic repose between the monumental outer movements. Its musical material is based on a
minuet intended for the ball scene of *Eugene Onegin*. In its original context,
it had the formal, slightly clumsy character of "battalion music" (Pushkin's
phrase) and was scored for brass band. Here in the sonata, however, the general tone is determined by the unusual indication *sognando* (dreamily); indeed, it sounds like an elegiac reverie. There is a relative paucity of material
in this movement; only three melodic statements appear repeatedly, in
different keys and registers, suggesting changing orchestral colors.

The texture of the opening was transferred unchanged from the brass
band scoring of the original. The three voices in the right hand play mostly
in parallel motion, while the simple three-note formula in the bass remains
unchanged for eight bars. (The sonority of the brass band might have
evoked a nostalgic sentiment in Prokofiev: such bands, playing in public
gardens, were a common summer entertainment in the Russia of his

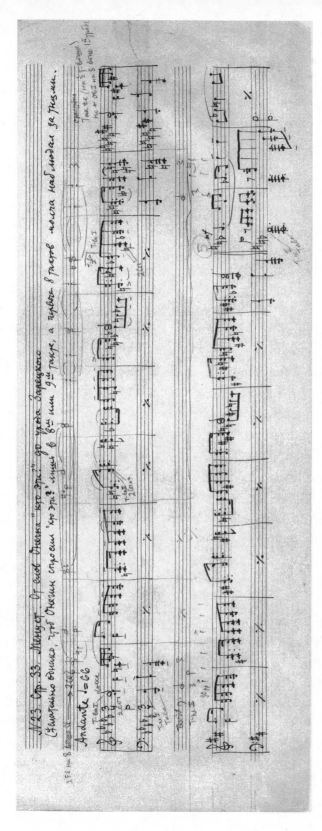

Fig. 5 *Music for the projected theater production of Eugene Onegin, op. 71 (manuscript). Russian State Archive for Literature and Art (RGALI). Reproduced by permission of the Estate of Sergei Prokofiev.*

youth.) In m. 9 (00:28), there is a shift to a new key a half step higher. Here the bass plays the same accompanying formula as before, but instead of keeping pace with the melody it lags behind absentmindedly.

In m. 17 (00:55), another tonal shift introduces a long new melody. It has a more songful, less dancelike character than the first theme, which returns in m. 27 (01:26). This time, fragments of the melody appear in different registers, as if various groups of orchestral instruments were passing the melodic line to each other. (Prokofiev used the same technique in the slow movement of the Sixth Sonata; see m. 57 [Disc 2, Track 6, 03:32].)

In m. 35 (01:51), a soothing, gently rocking theme is introduced. The tonality shifts back to D-flat major in m. 43 (02:19), mirroring the earlier modulation in the first theme. In m. 47 (02:32), the opening theme is heard in the bass against the new background of ascending pairs of sixteenths in the right hand. The melody is taken over or imitated by different voices in mm. 49 (02:38), 51 (02:44), and 52 (02:47). In the following section, starting in m. 57 (03:04), the rocking motive is combined with elements of the singing melody first heard in m. 17 (00:55).

The first theme appears again in m. 66 (03:36), surrounded by a shimmering, lilting rhythm and anchored by the dominant pitch of A-flat. The coda, which again is suggestive of orchestral sonorities, starts in the upbeat to m. 74 (04:02). A calm farewell reappearance of the main theme in m. 78 (04:19) concludes the movement.

THIRD MOVEMENT: VIVACE (DISC 3, TRACK 3)

After the dreamy second movement, the sonata's finale bursts in with great energy. Its forging-ahead motion recalls the opening of the Sixth Sonata's last movement. While the finale of the Sixth Sonata is full of nervous anxiety, however, its counterpart in the Eighth exudes a confident, controlled quality. The movement is in a sonata-rondo form, with an extensive episode in the middle and a coda.

The harmonic language of the movement is very clear. Perhaps no other movement in Prokofiev's sonatas displays so many major chords free of ob-

Ex. 8.2 Alexander Nevsky, *"The Battle on Ice"*

scuring dissonances. The light and confident motion of the first theme, based on a trumpetlike call in B-flat major, echoes the depiction of the victorious Russian army in *Alexander Nevsky* (Ex. 8.2). However, the first theme also includes a somewhat apprehensive subject in E minor (m. 9, 00:11). Notice the tritone distance between the tonalities of the two subjects; Prokofiev often employed this juxtaposition. Another of his favorite tonal relationships, that of the semitone, was used abundantly in the second movement. It also appears a bit later in the finale, when a short connecting passage (mm. 38–41, 00:49–00:54) establishes the key of B major in m. 42 (00:54), introducing the second theme. Its boldly etched melody encompasses an increasingly expansive range. Prokofiev masterfully doubles it in secondary voices, which then veer off to become independent lines (another favorite technique of his; we hear it, for instance, in the second movement of the Seventh Sonata). Note the impassioned section based on a three-note intonation later in the theme (m. 49, 01:04); this motive becomes very important

Ex. 8.3a Sonata No. 8, mvt. 2

Ex. 8.3b Sonata No. 8, mvt. 3

in the subsequent development section. Sweeping, surging arpeggios (mm. 71–78, 01:34–01:45) precede the return of the first group of themes. This time they appear in reversed order: the second subject in m. 79 (01:45) in E major, and the first one in m. 85 (01:54) in the original B-flat major. The concluding passage that follows (mm. 93–100, 02:04–02:14) firmly reestablishes the home key of B-flat major.

The fanfares in mm. 101–6 (02:14–02:23) announce the central episode of the movement in the key of D-flat major. This section is a waltz, but it is not one of Prokofiev's tenderly lyrical waltzes, like the B-minor "Natasha Rostova" waltz in *War and Peace*. Nor is it a warm and amorous one, exemplified by some of the waltzes in *Cinderella* or by the slow movement of the Sixth Sonata. This one is more brilliant, more "official," and less personal. Its subject is based on the pitches we have heard in the beginning of the second movement: A-flat, G, and D-flat (see Exx. 8.3a and 8.3b).

A short formulaic motive is heard (*a* in Ex. 8.4) against a background of repeated A-flats (m. 107, 02:24). Then a longer melody (*b* in Ex. 8.4) is introduced in the bass line (m. 111, 02:28) and is imitated in the tenor voice. The three-note motive returns in an altered form, which includes an audacious melodic leap (mm. 121–22, 02:38); it is immediately imitated in the bass with an even bigger jump. All this sets the stage for the main theme of this section (*c* in Ex. 8.4), an energetic, bold melody in the treble voice that ap-

Ex. 8.4 Sonata No. 8, mvt. 3

pears in m. 137 (02:54). The melodic material reappears in a kaleidoscopic
fashion, leading us to a brilliantly festive climax (m. 185, 03:42). The composer uses the whole range of the piano to re-create the glittering frenzy of a
ball.

In m. 208 (04:04), the atmosphere darkens as the ominous fanfares of
the transitional episode (see mm. 101–6, 02:14–02:23) are superimposed
over the waltz's three-note motive. After a whistling upward run (mm. 223–
24, 04:19), the ostinato motive moves to the low register, where it stomps
about with sinister ferocity. Out of this comes the two-note intonation of the

Ex. 8.5 Sonata No. 8, mvt. 3

descending ninth (m. 233, 04:28; Ex. 8.5). We recognize it as deriving from the opening of the first movement's second theme (see m. 61, 03:47, Track 1). Eerie, flutelike squeals in the high register intensify the infernal character of this dramatic section.

The satanic dance subsides to a mysterious *pianissimo,* in which only the ostinato formula is repeated in the bass. Against this background, the first movement's second theme reappears in m. 289 (05:21) like an apparition. Heard in a high register, it has a ghostly, plaintive character. After the last echoes of this episode die away, the music of the exposition timidly returns. The transition (m. 343, 06:33) is based on the three-note motive first heard in the middle of the second theme (m. 49, 01:04). Prokofiev's marking of *irresoluto* (indecisively) is very unusual for this composer. The music gradually becomes bolder and more impassioned, leading to a reminiscence of the first theme's second subject (m. 359, 07:28). In m. 367 (07:40), this material is presented in full, heralding the arrival of the recapitulation.

The first theme's initial subject is heard again in m. 380 (07:56). In the exposition, the tonalities of the first and second themes were a half step apart (B-flat major and B major), but here in the recapitulation the second theme (m. 404, 08:27) appears in E major, a tritone away from B-flat major.

The triumphant coda (m. 458, 09:42) is full of bell chimes and jubilant trumpet calls. A variant of the second theme (m. 466, 09:53) is presented with earthy, folksy stomps. Brief reminiscences of the second subject of the first theme (mm. 486–89, 10:24–10:30) vigorously conclude this highly effective and energetic movement.

Master Class

FIRST MOVEMENT*

Because of the first movement's expansive dimensions, the pianist's ability to sustain a long melodic line is essential. The first theme lasts 34 bars and consists of four period-like phrases. While it is necessary to recognize the special qualities of each of these statements, one should feel the theme as being a unified whole. Another issue of concern in the opening is sustaining the long notes in the bass line, as using the pedal may blur the moving middle voices. The pianist should have a highly sensitive touch and adjust it to the changing nature of these weaving lines: to treat them melodically when they move stepwise (a in Ex. 8.6) and to allow them to blend into harmonies when they form arpeggios (b in Ex. 8.6). Maintaining the legato in the melody requires a careful choice of fingering, often making a change of fingers while on the same key. The great range covered by the first phrase makes evenness in the sound across different registers especially important. Make sure that m. 3, for instance, does not sound thin or percussive compared with m. 1. Pay attention to the dashes in mm. 10 and 14 and play these notes expressively, deep into the keys, perhaps even stretching them a little. (In some editions, the dashes over the last four eighth notes in the top voice in m. 14 are missing.)

As the key of the third sentence (m. 18) changes to E-flat major, find a new color for the sound. Some editions have a misprint in m. 18: the melodic line

---

*Prokofiev never gave metronome indications for his sonatas. However, the episode "Lisa" from the music for the projected film *The Queen of Spades*, on which the first theme of this movement is based, bears the indication ♩ = 63.

Ex. 8.6 Sonata No. 8, mvt. 1

should have F on the third beat, not A. This is what the manuscript for the film music, mentioned above, shows, and this is how the sonata was recorded by both Gilels and Richter. When the theme returns in the recapitulation, all editions show the F (m. 223).

Play the bridge theme (m. 35) *dolce;* the legato here should not sound forced. Use a light touch as well as pedal to help sustain the chords. Play the octave Cs in the left hand (m. 40) like a distant horn call. When the sixteenths appear in m. 42, do not let them sound overly articulated. Use an overlapping legato (i.e., slightly delay the release of each note). It will allow you to use the pedal sparingly and to produce a sound that is transparent but not dry. In the polyphonic passage in mm. 54–59, phrase clearly in each voice, making the upbeats in the outer voices lead into the downbeats. In mm. 59–60, follow the line of the five descending Ds.

In the second theme (m. 61), play the recurring three-note motive hauntingly, while the fifth in the low bass should resonate mysteriously, like a tam-tam stroke. The melody in the top voices should be played with a fluid legato. Treat the first two phrases as one long line extending from m. 61 through m. 64, spanning the interruption in m. 63. This is the first of three phrases that compose the bigger statement, the second one lasting from the pickup to m. 65 through the end of m. 66. (The octave Gs on the downbeat of m. 67 belong to the middle voice.) The third phrase starts in the second half of m. 67 and ends at the end of m. 71. Play the eighth notes expressively but do not use too much pressure.

In the passage starting with the upbeat to m. 79, do not let the top melody sound shrill. The tempo relationship between mm. 82 and 83 should be, approximately, $\quartnote = \dottedquarternote$. The line in the left hand of m. 83 resolves in the next bar into G in the right-hand part. The "cuckoo call" in mm. 84–87 should have the same inflection every time it is heard.

The energetic beginning of the development section should be played evenly, without making the hand changes audible. Be sure to phrase well when the first theme appears in augmentation in mm. 100–107. Using overlapping legato in the right hand will allow a more sparing use of the pedal and, as a result, a more transparent sonority. The unexpected slowing of the tempo in m. 111 requires creating a more reflective mood, before the restless motion returns in m. 116. Here again, the left hand plays a long melody through m. 123. I treat the three C-sharps in m. 118 as if they were in parentheses.

From m. 123 until m. 190, the dynamic markings never go below *forte* and often reach *ff* and *fff*. In spite of this, the pianist should avoid excessive banging and the monotony of relentlessly loud playing. Find places where the music justifies bringing the dynamic level down.

Play the melody of the middle voice in m. 127 with an "out of the piano" stroke, imitating the sound of a brass instrument, and shape it well as it passes from one hand to the other. In m. 130, I recommend starting the left-hand phrase on the second beat more softly and making a crescendo to the downbeat of the following bar. Start the similar phrase in m. 131 softer as well; this time, however, the crescendo needs to be spread over two bars to reach *fortissimo* on the second beat of m. 133.

Play the *fortissimo* passage in m. 133 with an expressive legato, phrasing toward the downbeat and making the imitation in the tenor voice meaningful. Play the chimelike texture in mm. 137–39 with "out of the piano" arm strokes. In response to the indication *marcatissimo*, play the thirty-second notes in m. 140 non legato.

In the long section beginning in m. 141, notice the different agogic indications given to various melodic lines: some of them are marked with dashes (–), others with dashes and dots (⁻.) or conventional accents (>). Also pay attention here to the dynamic marking of *forte*, not *fortissimo*. This phrase, as well as its augmented versions in the left hand in mm. 149–50 and 159–60, should be well shaped. The runs in the left hand in mm. 151 and 161 should sound quasi glissando. The texture in mm. 155–58 and 165–67 is quite sparse; make sure it does not sound dry. Play the melody in the right hand expressively and the chromatic fast notes in the left hand with a "sticky" legato.

In mm. 159–60, bring out the thumb in the left hand to highlight the melody in the chords. In the second theme, which appears in m. 169, you should produce an opulent sound, chimelike in the chords and warmly singing in the melody. In the huge crescendo in mm. 181–82, the right hand climbs up quite high; make sure it does not sound thin or percussive. In the following *Andante* (beginning in m. 183), choose a tempo that is deliberate enough so you do not have to slow further for the triplets in m. 187. This whole passage should be felt in two, with the arpeggios (m. 183 and later) and runs (mm. 187 and 189) soaring like gigantic waves; they do not need to be excessively articulated. The repeated chords, starting m. 187, should be sonorous but not hard. When the music dies down to *pianissimo*, I suggest playing the repeated notes, marked *quasi Timpani*, without pedal.

The rhythmic relationship between mm. 195 and 196 is somewhat problematic. The way it is marked ($\downarrow. = \downarrow$) makes the episode in mm. 196–205 significantly slower than the similar one at the end of the exposition (mm. 84–89). This is how Sviatoslav Richter recorded it. However, Emil Gilels, who premiered the sonata, adopted a different strategy in his recording: prior to m. 194 he slowed the tempo considerably and then played mm. 194–95 twice as fast. This way the episode that follows sounds close to the tempo it had in the exposition. Instead of resorting to these unmarked changes of tempo, I prefer to amend the ratio above to one in which a dotted half equals the preceding quarter (i.e., $\downarrow. = \downarrow$). Whatever tempo one chooses, this passage leading to the recapitulation (mm. 196–205) should be played as if under a spell, without ever letting it sound boring.

The recapitulation of the first theme, starting in m. 206, has the same character as in the beginning, whereas the bridge section (m. 231) is slower and less fluid than in the exposition. Make the octave Fs in the left hand in m. 236 sound like a distant horn call, as you did in the similar place in the exposition. Let the last phrase of the second theme (mm. 259–60) sound like a wistful question.

The beginning of the coda (m. 261) is reminiscent of the way the development had started. The melodic line in the bass in mm. 273–74 and 276–77 should be played with severe determination. A descending chromatic line of fifths in the left hand is added in m. 275 to the material of the bridge section. It should sound like a light and sonorous ringing of bells; play this progression smoothly, without marking every fifth in the left hand. In mm. 278–79, I recommend bringing out the melodic line, as shown in Ex. 8.7.

The ascending scalar runs in mm. 290–91 should sound like menacing

Ex. 8.7 Sonata No. 8, mvt. 1

trombone glissandos. In contrast, the melodic bass line in mm. 293–94 should be played with a deep, soft touch evoking the sound of low strings. The B-flat major chord in the last bar should have the color of woodwinds.

I can offer only a few practical recommendations regarding this movement. Everything here depends on how successful the pianist is in evoking different orchestral colors as the themes appear each time in a different register, key, or within a different texture. Another difficulty is in building an almost hypnotic, dreamy (*sognando*) atmosphere without making the music sound static or repetitive.*

I suggest phrasing the first theme in a way that treats the three last eighth notes in mm. 2 and 3 and in all similar places as an upbeat to the next downbeat. This approach will better connect the bar's third beat to the next bar and enhance the feeling of a dance. Change the color when the tonality shifts up a half step in m. 9. The offbeat bass notes here should be played with a light touch. Play the new melody in m. 17 with a warm singing tone, while paying attention to all accompanying voices. In m. 27, make the different registers sound like different groups of instruments. The long line, however, must not be fragmented.

The new episode starting in m. 35 introduces a lilting rhythmic figure (Ex. 8.8), which I treat iambically, that is, by playing the first of the linked notes more lightly than the second. The low bass notes provide a gentle foundation. The arpeggios in both hands in mm. 38 and 42 should be airy and played without excessive articulation of every note. Change the color to respond to the modulation in m. 43. Play the sixteenths in the left hand here as smoothly as possible.

In the next episode, starting in m. 47, play the accompanying sixteenths

*The tempo of the minuet in the music for *Eugene Onegin*, the source of the material for this movement, is given as $\downarrow$ = 66. The character of the sonata's movement is so different from its original source, however, that this tempo cannot be considered binding.

Ex. 8.8 Sonata No. 8, mvt. 2

lightly and evenly, but with a warm touch. Make the imitations of the first
theme noticeable, and differentiate the color for each. The *pianissimo* in m.
57 should sound dreamy and smooth, while the two-bar reminiscences of
the singing theme in the left hand (mm. 59–60 and 63–64) should be
played very warmly. Make the run at the end of m. 60 sound whispery, light,
and even, but not at all virtuosic.

In the return of the first theme in m. 66, differentiate the sound of the
melody and the accompaniment. Pass the melody from one hand to another
unnoticeably; the gently ringing A-flats of the accompaniment should have
a soothing lilt.

In the coda (beginning with the upbeat to m. 74), give an individual color
to each of the different layers of sound. The ascending scale beginning in m.
78 should be even and smooth; it ought not to obscure the melody. Give the
feeling of a gentle and slightly ceremonial parting bow to the resolution in
the last bar.

THIRD MOVEMENT

The first theme needs clear articulation of every note. Avoid accenting the
first note of every beat, except where marked. The octaves in the left hand
should sound like pizzicato in the orchestra, while the chords in the left
hand in mm. 2–4 should be played tenuto, imitating French horns. The second subject (m. 9) is quite different from the first. Against the background
of the long-held chords (I think here again of French horns), the melody in
the bass should sound apprehensive and slightly spooky. In mm. 15–16,

play the fourths in the right hand legato, and do not make a crescendo until m. 17, as marked in the score. The *forte* passage in mm. 19–21 and the short connecting passage in mm. 38–41 should sound resonant and jubilant.

In the second theme (starting in m. 42), create a long melodic line with both hands and do not articulate the accompaniment of triplets excessively. The ascending arpeggios (mm. 45, 49, 51, and so on) should have a sense of direction, imitating the way they sounded at the beginning of the movement (mm. 2, 6, and so on). The three-note motives in mm. 49–52 should not sound separated from each other, but rather as part of the long melodic line. In mm. 57–58, bring out the imitation in the left hand. The octave passage in m. 62 should sound full, like the tutti of orchestral strings; there should be no "poking" into the keys by the fifth finger.

The arpeggio passages in mm. 71–78 should be played with well-articulated fingers, but not dryly. Use the pedal generously to create a resonant sonority, but keep changing it. In the transition to the middle episode, the fanfare imitations in the left hand should have an incisive and cutting-through sound quality.

I hear a change of character in the course of the following section: Having started as a brilliant waltz, it turns into a frightening *danse macabre* of evil forces. Other people may feel this ominous character from the beginning of the waltz. However, I find that my interpretation allows for more dramatic and psychological development and brings greater variety to this lengthy episode, which can easily become monotonous.

In the score, Prokofiev meticulously notes several different kinds of articulation for the waltz: non legato, regular staccato (·), and short staccato (▾). These differences must be audible. In addition, the half notes (mm. 113–14 and later) should be played tenuto. This section may sound stolid and monotonous because of its rhythmic homogeneity. To avoid this, one needs to give varied orchestral colors to the recurrent short motive and its imitations in different registers (mm. 108, 110, and so on), and to shape a long melodic line in mm. 112–16 and similar passages. Play the melody in m. 137 by imitating the fresh color of an oboe.

The section starting in m. 185 should sound festive and bright, like an or-

Ex. 8.9 Sonata No. 8, mvt. 3

chestral tutti; bring out the colors in different registers. The fanfares starting in the left hand in m. 208 should cut through the overall *fortissimo* like trombones. Each subsequent imitation should have a different sonority. Play the run in mm. 223–24 as a single gesture; no changes of hands should be heard. I voice the ominous passage that starts in m. 225 as shown in Ex. 8.9.

The whistling sixteenths in m. 234 and later should sound like a piccolo. Each of the imitations of this figure in the lower registers should have its own color. Play the chords in mm. 269–72 *tenuto separato*, to make them sound like three brass instruments.

The reminiscence of the first movement's second theme (m. 289) should sound warm and lyrical; avoid playing it too percussively or too rhythmically. In the wistful passage starting in m. 343, which is based on a fragment of the finale's second theme, one can use a little rubato, in response to Prokofiev's marking of *irresoluto* (indecisive). The indication *espressivo* in m. 348 calls for a warmer sound. With the crescendo in m. 353, the music becomes more impassioned. Do not let the melody in the top voice in m. 355 sound too thin.

The return of the apprehensive second subject of the first theme in m. 359 shakes off the nostalgic mood of the preceding passage. Establish the new tempo right away, playing the eighth notes evenly and clearly while making the chords sound like French horns. In addition, make the top voice in m. 367 sound like a new melodic line. As in the similar passage in the exposition, do not make a crescendo in mm. 373–74.

The material of the recapitulation closely follows that of the exposition and should be presented in the same manner. Thus, my earlier observations apply here as well.

In m. 449, the approach to the coda begins. Play it confidently, with long, clear melodic lines. The coda proper starts in m. 458. The *fortissimo sonora-mente* should sound mighty but not forced; the chords in the left hand should not break the long line. Let the repeated notes in m. 464 and from m. 477 on sound like a trumpet rather than a percussion instrument. The melody in the bass in m. 466 should have a folksy heaviness, without sounding rude. Make the same melody sound distinctly in the top voice in m. 470. The chiming sonority becomes progressively mightier and more majestic. A small cloud (mm. 486–87) is dismissed with the willful energy of the last two bars, which must remain strictly in tempo.

Sonata No. 9 in C Major, op. 103

Composed in 1947. First performed by Sviatoslav Richter on April 21, 1951, in Moscow. Published by Muzgiz in 1955. Dedicated to Richter.

This sonata was composed in 1947 but not performed until 1951, and not published until after Prokofiev's death. These delays, unusual given the performing and publishing history of Prokofiev's earlier compositions, are indicative of the composer's changed political fortunes. In the campaign against formalism launched by Communist Party officials in the early months of 1948, Prokofiev (along with Shostakovich) was implicated as one of the principal culprits.

The Ninth Sonata—in the key of C major—is notable for the simplicity of its style, as well as for the conciseness and clarity of its structure. It lacks the dramatic conflicts, complexity, and energy of the preceding group of "War Sonatas." The conservative musical language may be attributed partly to Prokofiev's premonition of the politically repressive times. More likely, however, it reflects his general turn to a greater simplicity, as discussed in the opening chapter. The dramatic worsening of Prokofiev's health may also have contributed to the relative lack of sheer motoric energy so typical of his music. Since early 1945, the composer had been plagued by medical problems that would haunt him for the remaining eight years of his life.

Richter later recalled his first reaction to the sonata:

It was Prokofiev's birthday [probably 1947], and he invited me to visit him for the first time at his dacha at Nikolina Gora. "I've something interesting to show you," he announced as soon as I arrived, whereupon he produced the sketches of his Ninth Sonata. "This will be your sonata. But do not think it's intended to create an effect. It's not the sort of work to raise the roof of the Grand Hall."

And at first glance it did indeed look a little simplistic. I was even a tiny bit disappointed.

. . . In 1951 he turned sixty. On his birthday Prokofiev was once again ill. On the eve of his birthday a concert was held at the Composers' Union and he listened to it over the phone. It was on this occasion that I played the Ninth Sonata for the first time, a radiant, simple and even intimate work. In some ways it is a *Sonata domestica*. The more one hears it, the more one comes to love it and feels its magnetism. And the more perfect it seems. I love it very much.[1]

While the sonata's musical language is more conservative than that of its predecessors, we do find here the new traits of a more intimate lyricism and introspection. Prokofiev also introduced several subtle innovations into the sonata's structure. The most prominent feature is the device of "previewing," when toward the end of each movement the material of the next is introduced.

Mira Mendelson-Prokofieva recorded her impressions of the Ninth Sonata in her diary (entry of September 29, 1947): "This sonata is very different from the three preceding ones. It is calm and deep. When I told [Prokofiev] that my first impression was of it being both Russian and Beethoven-like, he answered that he himself found both of these qualities present in it."[2]

A serene, meditative tone is indeed the signature mark of the Ninth. This is expressed strongest of all at the end of the work, when the opening theme of the first movement reappears. The texture of this ending, its spirit, and even its key cannot fail to bring to mind the conclusion of Beethoven's last piano sonata (op. 111).

Givi Ordzhonikidze observed another trait of the Ninth Sonata: the important role played by the imagery of childhood.[3] Throughout his life, Prokofiev turned to childhood-inspired, or childhood-related, themes: from the set of piano pieces *Music for Children,* op. 65; to the symphonic fairy tale *Peter and the Wolf,* op. 67; to the suite for speakers, boys' choir, and orchestra, *Winter Bonfire,* op. 122; to the oratorio *On Guard for Peace,* op. 124. In these works he highlights the emotional qualities associated with childhood—innocent simplicity, naïveté, pure lyricism, and carefree playfulness. These characteristics also figure prominently in later works that are not explicitly related to childhood by a program or a title, such as the Seventh Symphony or many pages in *Cinderella.* In the Ninth Sonata, these images are particularly prominent in the fourth movement.

Listening Closely

FIRST MOVEMENT: ALLEGRETTO (DISC 3, TRACK 4)

The first theme, a simple and diatonic melody in C major, is one of Prokofiev's melodies composed entirely on the piano's white keys. (This task amused the composer throughout much of his life. Among his most memorable "white key" themes are the opening of the Third Piano Concerto, the second theme of the second movement of the Fourth Sonata, and the second theme of the Third Sonata.) In the case of the Ninth Sonata, the simplicity of the melody—it uses only one black key toward the end—is enriched by chromatic accompanying voices. In the restatement of the theme (m. 11, 00:33), each phrase is anticipated by a few notes in middle voices. This way of introducing the principal melody is common in Russian folk songs. Prokofiev used it in the second theme of the Third Sonata as well (m. 58, see Disc 1, Track 6, 01:32).

In m. 20 (01:01), the bridge theme appears. Presented in unison, it conveys a slightly mysterious, austere mood. In m. 37 (01:39), the second theme is prepared by establishing a new rhythmic pattern of gentle, lullaby-like rocking. This and the distant tolling of bells create a melancholy atmosphere. A new lyrical melody appears in m. 41 (01:48). It is written in B minor, a half step from the home key, but is superimposed on a sustained bass note of G, the dominant of C major, making the tonality slightly ambiguous.

The theme sounds three times in different registers, as if the composer were trying to hold on to a beloved image.

The closing section is introduced in m. 61 (02:34). Written in the dominant key of G major, as required by convention, it is presented by two voices playing two octaves apart from each other. This texture alludes to the orchestral sound of woodwinds and helps to establish a pastoral, slightly wistful character. A more active episode in m. 69 (02:54) is the only moment of drama in an otherwise serene exposition. This brief turmoil quickly subsides, and the mood of introspection is reestablished by the end of the exposition in m. 76 (03:10).

The development begins with a harmonic pedal on G, which is either retained or implied for a long stretch until m. 93 (04:03). This initial section of the development is dedicated to elaborating on the first theme. The melody starts with narrow chromatic steps but expands into a lyrical soliloquy tinged with regret. At its end, intonations from the second theme (m. 91, 03:57) and distant calls deriving from the concluding section (m. 93, 04:03) herald the reappearance of the second theme in m. 95 (04:10). Accompanied by a turbulent motion in the bass, it ushers in a feeling of agitation. The tonality of the theme is unstable and often ambiguous, as it was in the exposition. The opening motive of the bridge section, superimposed on the second theme, intrudes boldly in m. 105 (04:26).

The closing theme, appearing in m. 107 (04:30), retains nothing of its original pastoral tranquility. Presented in a high, shrill register and accompanied by restless triplets in the left hand, it continues to build dramatic tension. Harmonic explosions in mm. 111 and 113 (04:36 and 04:40) are preceded by short runs. The latter derive from the opening of the bridge theme and are interspersed with fragments of the first theme in mm. 112 and 115 (04:38 and 04:42). The dark, foreboding atmosphere intensifies and reaches a climax in a dramatic chord in m. 119 (04:49). After this, a melody based on the first theme restores the general serenity.

In m. 124 (05:04), the home key returns and the first theme begins to reemerge, making this a logical place for a recapitulation. However, the pulsating bass on C and a generally tentative mood create an unstable, transitory feeling, making the listener wait for a real return, which happens in m. 134 (05:35). This kind of "false reprise" is a fairly common occurrence in classical sonata form. Usually in such sections the initial material presents itself in a tonality other than the home key, which is delayed until a "true" re- capitulation arrives. In a characteristically Prokofievian twist of the old form, here it is the false reprise that is written in the home key, while the sta- bility of the recapitulation is achieved only after modulating a half step lower to the key of B major. At this point the music regains the narrative intro- spective character of the beginning.

The first theme is shortened in the recapitulation, while the bridge sec- tion (m. 144, 06:07) is expanded, leading us to a brief lyrical monologue in m. 156 (06:32). In the ensuing transition, the bass line finally reaches the tonic of the home key of C major in m. 162 (06:49), when the second theme is heard. Similar to the way in which the theme appeared in the exposition, the mediant minor key (E minor) is superimposed on the tonic of the home key (C major) in the bass. The concluding section is restated in m. 176 (07:22), heralded by distant calls in two preceding bars; they are based on the dotted rhythm that begins this theme. The music assumes again its ini- tial pastoral tone. The more active second half of the concluding theme (m. 184, 07:41) leads us to unfamiliar material in m. 188 (07:48): fierce runs of triplets come as a rude disruption of the generally serene mood. This is an anticipation of the movement to follow.

The peaceful atmosphere is restored in m. 194 (07:58); the triplet runs subside, giving in to the prevailing tranquility.

SECOND MOVEMENT: ALLEGRO STREPITOSO
(DISC 3, TRACK 5)

The second movement is a quirky scherzo written in a simple ABA form. The key signature indicates G major, but the beginning and conclusion of the movement sound more like the Mixolydian mode, with D as the tonic. The texture of this scherzo is transparent, even sparse. The first theme be- gins with a frenetic run of triplets followed by hobbling, disjointed chords that end with a demanding exclamation (m. 4, 00:05). These chords lead to the second theme (m. 10, 00:11), which has a disturbing, nervous character produced by stomping chords in the low bass register and a hopping, stuttering melody. A restatement of the scalar run is followed by a new theme introduced in m. 21 (00:24). After a few measures it settles into a growling dialogue between two middle voices. Each voice's material consists of a short sputtering of fast notes followed by a sustained pitch. The soft repeated chords create the character of a quick, eerie march. The third theme is interrupted by the first theme's agitated triplets in m. 38 (00:45).

Unexpectedly, this emphatic ending of the opening theme is followed by a soothing transitional passage in a slower tempo (m. 45, 00:54). Two voices conversing with each other gently introduce the middle section in m. 51 (01:05). This section is written as a two-part invention and consists of a dialogue between two melodic lines. The right-hand part is based on arpeggiated harmonies and is marked by an elegiac lyricism, while the left-hand line moves chromatically and can be interpreted as an ironic commentary. (There is a distant resemblance between this section and the trio of the second movement of Beethoven's Sonata in A Major, op. 101.)

The intrusion of the scalar opening theme in m. 68 (01:52) ushers in the return of the A section, which is now structured differently. The first theme starts several times but never lasts more than two bars. The second theme does not appear at all, while the third theme, a mysterious march, is heard immediately after the initial scale of triplets (m. 70, 01:54). These structural changes create a slightly disorienting feeling.

Another attempt to launch the first theme is abandoned in favor of a new melody presented in unison by both hands in m. 90 (02:19). This offers a glimpse of the next movement's main theme. In the coda (m. 94, 02:24), the initial run returns with a vengeance two more times, first in the treble and then in the bass register. The new melody of the third movement appears in augmentation in m. 100 (02:32); it sounds in the low register and is followed by an ascending line. The nervously energetic character melts away, and the movement concludes in a pastoral mood, echoing the ending of the first movement.

THIRD MOVEMENT: ANDANTE TRANQUILLO
(DISC 3, TRACK 7)

The third movement, written in A-flat major, is a beautiful example of the lyricism of late Prokofiev. It possesses both noble tranquility and a dancelike lilt. The form of the Andante can be roughly described as ABA′B′A″ Coda with a strong variations component. The first A section presents an expansive theme with two variations, which contribute some textural differences but no significant changes in character, key, or harmonic language. In the first variation (m. 9, 00:41), Prokofiev uses his familiar technique of distributing the melody over different registers. The second variation (m. 18, 01:21) introduces a sustained dotted rhythm in the bass as a background to the main melody.

A sudden surge of energy heralds the beginning of the new section (theme B, m. 27, 02:05). Written in a faster tempo (*Allegro sostenuto*) and in the key of C major, the sonata's home key, this theme has a resonant, bright sonority, as well as a somewhat childish wide-eyed excitement. This episode builds on the dotted rhythm of the preceding variation and betrays a strong connection with the first theme. Ordzhonikidze described it as another variation of the main melody.[4] In this new section, the melody appears in both the upper and lower voices, while two middle voices provide an accompaniment that is both harmonic and rhythmic. Unexpectedly, alarming fanfares are heard in m. 41 (02:36). They are followed by a transitory section (m. 47, 02:51) whose rocking, soothing rhythm prepares the return of the first theme in the movement's home key of A-flat major.

The first theme comes back in m. 54 (03:30) almost exactly as at the beginning of the movement. It is followed by a variation in m. 64 (04:16), in which the melody is densely enveloped by a continual motion of sixteenth notes.

The *Allegro sostenuto* section returns in m. 73 (04:56), but this time the contrast with the preceding music is significantly less pronounced, with no change in tonality or dynamics. Here the B theme is prepared by a six-bar buildup, starting in the murky low register and gradually making its way up to a luminous *forte*. The mysterious left-hand accompaniment of quintuplets in the beginning of this section will be recalled in the last movement. In m. 79 (05:11), the B theme sounds very similar to its initial presentation. It is followed by a passage in which new music is played by the right hand against the background of sixteenths in the left (m. 87, 05:29). The polyphonic material of the right hand here strongly resembles the second movement's middle section.

In m. 92 (05:42), the opening tempo of *Andante tranquillo* returns. A continual gentle ringing creates a dreamy atmosphere, while the left-hand accompaniment recalls that of the first movement's second theme. Against this background, the last complete statement of the first theme is heard in m. 98 (06:11). The melody travels from the treble register to the low bass in a mood of slumbering calm. Suddenly, energetic new music is heard in *piano* in m. 108 (07:00), like the echo of a distant festivity. This anticipation of the next movement is followed in m. 117 (07:16) by the final recollections of the Andante's main theme.

FOURTH MOVEMENT: ALLEGRO CON BRIO, MA NON TROPPO PRESTO (DISC 3, TRACK 8)

The fourth movement is full of optimistic, cheerful energy. It is written in C major in a compact sonata-rondo form. The first theme, which was quietly previewed in the previous movement, is now heard in a brilliant and active *forte*. The humorous bridge theme (m. 10, 00:18) consists of soft limping chords interspersed with a loud group of four sixteenths. The latter rhythmic formula, derived from the preceding first theme, takes a more reflective turn in m. 18 (00:32) before reaching a somewhat formal cadence in m. 25 (00:46).

The second theme follows in the dominant key of G major. It belongs to the category of "youth" themes that we find in many of Prokofiev's later works, such as the oratorio *On Guard for Peace,* the suite *Winter Bonfire,* or the last movement of the Seventh Symphony. This type of music can come perilously close to the style of many run-of-the-mill "young pioneer" works by

Soviet composers (among the better-known of such compositions is Dmitri Kabalevsky's Third Piano Concerto). Prokofiev's talent, however, infuses this theme with a grace, humor, and originality that distinguish it from the forced optimism of many similar works. His playfully carefree melody is multifaceted; it changes rhythms and registers and varies the mood accordingly.

In m. 40 (01:14), the first theme returns. The atmosphere becomes quieter and somber immediately after (m. 46, 01:25), modulating to E-flat major and preparing for the next section in m. 54 (01:45). This episode introduces a new theme with two contrasting parts. The first is wistfully nostalgic, with an evocative calling intonation that keeps returning. Both voices are doubled in octaves, creating a peculiar organlike sonority. The theme's second half (m. 61, 02:05) is mysteriously hushed. The hands explore extreme registers at opposite ends of the keyboard; a short motive in the upper voice is imitated in other voices, sometimes in inversion. The melody's evocative beginning returns in m. 70 (02:26) to frame the episode. A short development brings back the second theme in m. 76 (02:42) and the bridge theme in m. 80 (02:50). This entire section sounds vaguely menacing compared with the preceding poetic episode.

The recapitulation starts in m. 88 (03:06), with the first theme exhibiting its initial energetic mood. In contrast, only the latter, more reflective part of the bridge section appears here, in m. 95 (03:20). The second theme, which is presented in m. 105 (03:38), receives a fairly extensive development starting in m. 114 (03:55).

Suddenly, in m. 121 (04:08), the exploration of the second theme stops in its tracks, giving way to a feeling of stillness and wonderment created by repetitive sonorities. Against the background of trill-like quintuplets in the left hand (we heard them in the third movement in m. 73, Track 7, 04:56) and of gentle syncopations in the right hand, the first movement's initial theme emerges (m. 128, 04:25). As mentioned earlier, its texture, register, and meditative tenor recall the last appearance of the main theme of the Arietta in Beethoven's Sonata in C Minor, op. 111. Hovering in the treble register like an apparition, the theme conveys a contemplative feeling. In m. 132 (04:41), the drone of the quintuplets stops, and the melody flows in an unhurried fashion. A new moment of stillness arrives in m. 135 (04:55), when the melodic flow gives way to distantly ringing bells. Prokofiev marks this passage *da lontano* (from afar). It is reminiscent of the similar bell tolling heard in the third movement (see m. 92, Track 7, 05:42). The narrative unfolding of the first movement's theme resumes in m. 143 (05:31), concluding the sonata with a noble, calm simplicity and in a spirit of wise acceptance.

Master Class

Sviatoslav Richter's recording contains several deviations from the sonata's printed score, which was published after Prokofiev's death. I had long suspected that Richter might have been following the manuscript, which was in his possession. However, I was in no position to confirm this until recently, when I had an opportunity to examine the manuscript. Thus, for the first time I am able to say with confidence that Richter's playing corresponds fully with the manuscript. Example 9.1 shows the variances between the published score and the manuscript. The composer and the pianist worked closely together, and the sonata was not published until after Prokofiev's death. Therefore, it seems more likely that the discrepancies in the printed score are due to misprints rather than to later corrections; the manuscript should thus be considered definitive. I regret that I could not consult the manuscript and correct these mistakes prior to my own recording of the sonata.

Regretfully, I must also report a misreading in my recording: in m. 84 of the third movement, the dotted eighth on the fourth beat in the right hand should be C-sharp, as printed, not C-natural. In addition, I cannot recall now the reasoning behind my playing the right hand in the sonata's last chord two octaves lower than is written, nor can I justify it.

FIRST MOVEMENT

Feel the pacing of the opening theme "in one." This will help in creating the feeling of an unfolding narrative. While the lines of the secondary voices need to be clearly etched, the top line should always prevail. Make sure that

Movement 1

Movement 2

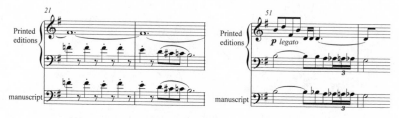

Ex. 9.1 *Sonata No. 9, discrepancies between the manuscript and published editions*

Movement 3

Movement 4

Ex. 9.1 Sonata No. 9, discrepancies between the manuscript and published editions, cont.

the passing of the middle voice from hand to hand in m. 5 does not create nervousness. Starting with the upbeat to m. 11, each phrase of the upper voice is anticipated by a lower voice. After the first two notes, the alto voice should yield prominence to the upper line without losing its distinctive color. In m. 18, the main melody is in the middle voice of the right hand.

In the bridge theme (m. 20), the tempo can become slightly faster. Create a mysterious character and play with a good, but not too deep, legato touch. Measures 23–26 have a more brooding mood, though they should still remain *piano*. In m. 27, the sonority of m. 20 returns, while m. 30 calls for a darker color. Return to the first tempo during the diminuendo in mm. 35–36. The light ringing tone of the bells in the right hand in mm. 37–40 prepares the dreamy, elegiac mood of the second theme (m. 41). Here I recommend using a warm touch in the right hand and a lighter, softer one in the left. Change the sonority of the melody in m. 47 and again in 57, as if the melodic line were taken over by different instruments. The concluding section (m. 61) has a light, pastoral character; play it with a transparent and slightly cool touch to evoke the sound of woodwinds. After the indicated *Poco meno mosso,* come back to the main tempo in m. 69.

The indication *con una dolcezza espressiva* (with an expressive sweetness) in the beginning of the development (m. 77) and the narrow chromatic intervals suggest a more intimate character than that of the movement's opening. Shape the phrases in mm. 81–87 in accordance with the slurs. The *espressivo* marking in m. 88 calls for a warmer, fuller-sounding upper voice; the slightly troubled repeated notes in the middle register should cut through the texture. The dotted rhythm from the concluding theme in mm. 93–94 should sound like a distant call.

It is better not to use much pedal in the second theme (starting with m. 95), in order not to obscure the motion of the eighth notes (and later triplets) in the left hand. The fragment of the bridge theme in the left hand in m. 105 must cut through with dramatic intensity. In m. 107, the concluding theme in the high register should sound expressive, with a slightly piercing woodwind sound. Use the pedal economically here. The explosions in the middle of mm. 111 and 113 should be preceded by short crescendos. Give fullness to the second theme in the bass in mm. 112–13 and mm. 115–16. Do not use too much pedal in mm. 116–17. Measure 118 should sound as an upbeat to the following bar, with the crescendo leading to the downbeat of m. 119. The last phrase of the first theme in the top voice in m. 120 should sound conclusive, indicating the end of the section. The diminuendo in mm. 122–23 leads from *fortissimo* to *mezzo forte,* not to *piano.*

The false reprise of m. 124 may be played in a slightly slower tempo. Change the pedal frequently so that the pulsation of the triplets in the bass remains clear. The recapitulation in m. 134 should have the warmth and narrative character of the movement's opening statement. The bridge theme (m. 144) should also evoke the mood it had when it first appeared in the exposition. The two melodic phrases elaborating on this theme's initial motive (mm. 150 and 153) should sound progressively more expressive and emotional, culminating in the short lyrical monologue in m. 156.

The second theme begins in the tenor voice in m. 163 and is taken over by the right hand in the upbeat to m. 166. Overlapping with the conclusion of this melody, the dotted rhythm of distant calls in mm. 174–75 precedes the closing theme in m. 176. Here it would make sense to pull back the tempo, similarly to the *Poco meno mosso* of m. 61. Return to the first tempo in m. 184. The agitated octave leaps in the melody here are carried over by the chords of mm. 188–89 and 190–91.

Play the runs of triplets in the left hand in m. 188 energetically but without heaviness. When they are taken over by the right hand in m. 192, the sound should suggest the whistling sonority of a flute.

In m. 196, play the F in the right hand sonorously, so that it remains audible prior to the resolution in the last bar. The final *ritenuto* in m. 197 should not be overdone; the rhythm in the second half of this bar should not be turned into a dotted one.

SECOND MOVEMENT

The precipitous (*strepitoso*) character need not cause us to take an unreasonably fast tempo; otherwise, mm. 27–37 will sound hurried and may lose their willful character. In m. 10, the quarter notes in the strangely hobbling new theme should not be played too short. Starting in m. 21, keep the dynamics of this enigmatic march precisely as indicated in the score. Play the transition to the middle section (m. 45) *poco espressivo,* using a gentle but not too deep touch. In mm. 49–50, listen to the line of D–C-sharp–B-sharp–C-sharp in the left hand.

In the middle section (m. 51), give each voice its own color. I recommend playing the left-hand line not as deeply as that in the right hand, with a slightly overlapping legato. Think in long phrases of at least four bars. In the second sentence of this theme (m. 60), the wide intervals in the melody justify more expressive playing.

The theme from the third movement (m. 90) should sound like a vision. Avoid introducing accents or making the rhythm too jumpy, both here and when the theme returns in m. 100. The chords in mm. 103 and 105 should lead to the next downbeat.

THIRD MOVEMENT

Feel the pacing of the first theme "in two," not "in four." I also recommend treating the second half of most of the bars as an upbeat to the next downbeat. Play the melody with a warm touch, imitating the sound of string instruments. In the left-hand part, the chords on the weak beats in the middle register should have a lighter sonority than the octaves in the bass. In the first variation (m. 9), let the parts of the melody distributed between different registers sound as one melodic line. The chords added parenthetically in m. 12 (and later in m. 21) should sound lightly, like woodwinds; they should not be confused with the main melody. Make sure, however, that in the last beat of m. 12 the two eighth notes C and B-flat in the right hand sound like parts of the principal melody. In the second variation (m. 18), make the ostinato figure in the bass dark and a little ominous; each sixteenth note needs to be slightly separated from the preceding dotted eighth note. Play the gentle runs of thirty-seconds in mm. 22–23 melodically, but not heavily and without a crescendo.

In the middle section (m. 27), the indication *Allegro sostenuto* cautions us against taking too fast a tempo. The general sonority should remain light and sunny; play the sixteenths clearly and transparently. The melody in the outer voices (m. 28) should not be too jumpy; feel it in two-bar phrases. Because of the difference in registers, the two outer voices must be balanced; make the top line sound warmer and the bottom line lighter. When these two lines diverge in m. 34, give prominence to the top voice. In mm. 35–39, follow the line of the upper voice, making the running sixteenths slightly less articulated. The fanfarelike chords in mm. 41–44 convey a slightly worrisome mood. In these fanfares, separate the sixteenths from the subsequent quarter notes.

In the return of the first tempo (m. 47), feeling the pacing in two will help to produce the needed lilt. After the *mezzo forte* in m. 50, the following *pianissimo* should sound mysterious. In the new variation of the main theme (m. 64), make the melody recognizable, but do not bring out single notes excessively.

In m. 73, do not play the sixteenths in the right hand together with the last notes of quintuplets; instead place the sixteenths earlier. In m. 79, the bass line does not double the top voice as it does in m. 28; for this reason the two lines should have different colors. Be careful not to overpower the melody in m. 83. The texture of the right hand in m. 87 is reminiscent of the second movement's middle section; it should be played with a similar touch.

Make the ringing in the right hand in m. 92 light and dreamy but quite clear. The long legato line starting in m. 105 should be smooth and light; do not sink too deeply into the keys. When the first theme of the last movement is "previewed" in m. 108, I suggest treating each consecutive bar (mm. 109, 110, and 111) as the entry of a new instrument. Avoid making a crescendo here; the whole presentation of this new theme should stay in *piano*. Achieve a very smooth, light legato in mm. 111–12. The last appearance of the third movement's main theme in m. 117 is marked *mezzo forte;* it is louder than the preceding passage. From here on, make a gradual descent into *piano,* but do not end softer than that.

FOURTH MOVEMENT

Play the first theme with a carefree energy but not too determinedly; do not turn it into a march. The chords in the left hand in mm. 3–4 should be played non legato, but their melodic contour must be heard. The register breaks in mm. 5–7 should not make the melody sound disjointed.

The bridge theme, too, should possess continuity in spite of the intrusion of groups of sixteenth notes in *forte*. Make sure that all four notes in these groups are played *forte,* not just the first one. In the upbeat to m. 18, the mood becomes slightly more tentative. In the cadence (mm. 24–26), listen as the low D in m. 24 resolves into G in m. 26. The tempo change in m. 24 should not be too drastic.

Feel the second theme "in one," and play it with light humor. In mm. 28–31, treat the increasing intervals in the upper voice melodically. The tempo change in m. 46 should not be too big. In this transition, follow the voice leading in the outer lines (Ex. 9.2). Do not take the *Andantino* in m. 50 too slowly either.

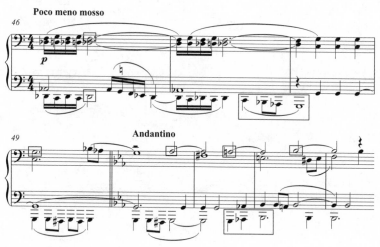

Ex. 9.2 Sonata No. 9, mvt. 4

The middle section should have the character of a warm evocation, slightly dreamy rather than intense. Make the difference between the two lines clear; the quarter notes in the low voice of each hand should sound slightly softer than the melody in the upper voice. I treat m. 58 as an extension of the previous sentence; the new phrase begins when the dynamics change to *mezzo forte*. In the difficult passage starting in m. 61, the objective should be for the eighth notes in both hands to sound legato, softly and evenly, avoiding dynamic swells. In addition, follow the voice leading in the outer lines, as shown in Example 9.3. The second theme starts in m. 76 as if from far away and then comes nearer in mm. 78–79.

The mood change in the middle of m. 121 justifies a slight slowing of the tempo. In the return of the first movement's main theme in m. 128, let the

Ex. 9.3 Sonata No. 9, mvt. 4

Ex. 9.4 Sonata No. 9, mvt. 4

melody sing gently, while the accompanying chords should remain light. Follow the bass line made out of the first notes of the quintuplets, but do not mark them excessively. In mm. 141–42, feel the cadence as shown in Example 9.4, before delivering the concluding statement.

Sonata No. 10 in E Minor, op. 137

Although Prokofiev included the Tenth Sonata in the list of his compositions, the draft of this sonata contains a mere forty-four bars. The manuscript of the draft is preserved in the Russian State Archive for Literature and Art. The first page, reproduced in Figure 6, was published in the book *S. S. Prokofiev: Materialy, Dokumenty, Vospominaniya* in 1961, while the second page has not been made public until recently.

This short sketch reveals a connection with the Sonatina in E Minor, op. 54, no. 1, written in 1931–32 in Paris. According to Mira Mendelson-Prokofieva, "[Prokofiev] had spoken of his desire to revise the sonatinas, op. 54, and to use them as the basis for two piano sonatas, the Tenth and Eleventh."[1] If completed, this would have been another sonata, after the Fifth, in which Prokofiev adjusted a work originally written abroad to his new taste for a greater simplicity of musical material.

Example 10.1 shows mm. 5–12 and 79–85 of the sonatina, which are incorporated in the draft of the sonata as mm. 11–16 and 21–26, respectively (see Fig. 6). We can see Prokofiev's uncanny ability to take material from the middle of a phrase and to incorporate it seamlessly into a new work.

The beginning of the sonata employs both hands playing in unison, similar to the opening of the Seventh Sonata. The second theme (m. 28 of the manuscript, 00:37) is reminiscent of the second theme of the first movement of Sonata No. 9 in its lyrical simplicity and haunting repeated notes.

Fig. 6 First page of the sketch for Sonata No. 10, op. 137 (manuscript). Russian State Archive for Literature and Art (RGALI). Reproduced by permission of the Estate of Sergei Prokofiev.

Ex. 10.1 Sonatina, op. 54, no. 1, mvt. 1

The surviving fragment is too short to enable us to speculate what the Tenth Sonata might have sounded like. Instead, I would recommend that readers become acquainted with the undeservedly neglected Sonatinas op. 54. (They are included in volume 5 of my recording of Prokofiev's complete piano works, CHAN 9017.)

Conclusion

TO BE A PROKOFIEV PIANIST

In the preceding chapters, we have examined each of the sonatas and discussed the challenges they present to their performers. We can now try to summarize the qualities and skills a pianist must possess in order to be a successful Prokofiev interpreter.

It is essential that a pianist meticulously observe the composer's indications regarding tempo, dynamics, and articulation. These are all crucial in creating full characterizations of individual themes and passages. Far too often one hears unidiomatic performances of Prokofiev's music in which speed and loudness seem to be the only parameters that matter to the pianist.

Prokoviev had a particular talent for creating a fully identifiable mood within the first notes of a piece, passage, or theme. Sometimes, especially in the later sonatas, this mood undergoes a gradual development or transformation. More often, though, it is juxtaposed against a contrasting image, the character of which is also established immediately. This stylistic trait typical of Prokofiev requires the performer to be always prepared for sudden emotional changes and to be able to flesh out a new image instantaneously, rather than unfold it gradually.

One of the most winning characteristics of Prokofiev's music is its indomitable energy. In expressing this quality, stability of tempo is particularly important. Rubato has no place in the motoric passages. Elsewhere, it should be used very sparingly, never compromising the overall steadiness of the musical pulse.

Prokofiev's virtuoso writing requires the pianist to have complete technical command; faultless finger and wrist technique is paramount. The execution of a broad range of articulation, particularly of the whole gamut of accents (see the description of Prokofiev's playing by Igor Glebov [Boris Asafiev], quoted in the chapter "Prokofiev the Pianist"), is not possible without the pianist's full control of touch. This mastery will also assure the dynamic precision necessary for effective interpretation of many of Prokofiev's works, especially his later sonatas.

In the lyrical passages, a pianist's ability to produce a long line and warm tone and to shape and mold the melody using dynamic shadings is essential. One of the most difficult tasks is finding how to communicate the shy, pure, and naive lyricism that is quintessentially Prokofievian.

There are numerous allusions to orchestral sonorities in Prokofiev's piano music. I strongly recommend that pianists study and listen to Prokofiev's orchestral works in order to acquire an aural image of these sonorities and of his highly individual instrumentation. Of course, one also needs a rich and varied touch to be able to create the illusion of orchestral colors on the piano.

Prokofiev's sonatas are among the high points of the piano repertoire of the twentieth century. Together they span the composer's entire creative path, reflecting all the stylistic variety of his music over the years. To do justice to these wonderful works, the pianist must possess a full command of the instrument, as well as a vivid imagination, unrelenting energy, and full emotional commitment. Mastering this repertoire is a challenging yet tremendously rewarding task.

GLOSSARY OF SELECTED TERMS
Compiled with assistance from Liam Viney

Alberti bass

An accompanying pattern based on *arpeggiation* of chords, characteristic of the keyboard music written by the Viennese Classical composers (notably Haydn, Mozart, and Beethoven). Named after Domenico Alberti (1710–1740), who used this accompaniment in his keyboard sonatas.

Arpeggiation

See *Arpeggio.*

Arpeggio

A chord whose notes are not simultaneously struck but instead sounded one after another, as typically played by the harp ("arpa" is Italian for "harp"). In Prokofiev's music, arpeggios mostly appear as fully written-out skips of three or more notes in the same direction, outlining a particular harmony.

Atonality

Music written without a sense of *key* or gravitation toward a single tonal center. See *Tonality.*

Augmentation

A process that involves expanding the rhythmic values of a melody, relative to its original form. Typically, augmentation in Prokofiev's music consists of doubling the rhythmic values of the original melody.

Chromatic, chromaticism

From the Greek word for "color," chromaticism involves the use of pitches foreign to the *diatonic* scale. The chromatic scale consists of all twelve pitches found in the traditional Western scale, equally separated by the interval of a half step. Chromaticism can be used to increase musical tension or for purely coloristic effect.

Counterpoint

The art of simultaneously combining two or more melodic lines so that each has independence and innate interest as well as the ability to work well in aggregation. The term is derived from the Latin "punctus contra punctum" (note against note).

Development

See *Sonata form*.

Diatonic

The use of only those seven pitches that are indigenous to the scale of the prevailing *key* at any given time.

Diminution

The opposite of *augmentation*, this process involves reducing the rhythmic values of a melody, relative to its original form. Typically, diminution in Prokofiev's music consists of halving the rhythmic values of the original melody.

Dominant

The fifth pitch of a major or minor scale. A dominant chord is a sonority built on this pitch. The dominant has special significance in tonal music because of its strong pull to the *tonic*.

Dyad

Two different pitches heard simultaneously.

Exposition

See *Sonata form*.

Harmonic pedal

See *Pedal point*.

Hemiola

A change in perception of two successive rhythmic groups of three even notes, when a composer treats them as three groups of two notes. Hemiolas were widely used by pre-Romantic composers, often in music connected with dance. Among later composers, Brahms employed them often.

Imitation

A polyphonic repetition by a voice of a melodic idea previously stated in another voice. See *Polyphony*.

Interval

The distance between two pitches, measured by the number of scale steps between them. After a unison, the next smallest interval is a second, followed by a third, and so on. The sound quality of some intervals is further identified as major or minor, others as perfect. An interval may also be augmented or diminished (made a half step larger or smaller than usual). One such interval of special importance is the "tritone." This term is commonly used to describe the interval of an augmented fourth (or diminished fifth), which spans the distance of three whole steps. Another important interval is the "octave," a span of eight notes. Pitches an octave apart share the same letter name and have the effect of the same note sounding in different *registers*. Passages of parallel octaves have been a mainstay of much piano music since the nineteenth century.

Inversion

When a melody, theme, or motive is inverted, it is, in effect, turned upside down. It retains the same sequence of intervals, but the direction of those intervals is reversed. This developmental technique results in a mirror-image of the original material, visually akin to the reflection of a mountain in a lake.

Key

Designation of a specific organization of pitches and chords within a major or minor framework, with a certain pitch functioning as a tonal center or *tonic*. See *Tonality*.

Mediant

The third pitch of a major or minor scale.

Meter

A perception of regular pulse in music. The specific arrangement of music into patterns of stressed and unstressed beats is indicated by a "time signature."

Mode

A specific ordering of pitches that form a scale, defined by the pattern of *intervals* between them. The most commonly used modes are known today as the major and minor scales. Rarer now are the modes that were widely used in European music until approximately 1600, such as the Phrygian, Lydian, Mixolydian, and others.

Modulation

A shift from one *key* to another during a section or phrase of music.

Motive

Sometimes used to describe the smallest identifiable unit of melodic material (e.g., the opening gesture of Beethoven's Fifth Symphony). The term can also describe a slightly longer melodic idea, but one that still does not warrant the label of "melody."

Octave

See *Interval*.

Ostinato

A rhythmic or melodic figure that is persistently repeated.

Pedal point
A term borrowed from organ music, describing a sustained or repeated pitch that is held while harmonies change around it. Pedal points are most often found in the bass register.

Polyphony
The simultaneous presentation of two or more melodic lines, as opposed to a texture characterized by melody and accompaniment (homophony).

Quintuplet
A group of five rhythmically equal notes (or notes and rests in combination), when the prevailing rhythmic organization suggests a group of four.

Recapitulation
See *Sonata form.*

Register
Refers to the relative highness or lowness of musical pitches.

Retransition
See *Sonata form.*

Scale
A collection of pitches with a specific arrangement of half and whole steps, depending on the type of scale.

Sequence
The immediate restatement (single or multiple) of a pattern (melodic, harmonic, or both), each starting at a successively higher or successively lower pitch.

Seventh chord
Any *triad* with an extra third added at the top, creating the dissonant interval of a seventh between the top and bottom pitches. The most common type of seventh chord is the dominant seventh, built on the *dominant* pitch. This seventh adds an extra dimension to the pull toward the *tonic* conveyed by the dominant.

Sextuplet
A group of six rhythmically equal notes (or notes and rests in combination), when the prevailing rhythmic organization suggests a group of four.

Sonata
An instrumental work of significant proportions. Sonatas usually consist of several movements, although one-movement sonatas exist (such as Prokofiev's Sonatas Nos. 1 and 3). It is common for sonatas from the late eighteenth century onward to cast at least one movement of a sonata in *sonata form.*

Sonata form (or sonata-allegro form)
According to the standard definition found in many textbooks since the nine-

teenth century—and the one that Prokofiev learned as a student—sonata form consists of three main sections. The first main section is known as the "exposition," where important thematic material is presented. The "first theme" or first theme group establishes a sense of *tonic*. A transitional passage called the "bridge passage" modulates and prepares for a "second theme" or group of themes. Many sonatas aim for contrast between the first and second theme areas through the use of variant *keys*—most often the *dominant*, or the relative major in a minor-key work. Contrast can also be created by imbuing themes with different affects (e.g., an energetic first theme may be followed by a lyrical second theme). Some sonatas have an additional third theme. The exposition normally ends with a "closing theme" or closing section.

The next main section is called the "development." Material from the exposition (or new material) is freely treated, fragmented, and manipulated. *Modulation* features prominently in the development sections of many sonatas. The end of the development may be signaled by a passage called the "retransition," which usually prepares the return of the tonic key.

The "recapitulation" restates the themes previously heard in the exposition, all in the tonic key. It is normally expected that all the themes will reappear in the recapitulation in the same order as they were heard in the exposition, although many deviations of this common practice are known, as is the case with many of Prokofiev's sonatas. The recapitulation may conclude with a "coda," a final section that enhances the sense of conclusion.

There are many variations of the formula for sonata form. One important expansion is the "sonata rondo," which combines elements of sonata form with those of a rondo. The latter is based on a succession of contrasting episodes, linked together by a recurring section (a "refrain").

Subdominant

The fourth pitch of a major or minor scale.

Time signature

See *Meter*.

Tonality

A system of musical thinking developed in the Western tradition, based on the feeling of centrality of one pitch over the others used in a composition. The other pitches have a hierarchical relationship with that central pitch, which is called the *tonic*. The word "tonality" is sometimes used synonymously with *key*.

Tonic

The first pitch of a major or minor scale, the *key*-defining note. The tonic chord is a *triad* constructed with the tonic note as its lowest-sounding note. A composition written in a tonal language will usually begin and end in the tonic. It is the single pitch that enables a piece of music written in a tonal language to sound complete.

Triad

A three-note chord constructed by superimposing two successive thirds (i.e., a third and a fifth above a pitch).

Triplet

A group of three rhythmically equal notes (or notes and rests in combination), when the prevailing rhythmic organization suggests a group of two.

Tritone

See *Interval*.

Variation

A variant of a previously heard statement, usually retaining certain fundamental qualities of the original material.

NOTES

Among various publications about Prokofiev, one of the earliest books remains the most essential one. S. I. Shlifshtein's compilation S. S. Prokofiev: Materialy, dokumenty, vospominaniya *[Materials, Documents, Reminiscences] (Moscow: Gosudarstvennoye muzykalnoye izdatelstvo, 1961) contains the first and still the fullest catalogue of Prokofiev's compositions, as well as a short version of his autobiography, selected correspondence, reviews, articles written by Prokofiev, and numerous reminiscences of those who knew the composer. Somewhat later, an abridged English translation of this book was published as S. I. Shlifshtein, ed.,* S. Prokofiev: Autobiography, Articles, Reminiscences *(Moscow: Foreign Languages Publishing House, n.d.). Some of the materials from the original 1961 publication later appeared in other English books, among them Bruno Monsaingeon's* Sviatoslav Richter: Notebooks and Conversations *(Princeton, N.J.: Princeton University Press, 2001), Neil Minturn's* The Music of Sergei Prokofiev *(New Haven, Conn.: Yale University Press, 1997), Sergei Prokofiev,* Dnevnik—27 *(Paris: Sintaksis, 1990), and Richard Buckle's* Diaghilev *(London: Weidenfeld and Nicholson, 1979). In quoting from these various books, I have selected those translations that seemed the most precise or idiomatic, citing the respective publications, or have provided my own translations, citing the original Russian source.*

While Prokofiev's autobiography was published in abbreviated form in the collection of 1961 and translated repeatedly, longer versions of it were published in Russian in 1973 and, in a second enlarged edition, in 1982 (S. S. Prokofiev, Avtobiografia *[Moscow: Sovetskiy kompozitor, 1982]). The translations for the quotations from this version are mine.*

The publication of two volumes of previously unknown Prokofiev diaries—Sergei Prokofiev, Dnevnik, 1907–1933 *(Paris: sprkfv [Serge Prokofiev Foundation], 2002)—has been one of the most significant recent events for Russian musicology. Quotations from this source are given in my translation. An English edition of the first volume appeared after this book was written (Sergey Prokofiev,* Diaries 1907–1914: Prodigious Youth, *trans. Anthony Phillips [London: Faber and Faber, 2006]).*

Preface
1. S. I. Shlifshtein, ed., *S. S. Prokofiev: Materialy, dokumenty, vospominaniya* [Materials, Documents, Reminiscences] (Moscow: Gosudarstvennoye muzykalnoye izdatelstvo, 1961), 189.
2. Ibid., 547.

Prokofiev: His Life and the Evolution of His Musical Language
1. S. I. Shlifshtein, ed., *S. Prokofiev: Autobiography, Articles, Reminiscences*, trans. Rose Prokofieva (Moscow: Foreign Languages Publishing House, n.d.), 25.
2. Ibid., 29.
3. Richard Buckle, *Diaghilev* (London: Weidenfeld and Nicholson, 1979), 289.
4. Shlifshtein, *S. Prokofiev: Autobiography*, 50.
5. Ibid, 64–65.
6. Ibid., 66.
7. Ibid., 73.
8. Dmitri Shostakovich, *Testimony: The Memoirs of Dmitri Shostakovich*, as related to and edited by Solomon Volkov, trans. Antonina W. Bouis (New York: Harper and Row, 1979), 36.
9. Shlifshtein, *S. Prokofiev: Autobiography*, 80.
10. Ibid., 106.
11. Ibid., 36–37.
12. Harlow Robinson, *Sergei Prokofiev: A Biography* (New York: Viking, 1987), 115.
13. Shlifshtein, *S. Prokofiev: Autobiography*, 79.
14. Robinson, *Sergei Prokofiev*, 392.
15. As related by Olga Lamm in her memoirs. See *Sergei Prokofiev: K 50-letiyu so dnia smerti. Vospominaniya, pis'ma, stat'yi* [Sergei Prokofiev: On the Fiftieth Anniversary of His Death. Reminiscences, Letters, Articles] (Moscow: M. I. Glinka State Central Museum of Musical Culture, 2004), 257.
16. Ibid., 474.
17. Shlifshtein, *S. Prokofiev: Autobiography*, 167–68.

Prokofiev the Pianist
1. Reinhold Glière, "First Steps," in S. I. Shlifshtein, ed., *S. Prokofiev: Autobiography, Articles, Reminiscences*, trans. Rose Prokofieva (Moscow: Foreign Languages Publishing House, n.d.), 146.
2. S. S. Prokofiev, *Avtobiografia* [Autobiography], ed. M. G. Kozlova (Moscow: Sovetskiy kompozitor, 1982), 237.
3. Shlifshtein, *S. Prokofiev: Autobiography*, 28.
4. Harlow Robinson, *Sergei Prokofiev: A Biography* (New York: Viking, 1987), 72.
5. Glière, "First Steps," 147.
6. Lina Prokofieva, "Memoirs," in Victor Delson, *Fortepiannoye tvorchestvo i pi-*

anizm Prokofieva [The Piano Music and the Pianism of Prokofiev] (Moscow: Sovetskiy kompozitor, Moscow, 1973), 235.

7. Mira Mendelson-Prokofieva, "O Sergee Sergeeviche Prokofieve" [About Sergei Sergeyevich Prokofiev], in S. I. Shlifshtein, ed., *S. S. Prokofiev: Materialy, dokumenty, vospominaniya* [Materials, Documents, Reminiscences] (Moscow: Gosudarstvennoye muzykalnoye izdatelstvo, 1961), 371.

8. Heinrich Neuhaus, "Prokofiev, Composer and Pianist," in Shlifshtein, *S. Prokofiev: Autobiography*, 237.

9. Delson, *Fortepiannoye tvorchestvo*, 245.

10. Shlifshtein, *S. Prokofiev: Autobiography*, 33.

11. Delson, *Fortepiannoye tvorchestvo*, 248. These quotes have been translated back from Russian.

12. Shlifshtein, *S. Prokofiev: Autobiography*, 52.

13. Igor Glebov [Boris Asafiev], "Pervoye vystupleniye Sergeia Prokofieva" [The First Performance of Sergei Prokofiev], in Shlifshtein, *S. S. Prokofiev: Materialy*, 324.

14. Igor Glebov, "Prokofiev—ispolnitel'" [Prokofiev the Performer], in Shlifshtein, *S. S. Prokofiev: Materialy*, 325–36.

15. David Oistrakh, "In Memoriam," in Shlifshtein, *S. Prokofiev: Autobiography*, 240.

16. Bruno Monsaingeon, *Sviatoslav Richter: Notebooks and Conversations*, trans. Stewart Spencer (Princeton, N.J.: Princeton University Press, 2001), 68.

17. Yakov Milshtein, "Prokofiev igraet v Moskve" [Prokofiev Plays in Moscow] (from *Sovetskaya muzyka*, 1962, no. 8, 49–50), quoted in Delson, *Fortepiannoye tvorchestvo*, 257.

18. Neuhaus, "Prokofiev, Composer and Pianist," 233–34.

19. Delson, *Fortepiannoye tvorchestvo*, 264–66.

20. Ibid., 252.

21. Detailed information on Prokofiev's recordings can be found in David Nice, *Prokofiev: From Russia to the West, 1891–1935* (New Haven, Conn.: Yale University Press, 2003), 369.

22. Ibid., 324.

23. Ibid., 325.

24. Monsaingeon, *Sviatoslav Richter*, 42.

Sonata No. 1

1. Vassily Morolyov (1880–1949), a veterinary doctor, Prokofiev's friend.

2. Neil Minturn, *The Music of Sergei Prokofiev* (New Haven, Conn.: Yale University Press, 1997), 74.

3. S. I. Shlifshtein, ed., *S. Prokofiev: Autobiography, Articles, Reminiscences*, trans. Rose Prokofieva (Moscow: Foreign Languages Publishing House, n.d.), 32.

4. Ibid., 27.

5. Sergei Prokofiev, *Dnevnik* [Diary], *1907–1918*, vol. 1 (Paris: sprkfv [Serge Prokofiev Foundation], 2002), 100.

6. Victor Delson, *Fortepiannoye tvorchestvo i pianizm Prokofieva* [Music for Piano and the Pianism of Prokofiev] (Moscow: Sovetskiy kompozitor, 1973), 164.

Sonata No. 2

1. Maximilian Anatolievich Schmidthof (1892–1913), student of St. Petersburg Conservatory, pianist.

2. Givi Ordzhonikidze, *Fortepiannye sonaty Prokofieva* [Piano Sonatas by Prokofiev] (Moscow: Muzgiz, 1962), 28.

3. S. I. Shlifshtein, ed., *S. Prokofiev: Autobiography, Articles, Reminiscences*, trans. Rose Prokofieva (Moscow: Foreign Languages Publishing House, n.d.), 31.

4. See Victor Delson, *Fortepiannoye tvorchestvo i pianizm Prokofieva* [The Piano Music and the Pianism of Prokofiev] (Moscow: Sovetskiy kompozitor, 1973), 169.

5. Ibid.

6. Shlifshtein, *S. Prokofiev: Autobiography*, 52.

7. Ordzhonikidze, *Sonaty*, 39.

Sonata No. 3

1. Boris Verin [Boris Nikolaevich Bashkirov] (1891–?), poet.

2. Piotr Petrovich [Pierre] Souvchinsky (1892–1985), musicologist and music critic.

3. Sergei Prokofiev, *Dnevnik* [Diary]—*27* (Paris: Sintaksis, 1990), 47.

Sonata No. 4

1. Maximilian Anatolievich Schmidthof (1892–1913), student of St. Petersburg Conservatory, pianist

2. Sergei Prokofiev, *Dnevnik* [Diary], *1907–1918*, vol. 1 (Paris: sprkfv [Serge Prokofiev Foundation], 2002), 648.

3. See S. I. Shlifshtein, ed., *S. Prokofiev: Autobiography, Articles, Reminiscences*, trans. Rose Prokofieva (Moscow: Foreign Languages Publishing House, n.d.), 27.

4. See Victor Delson, *Fortepiannoye tvorchestvo i pianizm Prokofieva* [The Piano Music and the Pianism of Prokofiev] (Moscow: Sovetskiy kompozitor, 1973), 181.

5. Prokofiev, *Dnevnik, 1907–1918*, 695.

6. E. K. Kulova, ed., *L. N. Oborin—pedagog* [Oborin the Pedagogue] (Moscow: Muzyka, 1989), 104.

7. Ibid.

Sonata No. 5

1. David Nice, *Prokofiev: From Russia to the West, 1891–1935* (New Haven, Conn.: Yale University Press, 2003), 195.
2. Sergei Prokofiev, *Dnevnik* [Diary], *1919–1933*, vol. 2 (Paris: sprkfv [Serge Prokofiev Foundation], 2002), 244.
3. S. I. Shlifshtein, ed., *S. Prokofiev: Autobiography, Articles, Reminiscences,* trans. Rose Prokofieva (Moscow: Foreign Languages Publishing House, n.d.), 64.
4. Nice, *Prokofiev,* 194.
5. Shlifshtein, *S. Prokofiev: Autobiography,* 176.

Sonata No. 6

1. S. I. Shlifshtein, ed., *S. Prokofiev: Autobiography, Articles, Reminiscences,* trans. Rose Prokofieva (Moscow: Foreign Languages Publishing House, n.d.), 168.
2. Bruno Monsaingeon, *Sviatoslav Richter: Notebooks and Conversations,* trans. Stewart Spencer (Princeton, N.J.: Princeton University Press, 2001), 74.
3. Harlow Robinson, *Sergei Prokofiev: A Biography* (New York: Viking, 1987), 377.
4. Monsaingeon, *Sviatoslav Richter,* 74.
5. Boris Alexeyevich Volsky (1903–?), a sound engineer, worked with Prokofiev while recording the music for the films *Alexander Nevsky* and *Ivan the Terrible.*
6. S. I. Shlifshtein, ed., *S. S. Prokofiev: Materialy, dokumenty, vospominaniya* [Materials, Documents, Reminiscences] (Moscow: Gosudarstvennoye muzykalnoye izdatelstvo, 1961), 534.
7. Givi Ordzhonikidze, *Fortepiannye sonaty Prokofieva* [Piano Sonatas by Prokofiev] (Moscow: Muzgiz, 1962), 91.
8. Robinson, *Sergei Prokofiev,* 377.

Sonata No. 7

1. Bruno Monsaingeon, *Sviatoslav Richter: Notebooks and Conversations,* trans. Stewart Spencer (Princeton, N.J.: Princeton University Press, 2001), 79–80.
2. Ibid., 80.
3. Givi Ordzhonikidze, *Fortepiannye sonaty Prokofieva* [Piano Sonatas by Prokofiev] (Moscow: Muzgiz, 1962), 102–3.
4. Ibid., 104.
5. This film has been released on videocassette (Kultur 1202) and DVD (Video Artists International 4260).
6. Harlow Robinson, *Sergei Prokofiev: A Biography* (New York: Viking, 1987), 400.

Sonata No. 8

1. Sergei Prokofiev, *Soviet Diary 1927 and Other Writings,* trans. and ed. Oleg Prokofiev (London: Faber and Faber, 1991), 101.
2. S. I. Shlifshtein, ed., *S. S. Prokofiev: Materialy, dokumenty, vospominaniya* [Materials, Documents, Memoirs] (Moscow: Gosudarstvennoye muzykalnoye izdatelstvo, 1961), 454.

3. Bruno Monsaingeon, *Sviatoslav Richter: Notebooks and Conversations*, trans. Stewart Spencer (Princeton, N.J.: Princeton University Press, 2001), 82.

Sonata No. 9

1. Bruno Monsaingeon, *Sviatoslav Richter: Notebooks and Conversations*, trans. Stewart Spencer (Princeton, N.J.: Princeton University Press, 2001), 83–84, 87.
2. *Sergei Prokofiev: K 50-letiyu so dnia smerti. Vospominaniya, pis'ma, stat'yi* [Sergei Prokofiev: On the Fiftieth Anniversary of His Death. Reminiscences, Letters, Articles] (Moscow: M. I. Glinka State Central Museum of Musical Culture, 2004), 66.
3. Givi Ordzhonikidze, *Fortepiannye sonaty Prokofieva* [Piano Sonatas by Prokofiev] (Moscow: Muzgiz, 1962), 136.
4. Ibid., 148.

Sonata No. 10

1. S. I. Shlifshtein, ed., *S. Prokofiev: Autobiography, Articles, Reminiscences*, trans. Rose Prokofieva (Moscow: Foreign Languages Publishing House, n.d.), 176.

CREDITS

The author and publisher are grateful to the music publishers who have granted permission to reproduce the following copyrighted material.

Alexander Nevsky, op. 78
By Sergei Prokofiev
Copyright © 1941 (Renewed) by G. Schirmer, Inc. (ASCAP)
International Copyright Secured. All Rights Reserved.
Reprinted by Permission.

Piano Concerto No. 3 in C, op. 26
Copyright © 1923 by Hawkes & Son (London) Ltd.
Reprinted by permission.

Piano Concerto No. 4 in B-flat Major, op. 53
By Sergei Prokofiev
Copyright © 1966 (Renewed) by G. Schirmer, Inc. (ASCAP)
International Copyright Secured. All Rights Reserved.
Reprinted by Permission.

Piano Concerto No. 5 in G, op. 55
Copyright © 1933 by Hawkes & Son (London) Ltd.
Reprinted by permission.

Piano Sonata No. 4 in C Minor, op. 29bis
Copyright © 1922 by Hawkes & Son (London) Ltd.
Reprinted by permission.

INDEX

Saint-Saëns, Camille: Piano Concerto No. *2*, 64
Schmidthof, Maximilian, 58, 84
Schoenberg, Arnold, 10, 36; Three Piano Pieces, op. *11*, 3
Schubert, Franz: Piano Sonata in B-flat Major, 171
Schumann, Robert: Piano Sonata in G Minor, 50; *Toccata*, 10
Scriabin, Alexander, 2, 4, 5, 36, 43, 50; Symphony No. *3* (*Divine Poem*), 77
Socialist Realism, 9
Shostakovich, Dmitri, 8, 130; *Lady Macbeth of Mtsensk*, 8; Symphony No. 7 ("Leningrad"), 18, 151
Souvchinsky, Piotr, 77, 102, 104
Stalin, Joseph, 8, 21

Stravinsky, Igor, 5, 8, 36, 62, 105, 118, 124; *Petrushka*, 62, 65, 124; *Rite of Spring*, 5

Taneyev, Sergei, 2, 10
Tcherepnin, Nikolai, 5
time signatures, 14; in Piano Sonata No. 7, 160; in Sonata No. *2* for Violin and Piano, 70

Ulanova, Galina, 155

Volkov, Solomon, 8
Volsky, Boris, 133

Winkler, Alexander, 35
World War II, 17–18

ABOUT THE AUTHOR

Born in Moscow, Boris Berman studied at Moscow Tchaikovsky Conservatory with the distinguished pianist and pedagogue Lev Oborin; he graduated with distinction as both pianist and harpsichordist. In 1973, he left the Soviet Union to immigrate to Israel. Since 1979 he has resided in the United States. As a concert pianist, Boris Berman has performed in over forty countries on six continents. His repertoire ranges from Baroque to the most recent contemporary compositions. His discography includes recordings with the Israel Philharmonic Orchestra under Leonard Bernstein and the Royal Concertgebouw Orchestra under Neemi Jarvi. Boris Berman was the first pianist to record all solo piano works by Sergei Prokofiev. His Shostakovich disc received the Edison Classic Award. Other recordings include complete sonatas by Scriabin, complete piano works by Schnittke, as well as works by Mozart, Beethoven, von Weber, Brahms, Schumann, Franck, Debussy, Stravinsky, Janáček, Berio, Joplin, and Cage.

In 2000, Yale University Press published Berman's book *Notes from the Pianist's Bench*. Named "Outstanding Academic Title" by *Choice* magazine, the book has been translated into several languages and is used as a required text in various conservatories and universities worldwide.

Boris Berman has served on the faculties of Indiana (Bloomington), Boston, Brandeis, and Tel-Aviv universities. Currently, he is Professor of

Piano at Yale School of Music. He was named Honorary Professor at Shanghai Conservatory. Berman conducts master classes throughout the world and is a frequent member of juries of international competitions. The web site www.borisberman.com contains more information about Boris Berman's performances, discography, and teaching.